ETHICS AND SEX

Ethics and Sex presents a systematic study of the nature and moral significance of human sexuality and of the major issues in sexual morality. The book is divided into two main parts. Part One gives a critical analysis of the key conceptions of human sexuality:

- the view of sex as bound up with procreation and marriage
- the romantic approach to sex
- the understanding of sex as body language
- the hedonist or "plain" sex view
- the traditional distinction between natural and unnatural sex and the notion of sexual perversion

Part Two discusses the most important issues in sexual morality:

- monogamy
- adultery
- prostitution
- homosexuality
- pedophilia
- sexual harassment
- rape

In this stimulating and often controversial book, the author argues for a "plainer" sex view and demonstrates that many of the prohibitions that make up the conventional sexual morality cannot withstand critical scrutiny and should be rejected. He claims that there are no sexual ethics, since sex has no particular moral significance.

Igor Primoratz is Associate Professor of Philosophy at the Hebrew University, Jerusalem. He is the author of *Justifying Legal Punishment* (1989 and 1997) and the editor of *Human Sexuality* (1997).

ETHICS AND SEX

Igor Primoratz

London and New York

First published 1999
by Routledge
11 New Fetter Lane, London EC4P 4EE

Simultaneously published in the USA and Canada
by Routledge
29 West 35th Street, New York, NY 10001

Routledge is an imprint of the Taylor & Francis Group

© 1999 Igor Primoratz

Typeset in Garamond by Routledge
Printed and bound in Great Britain by
TJ International Ltd, Padstow Cornwall

British Library Cataloguing in Publication Data
A catalogue record for this book is available from the British Library

Library of Congress Cataloging in Publication Data
Primoratz, Igor.
Ethics and sex / Igor Primoratz.
p. cm.
Includes bibliographical references and index.
1. Sexual ethics. I. Title.
HQ32.P75   1999
176–dc21   98–48882

ISBN 0–415–09333–3 (hbk)
ISBN 0–415–09334–1 (pbk)

CONTENTS

CONTENTS

CONTENTS

PREFACE AND ACKNOWLEDGMENTS

This is a study of two closely related subjects: the nature and moral significance of human sexuality, and the main issues of sexual morality.

In the first part, I present and take a critical look at the main conceptions of human sexuality: the traditional view of sex as meant for procreation and properly confined to marriage; the view of sex as bound up with love; the understanding of sex as a body language; and the hedonist or "plain sex" view. Against that background, I examine the distinction between natural and unnatural sex and the concept of sexual perversion. In the second part, I discuss the most important moral issues concerning sex: marriage, adultery, jealousy, prostitution, homosexuality, pedophilia, sexual harassment, and rape. (The problem of pornography has not been omitted as a result of any doubts concerning either its philosophical interest or its practical importance, but because of the usual limitations of space.)

I argue for a modified version of the plain sex view: the view that sex is basically just a source of a certain kind of pleasure and need not be bound up, either conceptually or morally, with anything else. I also try to show that we may be better off discarding the distinction between natural and unnatural sexual behavior and the idea of sexual perversion that usually comes with it. I further argue that most of the prohibitions that make up the conventional sexual morality cannot withstand critical scrutiny and should be rejected. In the final chapter, I suggest that sex has no particular moral significance and that, accordingly, there is no distinctively sexual morality. Moral questions raised by sex can and should be addressed in terms of those moral considerations that also apply elsewhere.

I am grateful for valuable help I received at various stages of this project from Professor John M. Finnis, Dr Mane Hajdin, Professor Richard D. Mohr, and Mr J. Martin Stafford. I also benefited from

ix

comments on the penultimate draft of the manuscript by an anonymous reader for Routledge.

My special thanks go to Professor Alan Soble, who read the penultimate version and made numerous and detailed comments. His queries, criticisms, and suggestions were of great help in the final revision of the book.

I am very grateful to Mr Richard Stoneman, Senior Editor at Routledge, for his sympathy, encouragement, and great patience over a period that proved much longer than we had anticipated.

I wrote several chapters while on sabbatical leave from the Hebrew University in 1996/7, during my tenure as Visiting Fellow in the Director's Section, Research School of Social Sciences, Australian National University, Canberra, and subsequently as Visiting Research Scholar, Centre for Philosophy and Public Affairs, Department of Philosophy, University of Melbourne. I wish to thank Professor Geoffrey Brennan, Director, RSSS, Professor Frank Jackson, Chair, Philosophy Program, RSSS, Professor C.A.J. Coady, Director, CPPI, and Professor Brian Scarlett, Head, Department of Philosophy at the University of Melbourne, for making that possible.

The chapters on sexual perversion, prostitution and pedophilia are based on my papers on these subjects published in philosophical journals. I wish to thank the editors and publishers for their permission to use that material:

Igor Primoratz, "Sexual Perversion", *American Philosophical Quarterly*, vol. 34 (1997), pp. 245–258. Copyright © *American Philosophical Quarterly*. Published by North American Philosophical Publications, Inc.

Igor Primoratz, "What's Wrong with Prostitution?", *Philosophy*, vol. 68 (1993), pp. 159–182. Copyright ©Royal Institute of Philosophy. Published by Cambridge University Press.

Igor Primoratz, "Pedophilia", *Public Affairs Quarterly*, vol. 13 (1993), pp. 99–110. Copyright © *Public Affairs Quarterly*. Published by North American Philosophical Publications, Inc.

ABBREVIATIONS USED IN THE NOTES AND BIBLIOGRAPHY

HS   Igor Primoratz (ed.), *Human Sexuality*, The International Research Library of Philosophy, Aldershot, Ashgate, 1997

P&S1   Robert Baker and Frederick Elliston (eds), *Philosophy & Sex*, Buffalo, NY, Prometheus Books, 1975

P&S2   Robert Baker and Frederick Elliston (eds), *Philosophy and Sex*, new revised ed., Buffalo, NY, Prometheus Books, 1984

POS1   Alan Soble (ed.), *The Philosophy of Sex: Contemporary Readings*, Totowa, NJ, Littlefield, Adams & Co., 1980

POS3   Alan Soble (ed.), *The Philosophy of Sex: Contemporary Readings*, 3rd ed., Lanham, MD, Rowman & Littlefield, 1997

SH   Edmund Wall (ed.), *Sexual Harassment: Confrontations and Decisions*, Buffalo, NY, Prometheus Books, 1992

SLF   Alan Soble (ed.), *Sex, Love, and Friendship: Studies of the Society for the Philosophy of Sex and Love 1977–1992*, Amsterdam and Atlanta, GA, Rodopi, 1997

I

THE BASICS

1

INTRODUCTION

Philosophers and sex

This book discusses a number of questions pertaining to human sexuality. Human sexuality gives rise to many interesting and important questions in several areas. The book will not deal with those that come up in sexology, psychology, sociology, or social and cultural history. This is a philosophical book; the approach will be ethical or, more broadly, philosophical.

When it comes to sex as a topic of philosophy, though, the surprising fact is that it is only comparatively recently that it has come to engage any stronger *and* sustained interest among professional philosophers. In this connection, it is instructive to refer to "The Metaphysics of Sexual Love" by Arthur Schopenhauer, written in 1844. In view of the unquestionable importance, indeed centrality, of sexuality in human life, Schopenhauer is surprised that philosophers should have ignored the subject almost completely, and left it to poets and novelists. The history of philosophy offers just a few exceptions to this general disregard, and they, in his view, do not amount to much:

> It is Plato who has been most concerned with it, especially in the *Banquet* and the *Phaedrus*; yet what he says about it is confined to the sphere of myths, fables, and jokes, and for the most part concerns only the Greek love of boys. The little that Rousseau says about our theme in the *Discours sur l'inégalité* ... is false and inadequate. Kant's discussion of the subject in the third section of the essay *On the Feeling of the Beautiful and the Sublime* ... is very superficial and without special knowledge; thus it is also partly incorrect. ... Spinoza's definition, on the other hand, deserves to be

quoted on account of its excessive naivety: *Amor est titillatio, concomitante idea causae externae* [Love is a titillation accompanied by the notion of an external cause]

(Ethics, IV, *Prop.* 44, *dem.*).[1]

Accordingly, Schopenhauer concludes: "I have no predecessors either to make use of or to refute ..."[2]

These remarks are somewhat cavalier. There is more on sexuality in Plato, Kant, and Rousseau than Schopenhauer is willing to acknowledge.[3] Furthermore, he could have mentioned a few others, at least if the subject is to be conceived broadly enough to include not only sexual attraction, desire, love, as such, but also social rules, practices and institutions pertaining to it. For instance, some utilitarians have discussed the institution of marriage, and offered either its justifications (Hume, Paley) or arguments for its abolition (Godwin). Still, Schopenhauer is right in the sense that, with a few exceptions, philosophers had not tended to show great and sustained interest in human sexuality before his time. Nor, indeed, for about a century afterwards.

This lack of sustained interest in sex as a philosophical subject, which characterizes Western philosophy through most of its history, can be explained in part by the influence of a strong metaphysical tradition, whose sources are in the teachings of Plato and the Pythagoreans, that tended to contrast the material and non-material, the body and the soul, and to extol the latter while disparaging the former. In that context, sexuality tended to be seen as purely physical, and accordingly to be treated as something of little value, if not downright bad. Another part of the explanation is the ideal of the philosopher's life, or even of good life in general, accepted by many philosophers in antiquity, and in later times too: the ideal of the life of Reason. This ideal, developed in particular by philosophers of the Stoic school, was based on the supreme values of rationality and inner freedom; both were seen as incompatible with and threatened by "passions" such as anger, fear, or sexual desire. The way of achieving inner peace and freedom and realizing the ideal of the life of Reason was one of fighting and subduing one's passions, including the sexual one. A good statement of this ideal is given by Epictetus:

> To-day when I saw a handsome woman I did not say to myself, 'Would that she were mine!' and 'Blessed is her husband!' ... Nor do I picture the next scene: the woman

present and disrobing and reclining by my side. ... And if,
though the woman herself ... is willing and beckons and
sends to me, and even touches me and comes close to me, I
still hold aloof and conquer ... this is a thing to be really
proud of ... Go to Socrates and see him reclining with
Alcibiades and making light of his beauty. Consider what a
victory, what an Olympic triumph, he won over himself ...
Great is the struggle, divine the task; the stake is a kingdom,
freedom, peace, an unruffled spirit.[4]

Christian philosophers of the middle ages, such as Augustine and
Thomas Aquinas, were heirs to this antisexual tradition of their
Greek and Roman predecessors. But they also wrote within the religious tradition that commanded "Be fruitful and multiply!" They
accordingly tried for a synthesis of the two, and developed theories
of sexuality which confined sex to heterosexual genital intercourse
within monogamous marriage.

In the seventeenth and eighteenth centuries the traditional world
view no longer held sway in philosophy. But the idea of the life of
Reason was still very powerful, and those committed to it tended to
think of sex as but one of the irrational distractions the philosopher
had to overcome if he was to be able to devote himself fully to his
vocation, rather than a legitimate subject of philosophical consider-
ation. Nietzsche points out that philosophers have tended to feel
"genuine irritation and rancour" against sensuality in general, and
the sort of sensuality bound up with sex, love, and marriage in
particular:

Thus the philosopher abhors *marriage* ... as hindrance and
catastrophe on his path to the optimum. Which great philosopher, so far, has been married? Heraclitus, Plato,
Descartes, Spinoza, Leibniz, Kant, Schopenhauer – were
not; indeed it is impossible to even *think* about them as
married. A married philosopher belongs to *comedy*, that is my
proposition: and that exception, Socrates, the mischievous
Socrates, appears to have married *ironice*, simply in order to
demonstrate *this* proposition.[5]

Those philosophers who did address the subject of sex at all were
for the most part content to merely prop up conventional sexual
morality by philosophical arguments. Philosophers so different as the
utilitarian Hume and the arch-deontologist Kant tended to advance

arguments with surprisingly similar and conventional moral conclusions, justifying the institution of monogamous marriage as the sole legitimate framework for sexual activity. There was one important exception to this in the century of the enlightenment: the Marquis de Sade radically repudiated the traditional view of sex and marriage, and forcefully expounded an alternative ideal of extreme naturalism and libertinism, which made his writings infamous to this day.[6]

The middle of the last century was the turning point. Schopenhauer both fully appreciated the intrinsic importance of the subject of sexuality, and did not feel committed to conventional morality. In his "Metaphysics of Sexual Love", mentioned above, he interpreted human sexual desire and love as but an expression of the blind will of the human species to perpetuate itself. And in his widely read and unabashedly misogynous essay on women, he criticized the traditional monogamous marriage as irrational and unfair, and did not flinch from advocating that it be replaced by polygamy. He argued that polygamy would not only be more in tune with the objective needs of the human species and would benefit men, but would also be good for women.[7]

An impetus towards a new understanding of sexuality and a reassessment of the rules of traditional sexual morality was given by the naturalistic philosophy of Schopenhauer and Nietzsche. Another important influence was the critique of the bourgeois society in general, and of bourgeois marriage in particular, by socialist and anarchist thinkers.

In the first half of the twentieth century, continental philosophers such as Jean-Paul Sartre (*Being and Nothingness*, 1943), Maurice Merleau-Ponty (*The Phenomenology of Perception*, 1945), and Simone de Beauvoir (*The Second Sex*, 1949) made important contributions to philosophical understanding of human sexuality. In Britain, Bertrand Russell's *Marriage and Morals* (1929) occasioned considerable debate by its argument for the liberalization of the institution of marriage and sexual morality in general.

But it is only since the mid-sixties that the philosophy of sex has come into its own: that human sexuality is widely recognized as a legitimate and indeed highly interesting and important subject of sustained philosophical investigation and debate. This development can be explained, in part, by the influence of certain social and cultural trends: the new libertinism of the anti-establishment currents among the young, the rise and expansion of contemporary feminism and the gay liberation movement, and the overall change in sexual mores, popularly known as the sexual revolution of the sixties, to which all these currents contributed. Within philosophy proper, the development of the philosophy of sex was made possible, above all, by the fact that by the late sixties and early seventies, the extreme version of the "linguistic turn" that had characterized philosophy in the English-speaking world for decades was being reversed. The view that moral, political and legal philosophy should confine itself to analysis of the basic terms or concepts of morals, politics, and law and leave moral, political, and legal issues to non-philosophers was losing ground, and a strong interest in the questions of moral, political, and legal norms and values was reasserting itself. Another factor may have been the influence of the continental philosophers mentioned above; their main writings were being translated into English and widely read in the English-speaking countries since the late fifties.

The period from the mid-sixties to late seventies was marked by the publication of several pioneering works in the philosophy of sex. In 1965 two systematic, book-length discussions of sexual morality were published: *Sexual Morality* by Ronald Atkinson,[8] and *Logic and Sexual Morality* by John Wilson.[9] Systematic studies of sexual ethics had been published before, of course, but they tended to take the point of view of particular religious traditions; Atkinson's and Wilson's works were the first philosophical books on the subject. The same period saw the publication of several pioneering papers, which have since been accorded the status of minor classics in the field: Thomas Nagel's "Sexual Perversion" (*The Journal of Philosophy*, 1968), Robert Solomon's "Sexual Paradigms" (*The Journal of Philosophy*, 1974), and Alan Goldman's "Plain Sex" (*Philosophy & Public Affairs*, 1977). By the mid-seventies, there was enough good material for the first anthology of contemporary philosophical writings on sex to be put together.[10] And the last two decades have seen considerable philosophical activity focused on the subject of sexuality. Numerous papers and quite a few books have been published, both on the nature of sexuality in general and on various specific issues, such as monogamy, adultery, prostitution, homosexuality, sexual harassment, pornography, or rape. An International Society for the Philosophy of Sex and Love has been active since 1977.[11] The philosophy of sex has clearly come of age.

Plan of the book

The first part of the book is devoted to the basics of the philosophy of sex. It focuses on two main questions: What is sex? How is natural or normal sex to be distinguished from unnatural or abnormal sex? With regard to the first question, I will look into four main accounts of sex to be found in the literature: the view of sex as meant for procreation; the view that it is, or ought to be, bound up with love; the view of sex as a type of language, used to express certain important feelings and attitudes; and the view that it is simply a source of pleasure. All four accounts are advanced primarily as ways of understanding the nature of sex; but each one also tells us something about the significance and value of sex in human life in general, and about its moral status in particular.

Talk of the nature of sex seems to entail the distinction between natural and unnatural, normal and abnormal sex. This distinction is very much in use both in our ordinary, everyday discourse about sex and in attempts of psychologists, sociologists and others to offer scientific explanations of some of its varieties. The negative side of the distinction is usually encapsulated in the idea of sexual perversion. This idea will be the subject of a separate chapter.

The second part of the book is devoted to the main issues in sexual morality. I will discuss the rights and wrongs of marriage, adultery, jealousy, prostitution, homosexuality, pedophilia, sexual harassment, and rape. I think that every one of these topics is very interesting in its own right; but their discussion is also bound to lead us back to certain wider problems in the philosophy of sex or to raise some important questions in moral and social philosophy. Thus marriage, adultery, or jealousy cannot be discussed without asking the more basic question about exclusivity in sexual relations. Thinking about prostitution inevitably brings up the distinction between intrinsically significant and merely instrumental social relations, as well as that between personal and impersonal social intercourse. The problems of sexual harassment and rape raise questions about the inequality and oppression of women.

Having discussed these issues of sexual morality, in the concluding chapter I will briefly reconsider the very idea of sexual morality. Is there anything special about sex from a moral point of view, so that there is, or should be, a specifically sexual morality? Or is sex as such devoid of any distinctively moral significance, morally neutral, so to speak, so that moral guidance regarding sexual behavior is provided by the same general moral rules and values that apply in other areas?

2

SEX AND PROCREATION

Sex, procreation, marriage

Today, the view is no longer generally accepted that the single most important fact for our understanding and evaluation of sex is that it makes procreation possible and that, accordingly, its proper place is within marriage. But it did reign supreme in the West for almost two millennia, in discourse about sex, at least, if not always in sexual practice. Even when it came to be questioned, it retained its central importance, for it served as the point of departure in discussions about sex. And if today it no longer exerts the influence it once did, it is still one of the main accounts of the nature and value of sexuality we have.

Historically, its main source is the Christian view of human nature and human sexuality in particular. This view was heir to the Old Testament idea of marriage as the proper institutional framework for carrying out the commandment "Be fruitful and multiply!". On the other hand, it was also informed by the Pythagorean and Platonic tradition of a negative attitude to the body, and the Stoic understanding of sexuality as one of the passions that are in constant conflict with the demands of reason.

The utterly negative view of sexuality characteristic of early Christianity is expressly stated, while at the same time its practical implications are circumscribed, in the famous passage of Paul's First Epistle to the Corinthians:

> It is well for a man not to touch a woman. But because of the temptation to immorality, each man should have his own wife and each woman her own husband. The husband should give to his wife her conjugal rights, and likewise the wife to her husband. ... Do not refuse one another except

9

perhaps by agreement for a season, that you may devote
yourselves to prayer; but then come together again, lest
Satan tempt you through lack of self-control. I say this by
way of concession, not of command. I wish that all were as
I myself am. But each has his own special gift from God,
one of one kind and one of another. To the unmarried and
the widows I say that it is well for them to remain single as
I do. But if they cannot exercise self-control, they should
marry. For it is better to marry than to be aflame with
passion.[1]

Paul believed that the second coming of Christ was imminent, and
accordingly felt that the commandment that humans should be
fruitful, multiply, and fill the Earth was no longer to the point. His
concession to human sexual needs was motivated solely by the
assessment that in many, indeed most people they are much too
strong to be completely suppressed. Several centuries later, Augustine
was bound to see things somewhat differently: in his account of
human sexuality the requirement of procreation receives a central
role. The negative account of human sexuality is elaborated and
connected with the dogma of the original sin by the doctrine that
sexuality expresses in a particularly telling way the basically sinful
character of the fallen human nature. The original sin was one of
rebellion against God's reason; part of the punishment for that rebellion is that our sexuality similarly rebels against our own reason,
and cannot be controlled by it the way, say, the movements of our
hands and feet are controlled and directed by it. Sexual lust, says
Augustine,

> asserts its power not only over the entire body, nor only
> externally, but also from within. It convulses all of a man
> when the emotion in his mind combines and mingles with
> the carnal drive to produce a pleasure unsurpassed among
> those of the body. The effect of this is that at the very
> moment of its climax there is an almost total eclipse of
> acumen and ... sentinel alertness. But surely any friend of
> wisdom and holy joys, who lives in wedlock ... would
> prefer, if he could, to beget children without this kind of
> lust. For he would want his mind to be served, even in this
> function of engendering offspring, by the parts created for
> this kind of work, just as it is served by the other members,
> each assigned to its own kind of work. They would be set

in motion when the will urged, not stirred to action when hot lust surged.[2]

This basic irrationality of human sexuality, its resistance to control by reason and will, accounts for the sense of shame and the need for privacy which are bound up with it. Thus sexual organs are called "shameful parts"; and even sexual intercourse between husband and wife, whose purpose is procreation, legitimate and respectable though it is, takes place in conditions of privacy. "What is the reason for this if not that something by nature fitting and proper is carried out in such a way as to be accompanied also by something of shame as punishment?"[3]

Given this inferior, embarassing, sinful and shameful character of sexuality, sex can be accepted only if, and in so far as, it is meant to serve an important extrinsic purpose that cannot be attained by any other means. It is legitimate when, and only when, it is geared towards procreation, and when it takes place within its proper institutional context, which is marriage. These views were further developed and modified in the writings of Thomas Aquinas, which offer the classic statement of pre-Reformation Christian sexual ethics. The central claim is that sexual activity is both to be understood and given its proper direction and scope in terms of the natural function or task of sexual organs. Now this function is clearly procreation. Sexual intercourse is therefore legitimate and proper when, and only when, it is geared toward procreation. In view of this, and in tune with the state of physiological knowledge of his times, Thomas then claims that the essential, defining element of this intercourse is the emission of semen. From this it follows that

> every emission of semen, in such a way that generation cannot follow, is contrary to the good for man. And if this be done deliberately, it must be a sin. Now, I am speaking of a way from which, *in itself*, generation could not result: such would be any emission of semen apart from the natural union of male and female. For which reason, sins of this type are called *contrary to nature*. But, if by accident generation cannot result from the emission of semen, then this is not a reason for its being against nature, or a sin; as for instance, if the woman happens to be sterile.[4]

11

The proper end of sexual intercourse is procreation; but procreation is not to be understood merely as bringing a human being into the world. It is rather a long process of raising the child until it reaches maturity and can live on its own. This means that when a person engages in sexual intercourse, he or she undertakes a commitment to see this process through to its successful completion. Now taking care of a child and bringing it up cannot be done very well in every environment. The best environment for nurturing and raising children is that of monogamous marriage. The requirement of bringing up the offspring is reason enough for marriage to be a long-term affair; but Thomas makes a stronger claim: marriage is for life. This is based, on the one hand, on the argument of fairness to women, who are assumed to be the obvious losers in divorce, and, on the other hand, on the "natural" superiority of men and subjection of women.[5]

Every one of these tenets has important implications. The apparently innocuous focusing of the discussion of sex on sexual *intercourse* and the definition of this intercourse in terms of procreation makes it possible for Thomas to see the defining element of sexual intercourse in the emission of semen. As Robert Baker and Frederick Elliston remark, "if ever a proposition appeared to be a metaphysical irrelevancy, [this] does. Yet this seemingly superfluous bit of abstraction can – and possibly does – have the mundane and tragically real effect of ruining the sex life of half of the population."[6] Incidentally, this approach is by no means merely an item of medieval metaphysics; sexual intercourse is still sometimes defined, both in everyday discourse and in law, from the same distinctively male point of view. Male arousal and satisfaction is thus acknowledged as an integral part of intercourse, while female arousal and satisfaction are relegated to its possible consequences.[7]

These claims of Augustine and Thomas Aquinas, taken together, make up an extremely restrictive sexual ethics. It is an ethics that confines legitimate sex within the bounds of heterosexual, monogamous, exclusive, indissoluble marriage, and thereby rules out sexual relations between any possible partners except husband and wife, as well as masturbation. Moreover, it is extremly restrictive within these narrow confines too. For it allows only for sexual relations between husband and wife that are intended to lead to procreation (Augustine) or, more permissively, for those that are "by nature ordained" toward procreation, i.e. to sexual acts that under normal circumstances can result in procreation (Thomas). Every other variety of sexual activity – petting to orgasm, oral sex, anal sex – is pronounced unnatural and morally unacceptable. Finally, it is an ethics of far-reaching gender inequality.

Of course, these views have undergone certain modifications since the Reformation. No major Christian church or denomination today teaches that men are "by nature" superior to women; most no longer maintain that marriage must be for life and that divorce is in principle unacceptable. But the central problem for all currents in Christianity has been to broaden the traditional sexual ethics so as to include aspects of human sexual experience not bound up with procreation. Given the fundamental tenets of Christianity, this expansion could not have been expected to acknowledge and legitimize sex as an important source of pleasure pure and simple; but it has allowed for the role of sex in expressing, enhancing, and even effecting, marital love and care.

The Catholic tradition, which is most conservative and therefore most instructive on the subject of this chapter, has made room for this by adding a "unitive" function of sex within marriage. According to the document of the church that is of central importance in this connection, the encyclical *Humanae Vitae*, the purpose of marriage is not only to provide a proper framework for procreating and bringing up the offspring, but also to realize God's design of love in humans. The love of husband and wife ought to be similar to God's love in that it is free and unconditional, total. But it also has to be "fully human", meaning "of the senses and of the spirit at the same time".[8] However, this innovation is of a rather limited significance; for the unitive function in itself is normally not enough to consecrate sexual intercourse. The two aspects of sex, the procreative and the unitive, are inseparably connected with one another by God's will, and must on no account be disconnected by humans.[9]

Objections to the procreation view

In so far as the procreation view is presented as part and parcel of the Christian faith, the first objection to it is that it is likely to be convincing, at best, only to those who accept this faith, while saying very little to anyone else. If it is disconnected from Christianity and presented as based on some philosophical version of theism, its appeal will still be limited to those who can embrace a theistic world-view. It will be found quite unattractive by those who do not share the same metaphysical assumptions concerning God and the world, the dualism of matter and spirit, body and soul, etc., and may not be convinced that we have a moral obligation to have children.[10] Moreover, even some Catholics find it difficult to accept some of the details of the procreation view of sex as described above. Let me mention some of the problems of the latter sort first.

The current statement of Catholic sexual morality seems to be plagued by a certain inconsistency. The addition of the "unitive" aspect of sex to its procreative purpose was meant to make this morality less narrow and restrictive and more in tune with the modern world. But these two functions of sex may not sit very well together. Marital love ought to be free and total, unreserved.[11] This love is to be expressed in sexual intercourse and enhanced by it. But it is also said that such intercourse must *always* be open to the possibility of procreation. It will not do for a married couple to carry out the commandment "Be fruitful and multiply!" by begetting a child or a number of children, and then conclude that if they do not want another child at the time, or any more children at all, they may conduct their sex life accordingly by making use of various means of birth control. The teaching that the two functions of sex, the procreative and the unitive, are inseparable, does not refer to the sex life of a couple as a whole, but to every single sexual intercourse: "... Each and every marriage act ... must remain open to the transmission of life."[12] Accordingly if, for social, economic, or health reasons, a married couple cannot afford a child at the time, or will not be able to afford any more children at all, their options seem to be either abstinence or sex plagued by the fear that it might result in pregnancy. If they choose the latter, it is not at all clear how their sexual encounters can be expected to express and enhance the free and total, unreserved conjugal love Catholic sexual ethics posits as an essential characteristic of matrimony.[13]

To be sure, this pressure is somewhat alleviated by the fact that Catholic sexual ethics does permit the use of one method of birth control: the rhythm (or "safe days") method. As *Humanae Vitae* puts it, sexual acts are not illegitimate "if, for causes independent of the will of husband and wife, they are foreseen to be infecund, since they always remain ordained towards expressing and consolidating their union."[14] (By the same token, sterility resulting from natural causes does not disbar a couple from having sex.) What is illegitimate is the deliberate prevention of conception. There is an "essential difference" between the rhythm method and such methods of birth control as the condom or the pill: while the former is merely the use of "a natural disposition", the latter amount to deliberate prevention of the natural process of conception by artificial means.

This stand is often criticized for arbitrarily denying legitimacy to the use of artificial means, i.e. devices produced by humans, in the field of sex, but not elsewhere. Why is it right and proper, say, to use certain pills in order to prevent disease, but wrong and improper to use certain other pills in order to prevent untimely pregnancy? This is all there is to it, since the deliberate intention to avoid conception is present in the use of the rhythm method no less than in the use of any other method of birth control.[15] This criticism is inaccurate and unfair, for the moral discrimination criticized is not based on the distinction between the natural and the artificial, but rather on the distinction between the intrinsic character of "safe days" intercourse and that of contraceptive intercourse. Since what are being judged are human acts, they ought to be considered as intentional, rather than merely physical acts. Now the description of an act of contraceptive intercourse as an intentional act must include the intention to avoid conception, as this intention is an integral part of the act. This is true whatever physical or chemical device is employed in order to avoid conception, and whether this is done before, in the course of, or after the act of intercourse. In an act of "safe days" intercourse, on the other hand, the intention to avoid conception is not an integral part of the act, as it would have been if the act itself had been interfered with; it is rather a *further* intention with which the act is performed, and which merely determines its timing.[16] Still, this does not seem to remove the problem. If "safe days" intercourse deliberately chosen with a view to avoiding conception is permissible, then the intention to avoid conception is not wrong in itself. But if so, it is not yet clear just why contraceptive intercourse should be condemned. As Jenny Teichman points out,

> the located difference is this. In safe-period sex a non-condemnable intention (to avoid generation) is a further intention, and in contraception a non-condemnable intention (to avoid generation) is embodied in the act (that is, makes it what it is). But how can an act which is *otherwise all right* be condemned on account of its embodying, as part of its intrinsic character, an intention which is *also all right*?[17]

These are problems peculiar to the most conservative, Catholic version of the procreation view of sex. This view is also plagued by some much more basic difficulties. Its main thesis is that we are to understand, evaluate, and morally circumscribe sex in terms of its purpose or function, which is procreation. But what does this thesis mean, and why should we accept it?

A purpose of X is always the purpose somebody has with regard to X; just whose purpose is it that sex should lead to procreation? Of course, in the traditional literature in which the procreation view of sex is presented and elaborated, the claim about its purpose is made within a theistic world-view, as a claim about God's purpose concerning human sexuality. Taken in this sense, the claim can have only a rather limited appeal, namely to the religious. And it is burdened with the usual difficulties of theistic ethics: How do we know what God's purposes are? And assuming we can find out what they are, just why are they his purposes? To take up the latter question first, if there is a reason why God has a certain purpose concerning our actions, then that reason is the ground of the value and binding power of that purpose, and appeals to God's authority are redundant. On the other hand, if the value and binding power of a purpose of God is based solely on the fact that it is God's purpose, that God has chosen it, without having a reason for the choice, we seem to be embracing an authoritarian ethics based on an arbitrary will. Moreover, we are committing ourselves to saying that we should be morally bound to do something completely different from what we hold ourselves to be morally bound to do, had God's arbitrary choice been different.

A standard way of propping up the claim that procreation is God's purpose with regard to human sexuality is to say that this is readily gathered if we just attend to nature. Nature is God's creation, and it reflects – as a whole and in its constituent parts – the design of its creator. Alternatively, the procreation view of sex can be disconnected from theism and advanced as a view suggested by nature itself, period. Procreation is simply the purpose nature has concerning human sexuality. The latter thesis would be considered by many as predicated on the dated, and discredited, teleological view of nature. But whether this claim is made within or without a theistic world-view, the idea that we can somehow discern the natural purpose of human sexual organs or sexual intercourse among humans from the facts of nature is not very helpful. If the relevant facts are what as a matter of fact most commonly happens in nature, then, as Joseph Fletcher says, they seem to undermine, rather than support, the main tenet of the sex as procreation view:

> . . .By the principle of statistical preponderance, the opposite belief – that nature does *not* intend conception – is more

tenable! In the 28-day menstrual cycle, only about six days are fertile and 22 are infertile. A woman can conceive, generally, from the ages of 14 to 50, or 36 years of 13 cycles each, giving 2,808 fertile days in the ovulation periods of her life as compared to 10,296 infertile days. Normal sexuality continues until about 66, thus adding 5,840 infertile days to the sexual span, which totals 18,944 days with only 2,808 of them, or 1 out of 7, fertile. If we grant that nature implants the sex drive and 'intends' intercourse ... and further that 'nature's intentions' are evident more in the rule than in the exception, it would follow that nature's purpose in sex is much more to contrive intercourse than conception.[18]

Finally, procreation is certainly not *the* purpose of human beings with regard to sex. They sometimes engage in sex with that purpose in mind, but more often than not they have sex although they do not or cannot intend it to result in conception, for purposes other than procreation. Sometimes they engage in sex while taking special measures to prevent procreation. Therefore, procreation is not *the* purpose of sex, since a purpose is always *somebody's* purpose, and there is nobody to whom this purpose can plausibly be ascribed as *the* purpose concerning sex.

The procreation view of sex does not fare much better if its main thesis is put in terms of function rather than purpose. How is the claim that procreation is the function of sex to be construed (other than as the claim that it is the purpose of sex, which I have just discussed)? It could be taken either as saying that procreation is (a) something proper to sex, or (b) something unique to sex, or (c) something that defines sex. Now (a) looks like a moral claim, (b) like an empirical claim, while (c) is a logical one. Neither (b) nor (c) are true, however; sex is not bound up with procreation, either empirically or logically. Sexual intercourse very often does not result in conception and procreation. On the other hand – although, of course, Augustine or Thomas Aquinas did not know that – procreation is possible without sexual intercourse, by means of artificial insemination. This means that (a) the moral claim that procreation is the right and proper result of sex, that sex ought to be geared toward procreation, cannot be supported either by (b) the empirical claim that procreation is unique to sex (which is how the Christian natural law tradition, epitomized in Thomas Aquinas, has tended to support it), or by (c) the logical claim that procreation defines sex.

17

(I am putting aside the well-known problems involved in attempts at drawing a moral conclusion from non-moral premises, which would have to be addressed at this point if either of the two non-moral claims about sex were true.) Why, then, should we accept it?

Here the argument typically takes the line exemplified by Peter A. Bertocci's thesis that there is an "inner progression of love" which begins with sex and leads up, successively, to love, marriage, and family complete with children.[19] Bertocci's argument has two stages: he offers a critique of sex not bound up with love, marriage and children; against this background, he tries to show that there is indeed a progression from sex to family. Sex pursued solely for its own sake is not progressive and enriching: it leads to nothing beyond itself. Nor is it very successful on its own terms: it is not truly, permanently satisfying. The sexual hedonist is doomed to an endless, ultimately frustrating and depressing search for novelty and variety. In this connection, Bertocci remarks:

> Many sexual perverts are products of this chase for new forms of pleasure. They teach us that sexual expression for its own sake brings diminishing returns. I am not, of course, trying to say that every incontinent person becomes a sex pervert, but he invites trouble for himself and others when he tries to find in sex what sex as such cannot give him.[20]

Moreover, when sexual satisfaction is sought for its own sake, one's actions are self-seeking, and one relates to others in instrumental, exploitative ways.

But sex can, and should, have a different meaning and role in human life. If it is allowed to express and develop its distinctively human potential, sex will evolve into love, love into marriage, and marriage into full-fledged family. Each of the first three stages of this process requires the following one to protect and nourish it. "Sex without love, love without marriage, and marriage without creative commitments to children (or the equivalent) are in constant danger of vanishing away."[21] What is no less important, each of the earlier stages needs the following one in order to develop into the best, the richest it can be. Finally, letting sexual desire lead us beyond itself proves to be wise from a more comprehensive hedonistic point of view too: "persons enjoy deeper, more lasting, and more profound satisfaction when the normal experience of sex lust is not primarily an end in itself but a symbolic expression of other values."[22]

The response to this can be three-pronged. One might wonder whether all Bertocci's empirical claims concerning sex, love, marriage and procreation are true. Each of the connections that make up his "progression of love" has been questioned. It has been argued that sex not bound up with love and all the expectations and commitments love involves is actually better *as sex*.[23] The institution of marriage has been criticized, among other things, as detrimental to, rather than supportive of, love.[24] Finally, the wisdom of having children has been questioned, if personal happiness is what one is after.[25] It should be noted that Bertocci himself is more circumspect on the last stage of his progression than on the preceding ones. His claim is that if a marriage is to be stable and secure, and if it is to be as good and flourishing as it could possibly be, the spouses ought to have a commitment to somebody or something beyond their own relationship. Now children are an obvious candidate for such a commitment, but there are certainly other possibilities; indeed, as we have seen, Bertocci speaks of a commitment to children "or the equivalent". If so, then procreation is not necessary after all for stable, healthy, fulfilling and flourishing sexual experience, love, and marriage. The last and crucial link in his chain binding sex, love, marriage and procreation turns out to be much too weak.

But even if, for the sake of argument, we were to grant all the empirical claims that prop up Bertocci's progression thesis, the case for the procreation view of sex would still not have been made out. For that view is a *moral* view, a view meant to generate a large set of *moral* requirements and prohibitions. And all that Bertocci's progression from sex to love to marriage to family actually tells us is that if we are to make the most of what human sexuality has to offer – both in the sense of getting the most out of it, and letting it bring out the most of what we have it in us to be – we should not pursue sex solely for its own sake. We should rather let it evolve into something beyond itself, generate experiences and involve us in relationships of a different order. Now this sort of guidance is merely prudential; there is nothing specifically moral about it. And those who ignore or reject it and choose to conduct their sex lives in a different way may be making a mistaken or unwise decision, but not necessarily an immoral one.

It might be objected that this response assumes too narrow an understanding of morality as nothing but a set of injunctions and prohibitions, rights and duties. Surely there is more to it: surely it also includes various conceptions of the human good, ideals of human flourishing. And Bertocci's account of sex should be seen as one such conception, one such ideal, relating specifically to human sexuality. It tells us that by letting the experience of sex evolve in accordance with its inner possibilities into something larger, more lasting, more fulfilling – a loving relationship, a marriage, a family – we will be achieving something of greater value than sexual satisfaction pure and simple. And the significance of that is not only prudential, but also moral.

However, if this is the true import of Bertocci's argument for the procreation view of sex, then we should be clear that it does nothing to support that view as it is usually understood: as a view that offers guidance at the basic level of morality, that confines legitimate, morally acceptable sex within the narrow bounds described above, while pronouncing every other type of sexual behavior improper and impermissible. Unlike moral rules and prohibitions, which apply generally and are backed up by moral condemnation and other sanctions, ideals are a matter of personal choice, and while those who live up to them may be praised, those who do not need not, indeed cannot be condemned. Accordingly, the prohibitions that make up the traditional view of sex as something that must be bound up with procreation are no longer to be considered as applying to all and sundry. Those who go against them may at most be said to be missing a worthwhile and rewarding option. But that option is admitted to be but one among several coexisting and legitimate options concerning human sexuality: merely *a* sexual ideal, not *the* ethics of sex.

3

SEX AND LOVE

Sex with love

While there is no dearth of philosophical literature expounding, elaborating and defending the procreation view of sex, it is only recently that one of its main competitors, the account of sex as bound up with love, has been given a detailed, systematic, and philosophically sophisticated account. I am referring to Roger Scruton's book *Sexual Desire*,[1] which will be the subject or the point of departure of most of the discussion in this chapter.

Scruton sets out to develop a philosophical theory of human sexuality and at least an outline of sexual ethics that is to be based on it. The emphasis is on the word "human", and that determines the philosophical nature of the enterprise. If the aim were to describe and explain animal sexuality, the proper approach would be that of science. But no scientific concepts and methods can capture the distinctively human experience. For that we need philosophy: we need to deploy the concepts and methods of phenomenological description and conceptual analysis. Only such concepts and methods can help us towards understanding what it is to undergo sexual arousal, to feel sexual desire, to experience erotic love and to engage in sexual intercourse, as human beings.

The first three are the basic phenomena of human sexuality. They are also distinctive to it. Scruton's main thesis is that they are all "purely human phenomena"; more specifically, that "they belong to that realm of reciprocal response which is mediated by the concept of the person, and which is available only to beings who possess and are motivated by that concept."[2]

While these claims might be thought innocuous as far as erotic love is concerned, they are much less compelling with regard to the other, more basic sexual phenomena: arousal and desire. Thus arousal tends to be described in scientific texts as a rather simple matter: as a bodily state common to humans and animals, and characterized by a certain tension in the body and its sexual parts in particular. This tension is released through sexual intercourse; the release brings sexual pleasure, which is for the most part localized in these parts too. But matters cannot be so simple; if they were, the phenomenon of sexual frustration would be very difficult to explain. For this understanding of arousal suggests that sexual desire is nothing but desire for a type of pleasure that can be achieved by masturbation as well as by intercourse.

When talking about humans and their pleasures, however, we need to distinguish two types of pleasure. Some pleasures are simply pleasures of sensation, like that of a cold drink after some physical exertion in the summer sun; others are "intentional", meaning *directed at* an object, like the pleasure of looking at something beautiful. Pleasures of the former type are located in the body; they are passive, something we experience rather than do; and they are not intentional. They are common to humans and animals. Pleasures of the latter type cannot be located so simply; they are active, i.e. they are something we actually do, rather than merely undergo; and they are much more complex since, unlike pleasures of mere sensation, they also involve thoughts. Thus they are distinctively human.

Now while the sexual act performed by humans does involve pleasures of mere sensation, there is much more to it. It is not mere experience, but an activity involving intentional pleasure and thoughts pertaining to it. This has important implications for our understanding of sexual arousal:

> ... It would be quite extraordinary if the caresses of one party were regarded by the other as the accidental causes of a pleasurable sensation, which might have been caused in some other way. Sexual arousal is a response, but not a response to a stimulus that could be fully described merely as the cause of a sensation. It is a response, at least in part, to a thought, where the thought refers to 'what is going on' between myself and another. ... The thought involves the following idea: It is *he* who is alertly touching me, intending my recognition of his act ... The subject's pleasurable sensation is entirely taken up by this thought and ... projected by means of it towards the other person. This is brought out vividly by the possibility of deception. Someone may discover that the fingers which are touching

him are not, as he thought, those of his lover, but those of an interloper. His pleasure (in the normal case) instantly turns to disgust....³

When aroused by another, one does not respond merely to his or her body, but to him or her as a person. The other's body is the focus of arousal, not simply as body, but rather as the embodiment of the particular person he or she is. Moreover, sexual arousal does not point beyond that individual; it is not transferable to another, who might do just as well.

This summary of Scruton's account of sexual arousal already adumbrates the main elements of his description of sexual desire. Sexual desire is a personal attitude. Now personal attitudes are for the most part directed to persons as such, i.e. they abstract from their embodiment. Desire is one of the few exceptions:

> Although people are essentially embodied for us, and although we always respond to them *as* embodied, it is only occasionally that their embodiment is *itself* the object of our interest, just as it is only occasionally that I am interested in the buildings of my university, rather than in its institutional procedure. It is only in desire, in certain tender forms of love, and in the tender hatred of sadism, that you must be, for me, through and through revealed in the flesh that harbours you.⁴

The relation between a person and that person's body is notoriously difficult to analyze. It is a relation both instrumental and constitutive: one *has* one's body, but one also *is* one's body. When talking of embodiment, we must keep in mind both aspects, and the inevitable tension between them.

Like the sexual arousal which gives rise to it, then, sexual desire is intentional, directed at an object. Its object is another person as embodied. Moreover, and most importantly, this intentionality of sexual desire is "an inherently individualizing intentionality": its object is not just *any* other person, or *any* other person of a certain type, as embodied. It is always directed to *the particular person in his or her individuality*.

> ...Whatever one wants to do *with* the object of desire, his 'being who he is' (in some individualising application of that phrase) enters essentially into a description of what is

wanted. It is Elizabeth or Albert who is wanted, and not just any person, answering to whatever description.[5]

But what, exactly, *is* wanted of the embodied person one desires? Not mere orgasm – the scientific approach to sexual desire, exemplified by Freud and by reports of Kinsey and other sexologists, misses both its interpersonal character and its essentially individualizing orientation. If we are to answer this question, Scruton argues, we must attend to "the course of sexual desire" in its several stages.

It is not easy, he says, to state what the person I desire sexually ought to do in order to satisfy me and my desire. To be sure, sexual desire, emerging from arousal, tends to focus on the other person's distinctively sexual parts. However, they are not significant in themselves. They are "interesting only on account of [their] dramatic role. A woman is interested in her lover's sexual parts because she wishes to be penetrated by *him*, and to feel him feeling pleasure inside her. The penis is the avatar of his presence, and the ground that it crosses in entering her is at once overrun and occupied by the man himself."[6]

Sexual desire does, indeed, aim at sex. But this should not be taken to mean that it simply aims at sexual intercourse, complete with its consummation in orgasm. Its aim is "union with the other" as the particular individual he or she is. This, on Scruton's analysis, involves two things: mutual arousal and mutual embodiment. Obviously, it all begins with arousal. But if not initially, then at a further stage, sexual arousal is, or should be, mutual: one is aroused not only by the presence of the other, by the other's body, but also by the other's arousal directed at oneself. Sexual desire is after reciprocal arousal, arousal recognized and responded to by arousal. The parties to this mutual arousal are embodied persons. Each seeks to impress their own embodiment upon the other, to reach and know the other as embodied, and to see themselves as embodied, aroused and desiring through the eyes of the other embodied, aroused and desiring person.

To be sure, "the aim of sexual desire does not stop short at 'union'. There is the further and developing project of sexual pleasure." But this does not mean that this pleasure, and orgasm as its peak, is the ultimate end of desire. "Although the experience is all-important, it is not part of the aim or project of desire. For it has no root in the thought upon which desire is founded, and plays no part in the continuation of the aim of union. In a very important sense, it is an *interruption* of congress, from which the subject must recover…"[7]

24

There are two further stages of "the course of desire": intimacy and love. The "project of intimacy" – of particular closeness, sympathy, and concern that sets the persons involved apart from everyone else – is suggested already in the first glances of desire, and naturally (although not inevitably) evolves from it. Finally, desire naturally (but, again, not inevitably) finds its fulfilment in love:

> Just as sexual pleasure tends to intimacy, so does intimacy tend to love – to a sense of commitment founded in the mutuality of desire. For the person who is compromised by his desire for another has acquired a crucial vulnerability: the vulnerability of one who has been overcome in his body by the embodied presence of another. This vulnerability is finally assuaged only in love ... It is through studying erotic love, therefore, that we shall be able to characterise in full the intentionality of desire.[8]

Sexual desire is often sharply distinguished from love, indeed contrasted with it, both conceptually and in terms of their respective significance and value. How, then, can they be integrated in this way? Scruton argues that desire and acts that express and satisfy it can express love too. They can do that since sexual contact has the same epistemic character as sexual arousal: it can be *felt* to express erotic love, and therefore it can also be *meant* to do so.

As for the "course of love", Scruton traces it as a process of "mutual self-building" in which love grows, while desire withers with time, eventually to be replaced by a love that is no longer erotic, but rather anchored in trust and companionship.

These, then, are the main tenets of Scruton's philosophy of sex. They provide the basis for his account of a wide array of sexual phenomena and for his theory of sexual morality.

Among the sexual phenomena Scruton interprets in the light of his understanding of the nature of sexual desire, two in particular are important in the present context: obscenity and perversion. Obscenity does not reside in our sexuality – our bodies, sexual parts, or sexual acts in themselves – but in the way they are seen or represented. It is a way of seeing or representing them that dissociates them from the person embodied in them, and focuses on their "fleshy reality". By doing so, obscenity denies the individualizing intentionality of sexual desire distinctive of human sexuality, and therefore can be likened to zoophilia. It can also be likened to necrophilia. For "in obscenity, attention is taken away from embodiment towards the body; the body rises up and inundates our perception, and in this nightmare the spirit goes under, as it goes under in death."[9] Similarly, sexual perversion is "all deviation from the unity of animal and interpersonal relation", "the complete or partial failure to recognise, in and through desire, the personal existence of the other."[10]

One of the things Scruton shares with the traditional sexual ethics, discussed in the preceding chapter, is the view that "sexual perversion" is a morally loaded term. Thus his conception of perversion is an important link connecting his theory of sexual desire with his account of sexual morality. This account, too, looks quite traditional in most of its prescriptions and proscriptions. Indeed, one of the express aims of Scruton's book is to provide a specifically sexual morality, similar to the traditional sexual ethics in its contents, but with different foundations: based on his theory of sexual desire, and on an Aristotelian approach to ethics focusing on a conception of human flourishing and on virtues which make possible, or express, that flourishing.

In such an ethics, of course, the pride of place belongs to the capacity for erotic love. The claim that this is *the* sexual virtue generates a series of judgments about other sexual virtues, such as chastity, modesty, and fidelity, and such sexual institutions as prostitution or marriage. The latter is presented as the ultimate destination of the "course of desire": human sexual union is said to "crave for its institutional realisation".[11] The same claim also generates judgments about sexual vices, i.e. habits that jeopardize the capacity for erotic love. Thus it turns out that "a whole section of traditional sexual morality must be upheld."[12] Actually, this is an understatement; for Scruton does not endorse a mere section, but almost all of that morality. He does not underwrite the traditional rejection of non-procreative sex in general, and contraception in particular, and is also willing to allow for oral sex, at least between heterosexual partners and when performed as an integral part of "the course of normal desire". But all the other prohibitions that make up the traditional sexual morality – including those on masturbation, adultery, promiscuity, prostitution, pornography, and homosexuality – are explicitly or implicitly endorsed.

Objections to the sex with love view

The above is a mere outline of Scruton's detailed, rich, philosophically sophisticated and often provocative statement of the view that distinctively human sex is bound up with love. But even an outline should be enough to expose at least the most important of its many difficulties.

The first, which is the root of most others, has to do with Scruton's claim that sexual arousal and desire are characterized by individualizing intentionality: that they aim at the unique, irreplaceable individuality of the other person, as present in, and accessible through, his or her body. Is that true of sexual arousal and sexual desire as such? The phenomenon of unfocused sexual desire, sexual hunger not directed at anyone in particular but felt as hunger and desire none the less, would seem to present an obvious counterexample to Scruton's central thesis. Scruton attempts to deal with it by interpreting it as something less than, and merely pointing in the direction of, sexual arousal and desire. Arousal may originate "in highly generalised thoughts, which flit libidinously from object to object. But when these thoughts have concentrated into the experience of arousal their generality is put aside; it is then the other who counts, and his particular embodiment."[13] As for "the sailor who storms ashore, with the one thought 'woman' in his body," he actually does not *desire a woman*, whatever he may be thinking and saying. We can understand the state he is in only in the light of "the transition that occurs when the woman is found and he is set on the path of satisfaction. For now he has found the woman whom he wants ...Until that moment, he desired *no* woman. His condition was one of desiring to desire."[14]

This is surely contrived and implausible. We are much closer to the truth of the matter with W.J. Earle, who argues that it is just the other way around:

> Instead of sex being *ab initio* and naturally personal and secondarily subject to a process of corruption, debasement, perversion, degradation, described as 'depersonalization', sexual desires never have the whole or integral persons as their objects. Sexual desires are always part-orientated though we try, because we are held captive by the myth of personal sex, to glue our desires to persons. The glue we use we manufacture out of a confusion of sexual desires with genuinely person-requiring relations like love, fidelity, and loyalty ...[15]

By making sexual arousal and desire essentially individualizing, Scruton sets them on their way to the later stages of his "course of desire" – intimacy and erotic love. But in doing so, he pays a considerable price: he ends up with an account that is oddly out of touch with a wide range of admittedly not very attractive, but nevertheless real and all too human sexual experience to be found in our culture: the type of sexual experience sought by people who hang out in bars or on street corners in wait for a pick-up, go to sex-shows, resort to prostitutes, or peruse pornography. And it is equally out of touch with much, or most, sexual experience of many pre-literate cultures, or of more developed but strongly patriarchal cultures where marriage is typically polygamous.[16]

At this point, Scruton might bring up his illustration of the irreplaceability of the particular other in sexual arousal and desire I have already cited. But that illustration cannot help much, since it is question-begging. One is indeed put off by discovering that the caressing hand is not the hand of one's lover, as one thought, but rather of an interloper. But that is precisely because one had expected to be touched by *one's lover*; the individualizing intentionality is already built into the situation. If this sort of thing were to happen at a sex orgy, however, the reaction would more likely be one of added excitement, heightened pleasure and the like. Scruton also finds it incomprehensible that somebody could be aroused by one person, and then be capable of having sexual intercourse with another. But that is a phenomenon fairly well known in quite a few cultures, including our own.

Of course, Scruton might respond to all this by saying that sexual experiences involving replaceability of this sort, and sexual experiences that do not accord with his model of individualizing intentionality in general, are not cases of sexual arousal and desire, but of something else – say, cases of mere animal-like sexual stirring and appetite. This would not sit well with his proclaimed aim of providing a phenomenological account of human sexuality: it would suggest that his enterprise is purely normative, rather than, as he maintains, descriptive first and normative second, insofar as the description generates certain norms. It would suggest that what he is doing is not so much presenting a phenomenological description of human sexual arousal and desire, but rather putting forward their persuasive definitions. Charles L. Stevenson, who introduced the term and provided the pioneering analysis of the procedure, pointed out that persuasive definitions are characteristically indicated by the application of adjectives such as "true" or "real" to the definiendum.[17]

And we do find Scruton occasionally speaking of "true" sexual arousal or desire, rather than of sexual arousal or desire *simpliciter*. That, in itself, need not be considered a flaw; persuasive definitions have their proper place and point. But, when offered above the counter, at least, such definitions are supported by argument showing the advantage of the proposed change in the way we speak about whatever is at issue. However, Scruton would be in a position to offer such an argument only after expressly changing the aim of his whole enterprise. Even then he would be at some disadvantage. Persuasive definitions obviously have to be very selective; but Scruton's persuasive definitions of "sexual arousal" and "sexual desire" might be thought unacceptably so: much too much culturally and historically parochial. For they would relegate beyond the pale much of what usually counts as sexual arousal and desire in our own culture, as well as most of what counts as arousal and desire in quite a few other cultures.

A related difficulty in Scruton's argument has to do with a certain equivocation of the term "interpersonal". What does it mean to say that human sexual experience is interpersonal? In one sense, the claim is innocuous: humans are persons, and in sex, like in everything else, this fact is in some way taken into account. Thus humans are, at least typically, interested in sexual access to other humans, rather than physical objects, or animals, or inflatable sex dolls, or the "fucking machines" Scruton mentions.[18] And in sex, like in everything else, there is a moral requirement not to ignore the fact that humans are persons, not to treat them as something other than, less than, persons. This requirement is sometimes termed the principle of respect for persons. But it is a different and not at all innocuous claim that sexual arousal and desire aim at the other human being as the particular, unique, irreplaceable individual he or she is, and that sexual interest in another human being that is not "interpersonal" in this latter sense is somehow less than fully human, indeed animal-like. And it is a different and quite problematic thesis that sexual experience that does not involve this individualizing intentionality is degrading and morally flawed. Scruton seems to be suggesting that in sex one has two options: *either* one "depersonalizes" the other, reduces the other to the mere "fleshy reality" of his or her body, virtually relates to him or her as to a sex doll or a "fucking machine", *or* one approaches the other's body as the embodiment of the unique, irreplaceable person he or she is, in a way that naturally evolves into intimacy and love.

But Scruton can face us with this choice only by sliding from the claim that in sex a human being relates, or should relate, to the other human being as *a* person, to the claim that he or she relates, or should relate, to the other human being as *the* particular, unique, irreplacable person the other is. In sex, as elsewhere, one is indeed morally required to treat the other as a person, i.e. to take into account in the appropriate way the other's thoughts, feelings, expectations, wishes, interests, and to ground one's intercourse with the other on the other's consent and co-operation, rather than on deception or coercion. But surely one can do that, while engaging the other with a view to a pleasurable sexual encounter and nothing more, and relating to the other as a sexually attractive partner and nothing more, without any hint of progress to the higher stages of Scruton's "course of desire" – that is, while relating to the other in an admittedly partial and instrumental way. Provided one does that with the other's informed and freely given consent, one is relating to the other as *a* person, and thus complying with the principle of respect for persons, although one is not engaging the other as *the* total, unique person he or she is.

The "course of desire" as portrayed by Scruton might remind us of Peter A. Bertocci's thesis about the "inner progression of love" I discussed in Chapter 2.[19] The similarities are clear, not only with regard to the main stages (although Scruton does without Bertocci's last stage of procreation), but also with regard to the work the thesis is expected to do. Both philosophers focus on an important possibility of human sexuality, and present their account of it as an account of human sexuality, period – and as one that generates a specifically sexual morality. But human sexuality offers other possibilities, no less human and equally morally legitimate, although, perhaps, less valuable from the point of view of certain conceptions of human flourishing. One might agree that, say, human sexual experience as described by Scruton – human sexual experience that relates to the other's body as to the embodiment of the whole unique personality of the other, and naturally evolves into the lasting commitment of intimacy, love and marriage – is indeed richer, more fulfilling, more worthwhile than casual sex. If one does, one will have reason to think well of those who live up to this notion of sex; they will be seen as living up to an ideal. But one will have no ground to condemn those who do not. For ideals cannot be legislated for universal guidance; they cannot generate moral prohibitions and cannot ground condemnation of those who choose to do otherwise.

This, however, is not how Scruton understands his account of human sexuality. Thus he maintains that "every developed form of sexual desire will tend to reach beyond the present encounter to a project of inner union with its object"[20] – a claim that is either trivial (if "developed form of sexual desire" is defined in terms of such a tendency), or clearly false (if such a persuasive definition is not assumed). And he makes it quite clear at the outset that what his theory of sexual desire is meant to ground is not merely a sexual ideal, but a robust sexual morality of *condemnation*: a sexual morality that is very close to the traditional sexual ethics in its contents and condemns, just as the latter does, a wide array of sexual behavior, including homosexual intercourse, fornication, and masturbation, "even though we all have an urge to do these things, and even though there may be no God who forbids them."[21]

Sex without love

Attempts to bind sex to love, either conceptually, or morally, or both, are very much an uphill struggle, because the combination does not seem to be an obvious and necessary one. On the contrary, one might argue, as Alan Goldman, for instance, has done, that such a combination must be plagued by an internal tension, since the two are quite dissimilar in several respects. Love tends towards permanence, at least in intent, while sexual desire is often fleeting. Love is usually considered exclusive, while sexual desire has often been characterized as tending to variety. The experiences and joys of love are cumulative, while the pleasures of sex are repetitive. Love is other-regarding, while sexual desire is basically self-regarding. Finally, there is a difference in importance: while the briefness of sexual pleasures contributes to their intensity, it also places them on the periphery of most conceptions of rational or good life, while love can, and often does, have a central place in such a conception. There is casual sex, but love is never casual.[22] And there are good practical reasons for attending to the differences and tensions between the two: "recognition of a clear distinction between sex and love in society would help avoid disastrous marriages which result from adolescent confusion of the two when sexual desire is mistaken for permanent love, and would weaken damaging jealousies which arise in marriages in relation to passing sexual desires."[23]

Being clear about this, however, need not lead us to embrace the facile view of sexual desire as necessarily inferior to love in all respects, and morally suspect as well. To take the latter point first, sexual desire not bound up with love – also termed "lust" – is often portrayed as cold, selfish, inconsiderate, manipulative and exploitative. That may provide an appropriately sordid background for celebration of sex with love, but is not at all an accurate portrayal. Love and lust are much more judiciously compared by those who, like Hume, can see kindness and good will in both – obviously, much stronger, more comprehensive, and lasting in the former, but "at least a momentary kindness" in the latter.[24] Furthermore, the moral picture is much more complex than those given to extolling love and denigrating lust like to suggest. As A.H. Lesser puts it,

> the problem is that the presence or absence even of genuine concern, tenderness and commitment does not guarantee the presence or absence of selfishness and exploitation. Lust is not by nature self-sacrificing, as love is; but it is not inevitably selfish, in the sense of disregarding the rights and feelings of others – as a desire, it is neutral, and it may or may not be satisfied in a selfish way. Genuine love can have a very selfish element – a desire to control and dominate another person spiritually in ways that are much more exploitative than the mere temporary use of his or her body. … Sexuality motivated by lust can still be harmless or beneficial; and love can lead to all kinds of cruelty and dishonesty.[25]

Moreover, there is no need and no justification for denigrating sex without love in non-moral terms, as a type of human experience, the way adherents of the sex with love view tend to do. They typically point out the differences between sex with and without love. The former is extolled as a distinctively human, complex, rich and fruitful experience, and a matter of great importance; the latter is described as merely casual, a one-dimensional, barren experience that satisfies only for a short while and belongs to our animal nature. These differences are taken to show that sex with love is valuable, while loveless sex is not. This kind of reasoning has the following structure:

A is much better than B.
Therefore, B is no good at all.

In addition to being logically flawed, this line of reasoning, if it were to be applied in areas other than sex, would prove quite difficult to follow. For one thing, all but the very rich among us would die of hunger; for only the very rich can afford to take *all* their meals at the fanciest restaurants.[26]

Of course, B can be good, even if it is much less good than A. Loveless sex is a case in point. Moreover, other things being equal, it is better to be able to enjoy both loving and loveless sex than only the former. A person who enjoyed sex as part of loving relationships but was completely incapable of enjoying casual sex would seem to be missing out on something. To be sure, when adherents of the sex with love view reject casual sex, they also claim that other things are not equal: that a person who indulges in loveless sex thereby somehow damages, and ultimately destroys, his or her capacity for experiencing sex as an integral part of a loving relationship. This is a straightforward empirical claim about human psychology. But, to the best of my knowledge, it is merely a popular piece of armchair psychology, rather than a psychological claim that has been established by research. Thus we have no good reason to accept it.

It has also been argued that sex without love is actually better, *as sex*, than sex as part of a loving relationship. That is the argument of Russell Vannoy's book *Sex without Love: A Philosophical Exploration*.[27] Vannoy attempts to show that erotic love is burdened by serious limitations and inner tensions, and that sex, if we are to make the most of what it has to offer, is best enjoyed when unencumbered with love. I do not want to take up this issue, though. It could be properly discussed only by looking into the nature, significance and value of love; and these large questions are beyond the scope of this book.

4

SEX AS LANGUAGE

A body language

Other philosophies of sex discussed in this book will strike the reader as quite familiar, at least so far as the central ideas and values are concerned. They are attempts at philosophical articulation of ideas and values that have been important parts of the Western moral tradition, of Western culture, for centuries, if not millennia: sex in the context of marriage and procreation; sex bound up with love; sex as a source of a distinctive type of pleasure. The view of sex discussed in this chapter differs in this respect – although it brings to the fore certain aspects of human sexual experience, it cannot be seen as a philosophical restatement of an established ethical or cultural tradition. It is rather the philosopher's philosophy of sex. Its main thesis is that sex among humans is best understood as a type of language.

This view is advanced in two papers by Robert Solomon. In developing his understanding of human sexuality, Solomon builds on the discussion of sex in Jean-Paul Sartre's *Being and Nothingness* and Thomas Nagel's "Sexual Perversion". On Sartre's account, what is at work in sexual desire and sexual relations is a search and competition for freedom, recognition, power. One generally attempts to exact from the other recognition of one's freedom by subduing the other. In sex, the subjection of the other takes the form of trapping the other in their flesh, reducing the other to flesh, a mere object. The means one employs in order to achieve this reduction of the other is one's own flesh. The other, of course, has the same project. Sexual encounter is thus construed as interpersonal communication with the body as the medium and mutual subjugation and degradation as the message.[1]

In his seminal paper "Sexual Perversion", Thomas Nagel draws

34

on Sartre's discussion, and in particular on his notion of "a double reciprocal incarnation",[2] in order to develop an account of human sexual encounter as a complex, multi-layered process of mutual perception and arousal. The object of sexual arousal and desire is not simply the other's body, but rather the other's arousal and desire as expressed in his or her body. Moreover, sexual desire is "a desire that one's partner be aroused by the recognition of one's desire that he or she be aroused."[3] So it turns out that sexual desire has a structure similar to that of the phenomenon of meaning as analyzed by H.P. Grice, where one intends to produce a belief or some other effect in the other by bringing about the other's recognition of one's intention to produce that effect.[4]

Against the background of Sartre's and Nagel's discussion of distinctively human sexuality, Robert Solomon has developed a full-fledged theory of sex as language.[5] While acknowledging the importance of the insights of his predecessors, he also points out the limitations of their views. Nagel says next to nothing about the contents of interpersonal communication that takes place in sex. He speaks of arousal, but that is too broad a term; we are told nothing about arousal as a specifically sexual experience. "Nagel's notion of 'arousal' and 'interpersonal awareness' gives us an outline of the grammar of the communication model, but no semantics."[6] Sartre does address the semantics, but what he offers is much too narrow and negative. "[His] notion of sexuality, taken seriously, would be enough to keep us out of bed for a month. Surely … something has been left out of account, for example, the two-person *Mitsein* that Sartre himself suggests in the same book."[7]

Solomon also rejects the view of sex as bound up with procreation. It cannot give a plausible account of sexual behavior that is independent of procreation, and sometimes even includes precautions against it. The hedonist view fares no better. It fails to explain why humans, who are not basically pleasure-seeking beings, accord sex such importance in their lives. Moreover, if sex is primarily about pleasure,

> the appropriate question is why we bother, given the enormous amount of effort and the continuous threats to our egos and our health, to attempt to engage in sex mutually instead of in solitude and in the safety and convenience of our own rooms. On this account it would seem that our sexual paradigm ought to be masturbation, and sexual release with other people an unnecessary complication.[8]

These crucial traits of sex among human beings – its great importance in human life, and the fact that it is something humans do or
experience with others – are best explained when sex is seen as a type
of body language: a language in which we communicate to others our
feelings and attitudes about them, and about ourselves too.

What feelings? Solomon's examples include gentleness and
affection; mutual recognition, "being-with", trust; anger and
resentment; shame, jealousy, possessiveness; superiority and depen-
dence; domination and passivity. Such interpersonal feelings and
attitudes are expressed in sexual behavior far more naturally,
succintly, and often elegantly too, than it would be possible by mere
words. Verbal expression of such feelings and attitudes is always
abstract, and often also clumsy.

One might be puzzled by the fact that one particular feeling does
not appear among Solomon's examples of feelings and attitudes apt
to be expressed in the body language of sex: that of love. Surely love
should be topping the list? Solomon maintains that it should not
appear on the list at all, for two reasons. Sexual attraction and
involvement need not be bound up with love:

> One may love another person with whom he or she is sexu-
> ally involved, but there are any number of attitudes he or
> she might take toward the person to whom he or she is
> sexually attracted, among which, unfortunately, hate, fear,
> resentment, anger, jealousy, insecurity, mastery, and compe-
> tition are probably far more common and more powerful
> than the rare and delicate threads of love and respect.[9]

On the other hand, when there is the feeling of love, it is not best
expressed sexually, since its sexual expression can hardly be distinguished from the sexual expression of some other feelings and
attitudes.[10]

The view of sex as language explains the two important facts
about sex mentioned above that elude the hedonist. If sex is a means
of communication, then it is an interpersonal activity. That explains
why mutual touch and intercourse, rather than masturbation, are
paradigmatic. And if sex is our best means of expressing feelings
and attitudes about others, and about ourselves, that are both highly
important and very difficult to express in words, that explains the
importance it has in our lives.

Having rejected the hedonist view of sex, Solomon nevertheless wants to acknowledge the hedonic aspect of sex. He does so by predicating it on the expressive character of sex:

> Whatever else sexuality might be and for whatever purposes it might be used or abused, it is first of all language. ... It can be enjoyable, not just on account of its phonetics, which are neither enjoyable nor meaningful in themselves, but because of *what* is said. One enjoys not just the tender caress but the message it carries; and one welcomes a painful thrust or bite not because of masochism but because of the meaning, in context, that it conveys. Most sexologists ... commit the McLuhanesque fallacy of confusing the medium with the message.[11]

These, then, are the main points of the understanding of sex as language. It shifts the emphasis in our thinking about sexuality from its physical and sensual aspects of reproduction and pleasure to interpersonal relations, roles, feelings, attitudes, and their expression in sex, by means of sex, as a language of the body. Sex is essentially a type of language: its grammar delineated by the body, the touch and the movement providing the phonetics, the gesture being the unit of meaningfulness, the bodily equivalent of a sentence. In terms of its contents, the view of sex as language is quite unlike other views of sex. In terms of its import, however, it is closer to the hedonist account than to the other two. For, unlike the procreation view and the view of sex as bound up with love, discussed in the preceding chapters, and like the hedonist account to be discussed in the next chapter, the view of sex as a type of language is offered as a way of understanding sex that has no particular moral implications. Understood as a body language, sex as such has no moral significance, positive or negative. What we will want to say on any particular sexual experience or interaction will depend on just what is being said in sex, by means of sex. But the fact that it is being said by means of sex is morally neutral in itself.

Objections to the language view

The plausibility of an understanding of sex as a type of language will greatly depend on the view of language that is assumed. One of the criticisms of Robert Solomon's account of sex as language has been that his view of language is seriously flawed, and that this inevitably vitiates his understanding of sex. That is the thrust of

Hugh T. Wilder's critique.[12] Solomon assumes a much too narrow instrumentalist and phonocentric view of language; as a result, his account of sex is one-sided and unconvincing. Its one-sidedness and insufficiency is displayed most conspicuously in its failure to account for the clearly sexual character of masturbation.

What Solomon has to say on masturbation is indeed quite peculiar. In his first paper, he says that it is "like talking to yourself", an activity "clearly secondary to sexuality in its broader interpersonal context".[13] In his second, more detailed discussion, Solomon argues that since there can be no private language, and sex is a type of language, there can be no private sex in the relevant sense, so that masturbation should be seen as "at best a borderline case". It represents "an inability or a refusal to say what one wants to say, going through the effort of expression without an audience, like writing to someone and then putting the letter in a drawer". Accordingly, "it is, in an important sense, self-denial."[14]

Solomon assumes that interpersonal communication is the essential purpose of language. He then claims that it is also the essential purpose of sex; thus sex turns out to be a type of language. Since masturbation does not have this purpose, it is considered not fully sexual, a borderline case at best. However, interpersonal communication is not the essential purpose of language: we talk to ourselves, use language to fill out embarassing silences, or to play a part in a ritual. These are perfectly regular linguistic activities, although the first is not an instance of interpersonal communication, while the second and third are not cases of communication at all, actual or intended.

In addition to being much too narrowly instrumentalist, the view of language Solomon uncritically assumes is flawed in that it is phonocentric: language is conceived as spoken rather than written. When talking about language, Solomon is actually talking only about speech. This, too, forces Solomon to take the stand on masturbation that he does. But while it may be plausible to understand speech as essentially interpersonal, it is clearly false that written language is essentially interpersonal too. Had Solomon truly offered an analysis of sex as a type of language, both spoken and written, rather than interpreting it as a type of speech, he might have come up with a less one-sided account. Why, then, does he opt for such a narrow approach? Hugh T. Wilder submits that it makes sense only, on the assumption that Solomon has some sort of grudge against diaries, journals, any manner of self-expression of personal (as opposed to interpersonal) feelings, as well as against masturbation. It may seem extravagant to be defending the writing of diaries as genuine linguistic activity, as extravagant, as I hope it seems, to be defending masturbation as genuine sex. After reading Solomon, both seem to be necessary.[15]

While Wilder's critique of the sex as language view shows this view to be much too narrow in an important respect, another objection displays it as much too inclusive in another respect. Solomon says that "between two people almost any activity *can* be fully sexual when it is an attempt to communicate mutual feelings through bodily gestures, touches, and movements."[16] This, it seems to me, amounts to a *reductio ad absurdum* of his view, for it shows it as an utterly implausible pansexualism of body language. A pat on the back expressing, say, sympathy or concern, between two exclusively heterosexual male friends, is an instance of interpersonal communication in body language that surely has nothing sexual about it; but it would have to be pronounced sexual if we were to accept Solomon's account of sex. Then again, some of the feelings and attitudes which, according to Solomon, are best expressed sexually, such as tenderness and trust, can be expressed in non-sexual ways quite as well, if not better. As Janice Moulton remarks, "a joint checking account may be a better expression of trust than sexual activity."[17] And they are definitely not best expressed sexually between an adult and a child; not every parent who expresses tenderness and trust in body language is a pedophile.

Nor is Solomon's attempt to account for sexual pleasure in terms of his language view of sex very successful. The fact that one's sexual touch expresses certain feelings for the other may well add to the other's pleasure; but sexual touch involved in merely casual sex is normally pleasurable too, as a *touch* of a certain type, rather than because of the meager emotive message it may carry. The phonetics of sex are indeed not *meaningful* in themselves, but because of what is said; but, *pace* Solomon, they are surely *enjoyable* in themselves.

Not all casual sex is sex with strangers, but sex with strangers is almost always casual. Now we normally do not have very much to say to strangers, whether in verbal or in body language; but it is not at all unusual for sex with strangers to be very exciting and pleasurable. On the communication view of sex, this is anomalous.

Solomon addresses this point, but his attempt to show that the anomaly is merely apparent does not succeed. He proposes to explain the pleasure of sex with strangers by the tension and excitement involved. But we are then told that "tension, arousal, and excitement, together with bodily sensuality, still add up to something much less than sexuality," and that we can come to understand what sexuality is only if we see it as a type of language.[18] This hardly takes care of the objection; indeed, it rather seems that Solomon is conceding the point.

Sex, according to Solomon, "is always personal and deeply revealing".[19] This generates another anomaly. Commercial sex is in the overwhelming majority of cases quite impersonal; indeed, its impersonality is one of the standard moral objections to it. How, then, are we to understand prostitution?

Now none of this is meant to deny the great communicative potential of sex, nor the value of pointing this potential out. It may even be true that we cannot fully comprehend some varieties of sexual behavior without understanding the communication they involve. Thus Solomon writes that "oral sex and anal sex ... carry unavoidable expressions of domination and subservience, though these surely need not be considered degrading ... and may be exceptionally expressive of tenderness and trust."[20] I am not sure about the inevitability of it, but otherwise Solomon certainly has a point. The trouble is that Solomon simply makes much too much of it. He is not content to offer what he has to say on sex as language as a description of an important possibility of sex, but presents it as a complete, exclusive account of sexuality. Sex can indeed be used as a medium for expressing thoughts, feelings, attitudes, but this possibility does not define it. After all, almost anything human beings do can be so used, but that does not make almost everything they do a language of some sort.

5

THE PLEASURE OF SEX

Plain sex

All three conceptions of sex considered so far insist on connecting it to something else, on understanding and evaluating it in terms of something else. One claims that sex is naturally directed toward procreation, and therefore ought to be experienced only in that particular variety that is normally open to the possibility of procreation, and within its proper institutional framework, monogamous marriage. The second argues that it can and ought to be bound up with the love of another person, and enjoins a set of requirements and prohibitions of its own. The third seeks to show that sex is essentially a language expressing some of our important feelings and attitudes about ourselves and others, a means of interpersonal communication. Each of these views is plagued with difficulties. But it could be maintained that their difficulties are ultimately a result of their unwillingness to take sex on its own terms, to try to understand and evaluate it simply as sex, rather than as part of, or a means to, something else.

If we are to understand and appreciate sex on its own terms, simply as sex, it seems that we should see it as a source of a distinctive type of pleasure. What else could it be? What else remains when we put aside its biological aspect and its romantic and expressive potential? This is just the claim of Alan Goldman's paper "Plain Sex", the best philosophical statement of the hedonist understanding of sex.

Goldman rejects all instrumental accounts of sex. Every such account subjugates sex to an extraneous purpose and thus misses its intrinsic nature. Moreover, such accounts usually have implausible implications in sexual ethics: they generate many restrictions which cannot be convincingly defended. While procreation may be "nature's" purpose concerning sex, it certainly need not be ours; by developing contraceptive techniques we have considerably restricted the role of "nature" in human sex anyway. The attempt to bind sex to love is burdened by serious tensions.[1] Sex and love are quite different matters and should be distinguished accordingly, both for the sake of clear thinking and for practical reasons, such as avoiding disastrous marriages that result from mistaking sexual attraction for love. And if sex were indeed a type of language, the moves that make up its vocabulary would be important only instrumentally, as efficient means of communication, and could have no significance in themselves. But that is surely not the case; if we focus on it and consider it without preconceptions, we readily see that sex is simply a bodily activity intensely pleasurable in itself. Although it can communicate many things, sex "can communicate nothing in particular and still be good sex."[2]

Central notions in Goldman's analysis of sex are those of sexual desire and sexual activity. Sexual desire is defined as "desire for contact with another person's body and for the pleasure which such contact produces". Sexual activity is "activity which tends to fulfill such desire of the agent."[3]

This definition of sexual desire seems to involve the person who has such desire and engages in deliberate and sustained pursuit of its satisfaction in what is sometimes termed "the paradox of hedonism". For the most part, we do not experience pleasure as a result of successful direct pursuit of pleasure, but rather in the course of doing things we like doing for their own sake, without any thought of the pleasure involved in doing them. A desire for pleasure as such and direct pursuit of pleasure are actually likely to prove self-defeating. Goldman grants that this is generally true, but argues that it does not apply in the case of sexual desire: the desire for contact with another's body is indeed the desire for the pleasure such contact gives. Sexual desire is thus a desire for another which is nonetheless basically self-regarding.

This notion of sexuality as essentially physical is quite narrow, when compared to other views of sex. But reducing sex to bodily activity is not tantamount to reducing it to genital activity. Actions such as kissing or caressing, when performed solely for the pleasure they give the agent, qualify as sexual actions independently of any attendant genital arousal. Genital arousal is not a necessary condition for an experience or activity to be considered sexual.

It might be objected that this analysis of sex is much too narrow in at least one respect. What one finds sexually attractive in another may not be solely, or even primarily, the other's body, but his or her personality. However, this does not call for a revision of the above account of sex, for

> it is not the contents of one's thoughts per se that are sexually appealing, but one's personality as embodied in certain manners of behavior. Furthermore, if a person is sexually attracted by another's personality, he or she will desire not just further conversation, but actual sexual contact. While looking at or conversing with someone can be interpreted as sexual in given contexts it is so when intended as preliminary to, and hence parasitic upon, elemental sexual interest.[4]

Unlike all other views of sex, which first superimpose some extraneous purpose on sex and then claim that that is just what sex is and ought to be, Goldman's account takes sex as it finds it. It tells us what sex as such, plain sex, is: an experience of desire for contact with another's body and the pleasure that contact produces, together with what we do that tends to satisfy that desire. All the rest − interpersonal communication, love, procreation, marriage − are possible uses of sex or additions to it, not something that belongs to its intrinsic nature. When superimposed on sex, love or procreation tend to generate all manner of moral requirements and prohibitions. Unlike the procreation view and the view of sex as bound up with love, and like the language view, Goldman's analysis presents sex in morally neutral terms. Sex as such has no moral import, positive or negative; particular sexual experiences or acts are accorded moral standing solely on the basis of considerations extrinsic to sex. To be sure, sexual pleasure, like other pleasures (or most of them, at least), is a good; but it is not a good endowed with moral significance. If there is an ethical doctrine implying that, since sexual pleasure is a good, the possibility of producing or amplifying such pleasure in oneself or another person entails a moral requirement to do so, so much the worse for that doctrine; for the suggestion is clearly ridiculous.

Plainer sex

Compared to the views of sex discussed in the preceding chapter, Goldman's down-to-earth approach to sex is truly refreshing. Against the background of attempts to wed human sexuality to procreation, or elevate it from a basically physical pleasure to the embodiment of love, or to a vehicle of interpersonal communication, Goldman's willingness to give us an unadorned account of sex has its obvious attractions. However, this account is plagued by one major difficulty.

Notwithstanding Goldman's criticism of other views of sex, he shares with them one assumption of crucial importance: that sexual experiences and activities are essentially interpersonal. This assumption makes it impossible for those views to give a plausible account of masturbation. Masturbation is best defined as sexual activity in which there is only one participant.[5] This definition precludes confusing talk about "mutual masturbation", and brings into sharp relief the problem masturbation poses for all the views of sex discussed so far: it is a sexual, but not interpersonal activity.

The view of sex as essentially a means to procreation condemns masturbation as a deviation from the natural purpose of the sexual organs and all sexual activity, as unnatural and immoral "self-abuse" for the sake of sheer bodily pleasure. The weight of the condemnation implied in the characterization of an activity as unnatural is such that Thomas Aquinas can say that masturbation is worse than adultery, incest, or rape. For these latter are violations of moral and legal rules established by human beings, and injure other humans, but are normally in accord with the natural manner of sexual intercourse. Masturbation, on the other hand, is in the same category as homosexuality and bestiality: these are "sins contrary to nature, whereby the very order of nature is violated, an injury is done to God, the Author of nature," and accordingly "in this matter ... gravest of all."[6] The view of sex as bound up with love condemns masturbation as a deviation from the proper focus of sexual desire on the beloved person. Roger Scruton writes that it offends against "the principle of personal encounter" which regulates normal sexuality by "creating a compliant world of desire, in which unreal objects become the focus of real emotions, and the emotions themselves are rendered incompetent to participate in the building of personal relations."[7] Therefore "it is wholly natural to us to perceive our own flesh as 'forbidden territory', like the flesh of our family."[8] The language view of sex is advanced as a morally neutral account of human sexuality and thus implies no moral disparagement of masturbation, but nevertheless suggests a bizarre interpretation of solitary sex as "an inability or a refusal to say what one wants to say", a sort of sexual self-denial.[9]

The same subject is a big stumbling-block for Goldman's plain sex view. If sexual activity is activity that tends to fulfill sexual desire, and sexual desire is the desire for contact with another person's body and the pleasure this contact gives the agent, how can masturbation be a sexual activity? And does the desire it embodies qualify as sexual desire at all?

Goldman assumes that the desire that leads to masturbation is the desire for contact with another person's body and the pleasure involved in that. This makes it possible for him to understand masturbation as an expression of sexual desire in his sense. He accordingly sees masturbation as similar to voyeurism or the perusal of pornography: these activities are said to qualify as sexual activities, but only as "imaginative substitutes for the real thing". When not performed as imaginative substitutes for sexual activities proper, such activities must be considered deviations.[10]

However, this is somewhat confused. Goldman is, in effect, giving masturbation the status of a borderline sexual activity. But however unsatisfactory in itself, this solution is still much too generous in terms of his own account. If an activity is a sexual activity by virtue of tending to fulfill sexual desire, then a borderline sexual activity is an activity that has at least some tendency toward at least partial fulfillment of sexual desire. But masturbation has no tendency whatsoever of producing even a partial satisfaction of sexual desire as defined by Goldman – the desire for contact with another person's body and the pleasure that contact involves. As Alan Soble points out in this connection, in general, if X is a substitute for Y, that presupposes a distinction between the two, rather than lack of it. "To eat soyburger as a beef substitute is not to eat hamburger, even if it tastes exactly like hamburger."[11] Accordingly, Goldman is committed to saying of all masturbation – masturbation performed as an imaginative substitute for sexual contact with another person, and masturbation which is not performed and experienced in these terms – what he expressly says of the latter: that it is simply a deviant activity.

This is a very unattractive thing to have to say, however, for two reasons. Masturbation is much too elementary, general and frequent a type of sexual behavior to be classified as mere deviation. And the view that masturbation is most of the time merely a substitute for "the real thing" is misguided too. This is brought out very clearly by Georg Groddeck:

> ...I should like to call attention to a strange distortion of the facts of which even men otherwise sensible are found guilty. They call masturbation a substitute for the normal sexual

act. Ah, what might not be written about that word 'normal' sexual act! But here I am dealing only with the idea of 'substitute'. ... In one form or another onanism accompanies man throughout his life, while normal sex activity only begins at a particular age, and often ceases at a time when onanism takes on again the childish form of a conscious playing with sexual organs. How can the one process be regarded as a substitute for another which only starts fifteen or twenty years later on?[12]

The source of this problem with masturbation is the assumption about interpersonal nature of sex, codified in the definition of sexual desire as desire for contact with *another person's* body and the pleasure such contact gives the agent. If we are not to deny the indubitably sexual character of masturbation, it seems that we must discard this assumption and adopt an even narrower, plainer view of sex. Sexual activity can then be defined as activity that tends to fulfill sexual desire, while sexual desire is sufficiently defined as the desire for certain bodily pleasures, period. This includes both sex with another person and solitary sex; the latter is not relegated beyond the pale, as some sort of imaginative substitute for, or deviation from, the former.[13]

What bodily pleasures? Not all such pleasures are of a sexual nature. The obvious way to be more specific here is to say that the pleasures referred to are pleasures experienced in the sexual parts of the body, i.e. the genitals and other parts that differentiate the sexes. This might be thought too narrow, though; sexual pleasure is in fact more diffuse, spreading over other areas of the body too. As we have seen, Goldman acknowledges this; he emphasizes that there is more to sexual activity and sexual pleasure than genital activity and the pleasure experienced in the genital area. But he disconnects the two much too sharply. It is true that a kiss or a caress performed solely for the pleasure it gives the agent need not be attended by genital arousal in order to be sexual. But we should add that if it is indeed sexual, then, *if* it is linked to some sort of arousal, that arousal will itself occur in the sexual parts of the body. The notion of sexual pleasure, then, can be specified as follows: it is the sort of bodily pleasure experienced in the sexual parts of the body, or at least related to those parts in that if it is associated with arousal, the arousal occurs in those parts. This implies that we cannot always determine whether a certain bodily pleasure and the action that gives rise to it – a touch, a caress, a kiss – is *by itself* of a sexual nature or not. But this implication seems quite plausible. Some of our bodily pleasures, and the actions that bring them about, are indeed somewhat ambiguous in this way: we can fully appreciate their import only when we situate them in a wider context of experience.[14]

As we have seen in the preceding chapter, Robert Solomon objects to the plain sex view that it cannot explain why people prefer sex with others to masturbation. The search after sex with others exacts a serious toll on one's resources. On the other hand, if it is only bodily pleasure one is after, one is better off on one's own; for sexual behavior research has shown that masturbation, rather than sexual intercourse, makes for the most intense orgasm. The same objection is likely to be advanced against the plainer sex view. But it does not show that either view is flawed. First, there is more to sexual pleasure (or any other type of pleasure) than sheer intensity. Sex with others may be preferred over masturbation because it is more pleasurable overall: masturbation may produce more intense pleasure, but the pleasure of sex with others may be better in terms of variety, or duration, or fecundity or, possibly, all three. Second, even if masturbation were indeed preferable to sex with others in terms of pleasure, one might still choose sex with others on account of the additional significance and value it may have, say as a means of interpersonal communication, or a way of expressing and enhancing love. For sex certainly can have considerable instrumental value in both these ways, and perhaps in others. But, as I have argued in the preceding chapters, the fact that sex can also be a medium of communication or a way of expressing and strengthening love need not, indeed should not, be mistaken for its intrinsic nature.

While it may not be very difficult to accept the argument that sex as such need have nothing to do with either love or interpersonal communication, the idea of disconnecting it from procreation too and understanding it solely in terms of sexual pleasure may be thought a different matter. Alan Soble finds the approach to sex in terms of sexual pleasure plausible, when taken to be stating sufficient conditions for identifying acts as sexual. But he argues that it fails as a definition of such acts, since it does not capture the necessary conditions for such identification. There are acts we would want to classify as sexual, although they do not involve sexual pleasure, such as those of the prostitute who experiences no sexual pleasure in plying her trade, or that of the woman who engages in coitus devoid of any pleasure in order to conceive a child. Moreover, if we adopt sexual pleasure as the criterion of the sexual nature of acts, we will no longer be able to use pleasure as a standard of the quality of sexual acts. "Consider the couple who have lost sexual interest in each other, and who engage in routine coitus from which they derive no pleasure. [The definition of sexual acts in terms of sexual pleasure] forbids us to say about this couple that they engage in sex but it is (nonmorally) bad sex."[15]

Accordingly, Soble offers an account that does not state a single necessary condition for classifying an act as sexual, and thus falls short of a definition of such acts. Instead, it gives us two alternative sufficient conditions for such classification. Sexual acts *either* produce sexual pleasure *or*, alternatively, are acts procreative in form, or acts that are their physiological or psychological precursors or concomitants. ("Procreative form" refers to the kind of acts that, in virtue of their biological nature, could, under appropriate conditions, result in conception, i.e. to heterosexual genital intercourse.) This two-pronged account accords due weight to the fact that "the procreative act is biologically and historically a central case of sexual activity."[16] The first prong explains why acts that give sexual pleasure are sexual acts, whether procreative or not; the second explains why procreative acts and their precursors and concomitants are sexual acts, whether pleasurable or not. And the account explains the connection between the two. There is

> a link between the sexual and the reproductive, a link that shows it is no accident that both [sexual pleasure] and [procreation] state sufficient conditions for acts to be sexual: some acts, not procreative in form, produce pleasure identical or similar to that normally produced by procreative acts. The similarity of the pleasure, despite the separation achieved by contraception, exhibits the enduring biological tie between sex and procreation.[17]

I do not find this case for a two-pronged account of sex convincing, and prefer to retain the view that focuses solely on sexual pleasure. Soble's objections to that view do not seem compelling. When discussing rape in this connection, he readily grants that one and the same act can be sexual for one of the participants without being so for the other, because it gives sexual pleasure to one but not to the other. But if one and the same act, the act of rape, can be sexual for the rapist, without being sexual for the victim, why not say the same in the case of prostitution? That, after all, is exactly how most prostitutes describe most, if not all, of what they do: *for them* it is work, rather than sex. Why not say the same of the woman who engages in coitus utterly devoid of pleasure for the sole reason of conceiving a child: that *for her* that is merely a reproductive act, although, of course, it may be a sexual act for the man? Finally, adopting sexual pleasure as a defining trait of sexual acts need not prevent us from assessing the quality of such acts in terms of that pleasure. Pleasure is a matter of degree, and we can evaluate sexual acts by determining *how pleasurable* they are. As for the couple who have lost sexual interest in each other but still engage in routine coitus, the less pleasurable it gets, the less valuable it is as sex. If, at some point, it becomes utterly bereft of sexual pleasure, would it be so odd to say that they were performing acts that for most people ordinarily involve at least a modicum of sexual pleasure, but that *they* were merely going through the motions, that *for them* there was no sex in it any longer?

6

SEXUAL PERVERSION

Inconsistencies of ordinary use

The distinction between "natural" and "unnatural", that is, "perverted" sex, has always been part of traditional sexual morality. Each of the four major philosophies of sex discussed in preceding chapters has its own account of the distinction; in two of them the distinction plays a highly important role.

In ordinary discourse, to say of a type of sexual behavior or forientation that it is unnatural or perverted is not only to say that it has certain important traits; normally it is also to condemn it, perhaps harshly, and also to imply that there is an objective reason, reason dictated by nature, that grounds the condemnation. Types of sexual behavior traditionally seen as unnatural or perverted would include homosexuality, sexual sadism, sexual masochism, exhibitionism, voyeurism, fetishism, transvestism, pedophilia, necrophilia, and zoophilia. The list is incomplete, but does include the main sexual perversions.

Not much more can be said in general, for a closer look at ordinary use displays considerable inconsistency. I have tried to establish the main contours of such use by inviting each class of students in my undergraduate course on sexual ethics over some years to answer a number of questions about the way they tend to use and interpret the term "sexual perversion". It appears that the term is indeed hardly ever used in a purely descriptive sense; it always seems to convey disapproval of some sort. But it is not clear of what sort. When the term is applied to pedophilia, necrophilia, or voyeurism, the disapproval tends to be moral; but when it is used to characterize fetishism, that does not seem to be the case. With regard to cases in which moral condemnation is implied, it tends to vary in seriousness: it is quite serious, indeed harsh, when the subject is pedophilia or necrophilia, but not very serious when it comes to voyeurism. Whether or not some sort of moral condemnation is implied, the term seems to express a clearly negative judgment of taste: most people tend to find most of the main traditional sexual perversions quite distasteful – but, again, in varying degrees. Moreover, there is often a suggestion of disorder or sickness on the part of those who exhibit perverted sexual preferences, which should be cured in their own best interest. Finally, the willingness to apply the qualification of perversion to sexual behavior seems to be related to the relevant statistical facts; but even here there may not be complete consistency. It is usually assumed that what is natural should also be typical or statistically normal. This assumption seems quite sensible. Accordingly, it could be expected that once we discover that a certain type of sexual preference traditionally labeled perverted is not at all quite atypical, characteristic of a tiny minority, but is much more widespread and can be found in a significant part of the population, we should withdraw the label. Something like that seems to have happened with homosexuality in quite a few Western societies. Still, it is a moot point whether, if a similar discovery were to be made with regard to, say, necrophilia or zoophilia, common usage would readily declassify it as perversion and take to depicting it as but another unproblematic sexual orientation.

Ordinary use is thus quite unhelpful, and there is not much point nor, indeed, much chance of success in attempting to formulate a definition of sexual perversion that would capture the meaning of the term in ordinary discourse. The major philosophical accounts of sex should be a different matter.

The main views of sex and the concept of perversion

There seems to be a strong connection between the notion of sexual perversion and that of unnatural sex. We would not say that a certain type of sexual behavior is a sexual perversion, but nevertheless quite natural for humans to engage in. This connection between the unnatural and the perverted is emphasized in particular in the traditional view of sex as bound up with procreation and marriage. This view condemns all but reproductive marital sex. The condemnation is based on the argument that procreation is the natural purpose or function of sexual organs and acts, which implies that types of sexual behavior condemned for not being in accordance with that purpose or function are also unnatural, abnormal, perverted.

This tying of the idea of sexual perversion to the notion of nature and the distinction between the natural and the unnatural seems to give the condemnatory moral use of the term a particular force, as well as a certain veneer of objectivity and, in certain contexts, of almost scientific authority. The immorality implied is not merely human, conventional, but rather seems to have a much more solid, objective ground. Nature itself condemns the perverted practice.

Of course, not everything the procreation view condemns is condemned as unnatural or perverted. For instance, adultery is, or can be, quite in accordance with the nature of sex as conceived in this tradition; it is wrong because it offends against the institution of marriage, which is claimed to be the sole appropriate framework for bringing up offspring. The same is true of pre-marital sex or rape. But every type of sexual behavior that is not meant for procreation (Augustine), or could not result in procreation under normal circumstances, whatever the intentions of the partners (Thomas Aquinas) is, indeed, considered unnatural, perverted, and *therefore* wrong. Thus, on both the former, "subjective", and the latter, "objective" interpretation of the procreation view of sex, all traditional perversions would count as such. In addition, the "subjective" version would pronounce masturbation, petting to orgasm, intercourse between partners at least one of which is sterile, intercourse on a "safe" day, or when some birth control device is employed, as well as oral and anal sex between heterosexual partners, to be unnatural, perverted, and therefore morally impermissible. The "objective" version of this view is slightly less restrictive: it would grant that heterosexual genital intercourse which, because of some "natural" cause such as sterility or the fact that it takes place on a "safe" day, cannot result in conception, is not unnatural. With regard to all the rest, it would not differ from the "subjective" version of the procreation view of sex.

One problem with this account of sexual perversion is that it is much too inclusive. It applies to all the main traditional perversions, which might be thought an advantage (although homosexuality is no longer considered a perversion as widely as it used to be). But it also classifies as unnatural and perverted some sexual practices which most of us cannot see in these terms, if only because we know that they are so widespread as to make it odd to call them unnatural (masturbation, petting to orgasm, contraceptive sexual intercourse, oral sex).

Another problem of this conception of sexual perversion is but a specific case of a basic difficulty plaguing claims about natural purposes or functions. Such claims have an appearance of factuality and objectivity. But when interpreted as factual, they are often easy to refute. As we have seen in an earlier chapter, sex is a case in point.[1] As a matter of fact, human beings engage in sex not only for the purpose of procreation, but also for the pleasure of it, or in order to express certain emotions and attitudes. As a matter of fact, sexual intercourse is well capable of doing all these different jobs. If it is claimed that, when having sex with any of the latter two purposes in view, people are deviating from the "true" purpose or function of sex, it becomes obvious that what is being put forward is not an ordinary factual statement, but rather a normative one. The veneer of objectivity and factuality is gone, and the need for a convincing argument showing just why sex not geared to procreation is unnatural, perverted, and therefore also immoral, becomes apparent.

Still another problem is a result of the expressly and emphatically moral character of the procreation view of sex and sexual perversion. Even if we could give some sense to the idea of procreation being the natural purpose or function of sex – perhaps by defining the natural function of sex as its biological function – the gap between the natural, thus defined, and the morally proper would remain. For it is not at all obvious that whatever is natural, i.e. biologically functional, is *ipso facto* morally good or required, and the other way around. Even if a certain type of sexual behavior or preference – say, homosexuality, or pedophilia – is indeed biologically dysfunctional and in this sense unnatural, it is not at all clear that it is also immoral, and immoral for just that reason. Actually, many would maintain that homosexuality is *not* immoral at all, however biologically dysfunctional it may be. On the other hand, most would agree that pedophilia is indeed morally unacceptable; but we should surely do so for reasons that have nothing to do with its being non-procreative.[2]

Of course, difficulties of the last type can be avoided by disconnecting the procreation view of sex and sexual perversion from its traditional theological underpinnings, and stripping it of its moral import. This has been done in Sara Ruddick's paper "Better Sex". Ruddick defines "natural sex" in terms of "the evolutionary and biological function of sexuality – namely, reproduction."[3] Her account is a restatement of the "objective", rather than "subjective" version of the traditional procreation view: what counts is not the intention to procreate, but the possibility of procreation. "'Natural' sexual desire," she maintains, "is for heterosexual genital activity, not for reproduction. ... It is so organized that it *could* lead to reproduction in normal physiological circumstances."[4] Accordingly, "natural" sexual desire has as its "object" living persons of the opposite sex, and in particular their postpubertal genitals. The "aim" of natural sexual desire – that is, the act that "naturally" completes it – is genital intercourse. Perverse sex acts are deviations from the natural object (e.g. homosexuality, fetishism) or from the standard aim (e.g. voyeurism, sadism).[5]

Ruddick emphasizes that this conception of natural and perverted sex is morally neutral. In cases where no extrinsic moral considerations apply, perverted sex acts are preferable to natural ones, if they are more pleasurable. To be sure, it is sometimes claimed that perverted sex is *less* pleasurable than natural sex. But "we have little reason to believe that this claim is true and no clear idea of the kind of evidence on which it would be based. In any case, to condemn perverse acts for lack of pleasure is to recognize the worth of pleasure, not of naturalness."[6]

But this account still faces other problems of the traditional procreation view: it is just as overinclusive as the latter. On Ruddick's account, just as on that of Thomas Aquinas, not only the main traditional sexual perversions, but also such common practices as masturbation, petting to orgasm, or oral sex, will have to be characterized as unnatural and perverted. While the former (with the likely exception of homosexuality) might be thought appropriate, the latter implication is surely quite unattractive.

The view of sex as bound up with love, like the traditional version of the procreation view, interprets sexual perversion as an emphatically moral notion. According to Roger Scruton, whose philosophy of sex was discussed in an earlier chapter as the best philosophical statement of that view, perversions are "all deviations from the unity of animal and interpersonal relation." By this, Scruton means all deviations from his account of sexual desire as characterized by "individualizing intention", i.e. directed at another human being as the embodied particular person he or she is. Sexual perversion is, thus, all impersonal sex. As such, it is "morally contaminated", since it amounts to "complete or partial failure to recognise, in and through desire, the personal existence of the other," and thereby sets our sexual experience apart "from our moral commerce ... in a realm that is free from the sovereignty of a moral law, ... in which the body is both sovereign and obscene."[7]

This account of sexual perversion might be thought to apply neatly to most traditional perversions. Zoophilia is so much removed from interpersonal sex that Scruton pronounces it "a paradigm of perversion."[8] Necrophilia "shows the process of perversion at its most accomplished, with the separation between sexual impulse and interpersonal emotion made absolute by death."[9] In perversions such as pedophilia or sadism the personality of the other is present, but only in a reduced or unacknowledged form. Homosexuality, on the other hand, does not qualify as a perversion, but that may be an advantage rather than a problem. However, the problem with this account of sexual perversion is that it is much too inclusive and indiscriminate. Under the heading of "depersonalized" and therefore perverted sex, it lumps together such practices as necrophilia or pedophilia, and types of sexual behavior that admittedly do not live up to Scruton's ideal of distinctively and fully human sex but, apart from that, have very little in common with the first group: casual and mercenary sex. Such sex is impersonal in the sense that the other is not engaged as *the* particular, unique person he or she is, but not in the sense of being reduced to something less than *a* person, and banished beyond the pale of moral concern.[10]

While the traditional procreation view and the view of sex as bound up with love accord a central place to the notion of sexual perversion and give it an emphatically moral interpretation, in the other two major philosophies of sex, the view of sex as language and the "plain sex" view, sexual perversion is no longer a moral concept, nor indeed one of central importance.

Robert Solomon is somewhat ambiguous about the idea of sexual perversion. Being a type of language, he argues, sex admits of breaches in communication, and that is where "what little is left of our conception of 'sexual perversion'" should be located. The concept itself is no longer a moral one, but rather a "logical category". Actually, we would be better off replacing the term by something like "sexual misunderstanding" or "sexual incompatibility".[11] But he then goes on using the term, and actually offers an analysis of its meaning in terms of his own theory of human sexuality.

Solomon distinguishes between perversions proper and "gross abuses" of sex as language. Perversions proper are various types of absence or breakdown of communication. They include traditional perversions, such as pedophilia, zoophilia, or fetishism, but also any kind of insincerity and deceit in sex – the nonverbal equivalent of lying – such as entertaining private fantasies, or "pretended tenderness and affection that reverses itself soon after orgasm."[12] Moreover, the language of sex, just as any other language, can be mastered poorly or well, and spoken with skill and sophistication, or in infelicitous, clumsy, or vulgar ways.

> It is because sex is a language that demands subtlety and artfulness that over-frankness and vulgarity are, if not perversions, at least gross abuses of the language, as very bad poetry might still be considered poetry. This explains, e.g., why overt propositions and subway exhibitionism are generally offensive, which is a mystery if one considers sex, as most people do, one of the 'appetites'.[13]

It might be thought that people have reasons other than the quasi-esthetic one brought up by Solomon to be put off by such things as subway exhibitionism. For one thing, their sense of privacy might be offended. But the main criticism of Solomon's account has to do with what he says of sexual perversions proper: that they are basically instances of unsuccessful communication by means of sex as a body language. This is too inclusive, and implies that much too much of what goes for common, everyday sex among human beings is actually perverted. In sex, as everywhere else, breakdown of communication among humans is a very common occurence. If every case of such breakdown is to count as perverted sex, the idea of perversion will no longer refer – as it presumably should – to something uncommon and strange.

On Alan Goldman's plain sex view sexual perversion is certainly an atypical sexual preference. Indeed, the distinction between natural and unnatural or perverted sex becomes a matter of statistics. The unnatural or perverted is a deviation from a norm, but the norm is merely statistical, rather than moral or esthetic. Goldman defines sexual desire as desire for contact with another person's body and for the pleasure such contact provides, and sexual activity as activity which tends to fulfil such desire of the agent. These definitions are meant to capture the central facts of human sexuality, rather than express some ideal superimposed on it. When somebody has a desire for something other than contact with another person's body – say, for merely looking at another's body, or at other people engaging in sex, or for contact with another person's clothes rather than body – and the satisfaction of such desire produces the kind of pleasure the overwhelming majority of human beings achieve through contact with others' bodies, the desire and the relevant activity are statistically abnormal and perverted. This notion of sexual perversion is disconnected both from moral considerations that apply to sex and from the idea of sex that is good *as* sex. The three distinctions – between natural and unnatural or perverted sex, between moral and immoral sex, and between good, i.e. pleasurable, and poor or bad sex, i.e. sex devoid of pleasure – are completely independent. Perverted sex may be more or less pleasant than natural sex, and moral or immoral as well. To be sure, some perversions (e.g. sadism or voyeurism) are clearly morally unacceptable; but that is not on account of being perversions, but rather because they offend against certain moral rules that hold for sexual and non-sexual conduct alike.

Goldman is aware that, in grounding his account of sexual perversion on the facts of human sexual behavior, he is deviating from the facts of usage of the term "sexual perversion". He does not deny that in ordinary usage the term is used to evaluate, and evaluate negatively, rather than merely describe. What he does deny is,

> that we can find a norm, other than that of statistically usual desire, against which all and only activities that properly count as sexual perversions can be contrasted. Perverted sex is simply abnormal sex, and if the norm is not to be an idealized or romanticized extraneous end or purpose, it must express the way human sexual desires usually manifest themselves. ... The connotations of the concept of perversion beyond those connected with abnormality or statistical deviation derive more from the attitudes of those likely to call certain acts perverted than from specifiable features of the acts themselves.[14]

This empirical account of the idea of sexual perversion makes its application relative – a function of changes in the field of human sexual preference and behavior. Goldman does not see this as a flaw: "It is not true that we properly could continue to consider acts perverted which were found to be very common practice across societies."[15]

It could be objected that, on Goldman's view, neither pedophilia nor necrophilia would qualify as sexual perversions. But this objection does not have great weight, as his definitions of sexual desire and activity can easily be amended so as to rule that out. There is another. If this is all there is to sexual perversion, the very notion of such perversion seems to have become redundant. If, properly understood, sexual perversion is merely a statistically abnormal, atypical, unusual sexual preference, and a preference that is atypical at a certain time, but need not be so at some other time, then the most accurate term may be simply "atypical" or "statistically abnormal" sexual preference. "Sexual perversion" has a very long history of condemnatory use, and it may not be possible to dissociate it clearly and definitely enough from that history and the rich connotations of extremely strange, incomprehensible, distasteful, and morally repellent sex it still has most of the time in ordinary discourse. If all that is to go by the board, so should the term itself. But this, too, is an objection with a limited weight. For instead of continuing to speak of sexual perversion, but using the term in his preferred value-free, purely statistical sense, Goldman could grant that the chances that others will reform their usage accordingly are very poor, and agree that the term itself should be dropped.

The immorality of sexual perversion

Some philosophers who have discussed the idea of sexual perversion take a stance opposed to that of Goldman's. They argue that we should preserve, and indeed emphasize and justify, its distinctively moral connotations.

One of them is Sara Ann Ketchum who, in order to develop a moral interpretation of sexual perversion, wants to break a connection acknowledged both in ordinary use and in almost all philosophical discussions: that between sexual perversion and unnatural sex. The aim of her analysis is to situate the notion of sexual perversion in an account of sex that is both good *as* sex and morally valuable, or at least acceptable.

Sexual relations are interpersonal relations. Such a relation may or may not be reciprocal, i.e. such that the parties have as objects of their awareness the other person's awareness. This reciprocity of awareness, again, may or may not be symmetrical. Finally, the symmetrical thoughts or feelings may or may not be capable of joint realization or satisfaction. For instance, A may be sexually aroused merely by B's body, without being interested in, or even aware of, any particular thoughts or feelings on the part of B. Such relation between the two persons is not reciprocal. A may be sexually aroused not merely by B's physical attractiveness, but also by certain thoughts or feelings by which B responds to A's arousal. That is a reciprocal relation. If B responds to A's arousal with annoyance, or embarrassment, or fear, then the relation is reciprocal, but asymmetrical. But if B is sexually aroused too, and aroused in response to A's arousal, the relation is both reciprocal and symmetrical, mutual.

It is also one of complementarity: the satisfaction of each side's arousal and desire is complementary with the satisfaction of the other's. Such a case would be one of good sex.

This conception of good sex requires that sex should involve communication and mutual consent. Reciprocity involves communication, while complementarity means that both parties desire the same and pursue it willingly, in concert. And "it follows from the requirements of mutuality and common objects of desire that to the degree that a sexual relation is a good sexual relation, each of the partners is getting good sex, since the relation is symmetrical."[16] Bad sex, on the other hand, is characterized either by non-reciprocal, or reciprocal but asymmetrical or non-complementary relations. Sex devoid of communication of thoughts and feelings, or involving communication of mutual hostility, contempt and the like, or non-consenusal sex would be examples of bad sex.

Perverted sex is a type of bad sex:

> The concept of perversion should be stronger than the
> concept of the merely bad. A perversion of x is not simply
> something which does not match up to the ideal, but, rather,
> a preference in which the ideal is reversed. ... If mutuality
> is a criterion of good sex, then universalizability will be a
> criterion of nonperverted sex. A person with sexual desires
> which are, in principle, nonuniversalizable − in particular, a
> sexual desire such that the lack of reciprocity or mutuality
> on the part of the other is part of the object of the desire −
> has a perverted sexual attitude or preference.[17]

Ketchum illustrates the distinction between perverted and merely bad sex with two types of rapists. One is indifferent to the wishes of his victims; he simply ignores the requirement of mutuality. Such a rapist will have sex with the person chosen whether that person consents or not. The other type is not indifferent to the victim's wishes, but wants the victim to reject his advances; he does not ignore the requirement of mutuality, but deliberately offends against it. Such a rapist may be called sadistic, since he desires an asymmetrical sexual encounter, and one that will be bad for the other person. The sexual preferences and behavior of the sadistic rapist are perverted, while those of the non-sadistic rapist are merely bad.

This analysis of sexual perversion has the advantage of being in tune with the usage of the word "perverse" in non-sexual contexts: to act in a perverse way in certain circumstances is to deliberately do the opposite of what the rules pertaining to such circumstances enjoin. In applying this general idea of perversity to sex, Ketchum assumes that the relevant rules would be, or include, moral rules. Now according to a view widely accepted in contemporary moral philosophy, moral rules apply to those actions that in some way affect others, and not only the agent. Hence Ketchum points out that her account "does not, and is not intended to, provide a framework for evaluating noninterpersonal sexual acts such as masturbation."[18] It does provide reasons for saying that such traditional perversions as sadism, pedophilia, voyeurism, or exhibitionism are indeed perverted. On the other hand, by confining the whole question of perversion to interpersonal contexts, it implies that some of the other traditional sexual perversions, such as necrophilia, zoophilia, fetishism, or transvestism, are *not* perversions. It might be thought that this is a rather unattractive conclusion to have to make.

To be sure, Ketchum might not worry about this. She might point out that her account of sexual perversion is expressly prescriptive, so that its implications cannot always tally with ordinary use of the term. Hers is a moral conception of sexual perversion, and it is quite appropriate that traditional perversions which we have no good reason to regard as immoral should not qualify, however strange, alien, or even repulsive they might be.

Ketchum argues that sexual perversion is not simply something that falls short of the sexual ideal, but "a preference in which the ideal is reversed." Accordingly, the term is to express moral condemnation significantly stronger than that of "merely bad." We might think that this is as it should be, if we take the defining trait of perverted sex to be its non-universalizability, its essential non-reciprocity or non-mutuality, *and* adopt sadistic rape as the paradigm, as Ketchum does. Sadistic rape is without doubt the worst type of perverted sex, thus conceived. However, by focusing too much on her chosen paradigm, Ketchum loses sight of the moral complexity of her subject. In the cases of sadistic rape, sadism, or pedophilia, very strong moral condemnation is called for. On the other hand, however, voyeurism and exhibitionism are also perverted, and for the same reason. But if the former is morally wrong, it is surely much less wrong than, say, sadism. And some might say that the latter is not morally wrong at all, however ridiculous, embarassing, or even disgusting it may be. Ketchum's account of sexual perversion implausibly lumps together all these as morally wrong, for the same reason, and in the same high degree.

Another important moral interpretation of the idea of sexual perversion is that of Donald Levy. Unlike Ketchum, Levy wants to preserve the connection between the perverted and the unnatural; he defines the former as a type of the latter. The unnatural or, more accurately, the unnatural as far as human beings are concerned, is defined in terms of basic human goods. Such goods are basic in that they are desired no matter what else is, since they are necessary for the achievement of any other goods. While those other, non-basic goods are many and varied, the list of the basic human goods is quite short: it includes life, health, control of one's bodily and psychic functions, knowledge (and the capacity for it), and love (and the capacity for it). Unlike non-basic goods, the basic human goods are desirable without qualification; one cannot have too much of such a good. And they help define human nature: "Any creature, however rational or articulate, who does not value the basic human goods is not human. ... Principled lack of concern for them by a creature is a sufficient condition of the creature's nonhumanity."[19]

Accordingly, it is unnatural for a human being to deny a person (oneself or another) a basic human good, except when that is done for the sake of another basic human good, e.g. when one makes a sacrifice in terms of one's health in order to persevere in one's pursuit of knowledge. But to act so as to deny oneself or another a basic human good (or the capacity for it) for the sake of attaining a non-basic good is, according to Levy, to act in an unintelligible and unnatural way. Pleasure is a good, but not a basic human good: it is not desired no matter what else is, one can have too much of it for one's own good, and a principled lack of concern for it would not strike us as incomprehensible, unnatural, non-human. When one sacrifices a basic human good (in oneself or another) for the pleasure of it, one acts in an unnatural, and also perverted way. To find pleasure in acting in a way that questions one's humanity is degrading, and immoral because degrading. Therefore all perversion is degrading and immoral. When the pleasure one finds in acting in an unnatural way is sexual, the perversion is sexual too.

How does this account apply to sexual preferences and behavior traditionally considered perverted? Levy professes to find its implications concerning homosexuality a moot point. I should have thought it clear that his account absolves homosexuality of the charge of perversion: it need not endanger any of the basic human goods. On the other hand, Levy tries to show that pedophilia and necrophilia would qualify as perversions. The pedophile is liable to damage the child's health or capacity for love, while the necrophile "has lost the ability to love another human being sexually."[20]

I suppose Levy would extend the latter explanation to zoophilia, fetishism, exhibitionism, voyeurism, and transvestism. It is not a good explanation, however, for several reasons. In order for a type of behavior to qualify as perversion on Levy's account, it must endanger, damage, or destroy a basic human good of the agent or someone else. But, first, one might take exception to Levy's inclusion of love (and the capacity for it) in the list of such goods. Levy is aware of this objection, but seems to think that it could be put forward only by someone who held that love was not a good at all, and tries to refute that view.[21] But that, of course, will not help much; for in order for love to carry the weight Levy puts on it, it is not enough that it should be a good; it must be shown to be a *basic human good*. And it is not at all clear that it is; it satisfies at best one of the three criteria by which Levy distinguishes between basic and non-basic goods. Perhaps there is no such thing as too much love (and capacity for it). But love is certainly not desired no matter what else is, as a precondition for attaining whatever else one might want. And a person who had no capacity and no concern for love would no doubt strike us as strange, but surely we would not find such a person utterly incomprehensible, alien, not really human. Second, there is a necessary and highly significant, but unacknowledged move from "love" to "sexual love" in Levy's explanation of the perverted nature of necrophilia and, presumably, other traditional perversions mentioned. Whatever one might think about Levy's claim that love (and the capacity for it) is a basic human good, to make that claim about *sexual* love (and the capacity for it) would obviously be quite implausible.

Moreover, Levy's argument fails even apart from these flaws in the theory of human goods that provides its basis. For to act in a way that shows that one has *lost* the capacity for sexual love of other human beings, and to act in a way that *endangers, damages,* or *destroys* one's capacity for sexual love of other humans, are not the same. Indeed, the former rules out the latter: one cannot endanger, damage, or destroy something one does not have in the first place. Now what Levy says, and can plausibly say, of necrophilia and other traditional perversions mentioned, is the former. That is, actually, a fairly common view of the necrophile, the zoophile, etc.: they resort to corpses, or to animals, etc., because they are psychologically incapable of engaging sexually other human beings, including sexually loving them. Their unusual behavior is the result, rather than the cause, of the lack of that capacity on their part. But if so, then what follows from Levy's attempted explanation of the perverted character of necrophilia is that necrophilia, zoophilia, fetishism, exhibitionism, voyeurism, and transvestism, are *not* sexual perversions.

A concept best discarded

In view of the inconsistent and, indeed, confusing use of "sexual perversion" in ordinary discourse,[22] and the difficulties plaguing philosophical accounts of such perversion, one might be tempted to conclude that the idea of sexual perversion should be discarded altogether.

Some philosophers have actually proposed just that. One was Marquis de Sade. He developed his notorious sexual libertinism as an alternative to the traditional view of sex as by nature (and God) ordained to procreation, and legitimate only within marriage. That view rules out a wide array of sexual practices as immoral, condemning with particular severity those that are considered immoral because unnatural, perverted. De Sade's moral philosophy does without God, but not without nature. However, his view of nature is quite different from that adopted by the tradition; it is tailored to generate the views on morality in general, and sexual morality in particular, which have made him infamous. The natural is the yardstick of the moral; but nature is merely the sum of natural laws, and everything that happens happens in accordance with these laws. That means that nothing that happens, nothing that people do, can ever be unnatural, perverted nor, indeed, immoral. Homosexuality, pedophilia, incest – and, of course, sadism and masochism – are neither unnatural, perverted, nor immoral and criminal, for nature is behind them all. Nature makes it possible for human beings to commit such acts, that is, allows them to do so. Moreover, nature is the real instigator, as it puts the inclinations to commit such acts in human beings. "... There is no extravagance which is not in Nature, none which she does not acknowledge as her own," says de Sade. Therefore "there can exist no evil in obedience to Nature's promptings ..."[23] Sexual preferences and acts traditionally depicted as unnatural, perverted, which are censured and punished as crimes against nature, are merely preferences and acts at odds with the conventional tastes in sex.[24]

Michael Slote, too, argues that the notion of unnatural or perverted behavior, including sexual behavior, is idle and should be dispensed with. Slote notes that "unnatural" and "perverted" have both descriptive and expressive meaning. The former has proven extremely difficult to capture by a definition, while the latter is easy to characterize: both words express horror. Whatever we may mean by saying of a type of behavior that it is unnatural or perverted, we always express our fear or horror of such behavior. It is this horror that points to the true descriptive meaning of these words in their ordinary use: to call a way of acting perverted or unnatural is to say that it is not to be found in nature, that it does not exist in nature. By banishing it from nature, we also banish it from our world. Both these claims are supported by the fact that people who are especially knowledgeable about human behavior are neither horrified by ways of acting most of us find horrible, nor given to calling such behavior unnatural or perverted, the way most of us do. Unlike most of us, they know, and are willing to acknowledge, that such behavior *is* to be found in nature, that it *is* part of our world.

But why should we be attempting to put those human acts that horrify us outside nature, outside our world? Because such acts are very strongly prohibited by society – and most of us nevertheless have certain impulses towards them, impulses which frighten us and threaten our self-image, and which we are extremely unwilling to acknowledge. As depth psychology tells us, most of us have some deep, unconscious, repressed desires towards incest, homosexuality, and possibly some forms of fetishism. We repress such impulses and keep them unconscious by determining that such behavior is unnatural or perverted. "By calling it 'unnatural' [and 'perverted'] we think of it as banished to a world other than ours, and this helps to reassure us that the impulse toward such behavior is not *in us*."[25]

Of course, all such claims are false, because there is no such thing as human behavior that is not part of nature or the human world. The ordinary notion of the unnatural or perverted is therefore inapplicable in principle. Those who employ it do so because they are ignorant of its inapplicability.

Slote's philosophical cum psychological account of the idea of unnatural or perverted sex is not convincing, for several reasons. One is given by James M. Humber. On Slote's theory,

> we would expect that as soon as a person consciously recognizes that he or she has an impulse to perform some 'threatening' sexual act, he/she would cease calling the impulse perverted. But this need not happen. Rather, a person can recognize that he or she has impulses to, say, incest or sadism, and consciously do all in her or his power to overcome these impulses *because* he/she believes the desires are perverted. And, if this is true, it is obvious that the person

is not using 'perverted' or 'unnatural' to mean 'without existence in reality'.[26]

Furthermore, Slote's claim that the terms "unnatural" and "perverted sex" express horror is not accurate in the general form in which he puts it forward. They do, when applied to perversions such as pedophilia, necrophilia, or zoophilia. When applied to other perversions, however, their emotive connotations are surely not so heavy. In calling fetishism or transvestism unnatural or perverted, we probably evince nothing stronger than distaste. When saying the same of exhibitionism or voyeurism, we may also be expressing embarassment, annoyance, and possibly anger too. But all these are a far cry from horror.

Finally, now that a good many tenets of depth psychology have been part of general education for decades, many of us probably do not find it all that difficult to own to the possibility of having had certain incestuous or homosexual impulses at some point in our lives. But most of the traditional sexual perversions are a different matter. I suspect that it is simply not true that many of us have or have had desires or impulses towards, say, necrophilia or zoophilia, and that no amount of depth-psychology analysis would succeed in bringing them to the fore. If so, Slote's thesis, plausible as it may be with regard incest or homosexuality, is not at all plausible with regard to other traditional sexual perversions.

Thus I cannot accept Slote's inapplicability thesis nor, for that matter, de Sade's simplistic naturalism in sexual ethics. But I do think that the idea of unnatural or perverted sex is best discarded. As we have seen, ordinary use is inconsistent and confusing. More importantly, none of the philosophical accounts discussed succeeds in giving the idea a plausible and helpful interpretation. And the philosophical accounts I have discussed cover between them the main lines of argument the subject seems to offer. When we put them aside, the descriptive content of the term amounts to no more than "unusual sexual preference or behavior". The term has rich evaluative connotations; but they tend to vary very much, not only in intensity, but also in quality. In view of all this, it can safely be said that the term serves no useful purpose. We should therefore simply drop it.[27]

The consigning of the concept of sexual perversion to intellectual and moral history need not prevent us from saying whatever needs to be said about the traditional sexual perversions. One of them, homosexuality, is sufficiently characterized as minority sexual behavior.

Others are more properly described as atypical, unusual, perhaps very unusual sexual behavior. As for their moral status, some, such as fetishism or transvestism, are surely morally indifferent. Others, such as pedophilia or necrophilia, do raise moral questions. But these questions are neither answered nor, indeed, best put in terms of the distinction between natural and unnatural or perverted sex.[28]

II

THE ISSUES

7

MARRIAGE, ADULTERY, JEALOUSY

Marriage: some defenses

Naturally enough, the institution of marriage – or, more accurately, heterosexual monogamous marriage – plays an important role in some major philosophies of sex, and hardly any in others. If sex is about procreation, marriage might well be thought the appropriate framework for bringing up offspring. If it is about love, that love may need to be given social recognition, protection, support, and marriage may well be the best way to provide all that. On the other hand, if sex is basically a body language, or a source of a certain type of pleasure, it is not obvious that it is connected in any interesting way to the institution of marriage.

In the classic statements of the procreation view of sex, those provided by Augustine and Thomas Aquinas, morally legitimate sex is possible only within the confines of marriage. In his treatise *The Good of Marriage*, Augustine argues that the great value of matrimony is based on several grounds. It provides the proper framework for begetting and bringing up children. It represses concupiscence, and harnesses it to the task of procreation, "so that marital intercourse makes something good out of the evil of lust." It fosters companionship between the spouses; if this were not an important good in its own right, "we could not speak of marriage in the case of old people, especially if they had either lost their children or had begotten none at all."[1] And it provides opportunities for the exercise of the virtue of fidelity. Since the marital bond symbolizes the bond between Christ and the Church, it must never be dissolved, even if it turns out that a spouse, or both of them, are incapable of carrying out the command to be fruitful and multiply, which is the paramount end of marriage.

Sex is acceptable only within marriage. When engaged in by

69

spouses for the purpose of procreation, it is fully legitimate. When the motive is not procreation but mere pleasure, sexual intercourse of a married couple has a different status: that of a lesser evil and venial sin.

> ...In the more immoderate demand of the carnal debt, which the Apostle enjoined on them not as a command but conceded as a favor, to have sexual intercourse even without the purpose of procreation, although evil habits impel them to such intercourse, marriage protects them from adultery and fornication. For this is not permitted because of the marriage, but because of the marriage it is pardoned. Therefore, married people owe each other not only the fidelity of sexual intercourse for the purpose of procreating children ... but also for mutual service, in a certain measure, in sustaining each other's weakness, for the avoidance of illicit intercourse ...[2]

Non-marital intercourse, i.e. adultery or fornication, is both a mortal sin and a crime that calls for punishment. At the other extreme, there is the ideal of complete renunciation of sex, for those who can live up to it.

Thomas Aquinas builds on some of the basic ideas provided by Augustine, and supports them by natural law arguments. In accordance with the natural purpose of sex, which is procreation, sex is permitted only in the form of heterosexual genital intercourse. Thomas is more lenient than Augustine: he does not require the intention to procreate, but only that the sex act should be of the type that, barring some "natural" obstacle such as sterility, could lead to conception. For, after all, "natural inclinations are present in things from God, Who moves all things."[3] Intercourse should take place in such circumstances that, if there is offspring, its proper upbringing could be assured. As Thomas sees it, "it is abundantly evident that the female in the human species is not at all able to take care of the upbringing of offspring by herself, since the needs of human life demand many things which cannot be provided by one person alone. Therefore, it is appropriate to human nature that a man remain together with a woman after the generative act..."[4] This shows the necessity of some sort of marriage. Now polyandry is ruled out by the fact that man naturally desires to know his offspring. Polygamy will not do because it would be too much for one man to have to provide for the children of several women.

Moreover, matrimony ought to be based on strong friendship, and one cannot develop and sustain such friendship with many people. Finally, experience shows that polygamy generates discord. Therefore marriage ought to be monogamous. It also ought to be for life. Since in marriage the husband naturally governs and the wife obeys, the wife is not in a position to divorce her husband. But since the wife cannot put an end to the marriage, neither can the husband; to give him this right would mean to make the relationship one of inequality. (Thomas does not seem to be aware of the inconsistency.) Moreover, divorce is not fair because the woman is always the loser: "with the disappearance of a woman's fecundity and beauty, she is prevented from association with another man."[5]

As can be seen from all the main papal pronouncements dealing with sex, marriage, and family, from *Casti Connubii* of Pius XII (1930) to *Humanae Vitae* of Paul VI (1968) to the *Letter to Families* (1994) and *Evangelium Vitae* (1995) of John Paul II, the basics of the Catholic teaching on marriage as set out by Thomas Aquinas have not undergone major change to this day. To be sure, today this teaching is no longer put in terms of a purely extrinsic meaning and instrumental value of marriage. It is rather conceived as a basic human good with a complex structure, involving the goods of conjugal love and of procreation and raising of offspring. The two are inseparable, so that "parenthood is essentially involved in the good of every marriage, even in that of an infertile couple."[6]

As for the main Protestant reformers, they were content to adopt most of the basic tenets of Catholic teaching. Thus Luther defines marriage as "the God-appointed and legitimate union of man and woman in the hope of having children or at least for the purpose of avoiding fornication and sin and living to the glory of God,"[7] adds companionship as a further good of matrimony, describes this companionship in extremely sexist terms, and rules out all non-marital sex as impermissible. Where Protestant ethics differs from the Catholic is in its acceptance of divorce and rejection of the ideal of continence and the requirement of celibacy for priests. And almost all major currents of Christian sexual ethics nowadays tend to drop, or at least de-emphasize and attenuate, the sexism of the traditional Christian thinking on marriage and sex.

The conception of marriage as having to do primarily with procreation and being the exclusive framework for legitimate sex has also been adopted and defended by some philosophers who were not committed to its traditional theological underpinnings. Good examples can be found in the writings of Hume and Kant, who are far apart on the most basic issues in philosophy, but both provide philosophical apologies for conventional monogamous marriage. Hume defines marriage as "an engagement entered into by mutual consent [which] has for its end the propagation of the species,"[8] and frames the question as one of choice between three options: polygamous marriage, monogamous marriage that allows for divorce, and indissoluble monogamous marriage, which is the traditional arrangement. In accordance with his view of the method of practical philosophy, he assesses these options in terms of their consequences for those concerned.

Polygamy has been recommended as "the only effectual remedy for the disorders of love, and the only expedient for freeing men from that slavery to the females, which the natural violence of our passions has imposed upon us." But it has serious drawbacks. It destroys the natural "nearness of rank, not to say equality," of men and women. "The *lover* is totally annihilated; and courtship, the most agreeable scene in life, can no longer have place...."[9] Furthermore, polygamy imposes crippling constraints on women, fosters jealousy, stands in the way of friendship between men, and can provide only poor education for children.

The possibility of divorce is a precondition of continued marital love. And divorce would seem to be the solution for those monogamous marriages where love has been replaced by disaffection and discord. But Hume brings up three objections. First, the fate of children of divorced parents is an unenviable one. Second, human beings do love freedom, but also can and do submit to necessity. Love does need freedom, but it is "a restless and impatient passion, full of caprices and variations," and is therefore best replaced by friendship, which is "a calm and sedate affection" that "rather thrives under constraint". Therefore "we need not ... be afraid of drawing the marriage-knot, which chiefly subsists by friendship, the closest possible. The amity between the persons, where it is solid and sincere, will rather gain by it: and where it is wavering and uncertain, this is the best expedient for fixing it."[10] Finally, it is actually dangerous to unite two persons as closely as husband and wife, without making their union complete and final; for the very possibility of separate interests leads to suspicion and discord. In the light of all this, Hume concludes that "the exclusion of polygamy and divorces sufficiently recommends our present European practice with regard to marriage."[11]

The apology of conventional marriage offered by Kant is different in method, but not in the conclusions reached. Kant sees sex as *a priori* morally suspect. His ethics states that the supreme law of morality prohibits the use of human beings as mere means, i.e. as things. But sex, on Kant's account, tends to be just that. Unlike "true human love", which promotes the happiness of the other and finds joy in that happiness, i.e. which is other-regarding, "sexual love" is self-regarding, a mere desire or appetite for the "sexual attributes" of the other. In sexually desiring another one disregards the fact that the other is a complete human being, a person; one is concerned only with the other's potential for satisfying one's desire. The other is thereby degraded: "as soon as a person becomes an Object of appetite for another, all motives of moral relationship cease to function, because as an Object of appetite for another a person becomes a thing and can be treated and used as such..."[12] The fact that sexual desire is mutual and results in a consensual sexual encounter makes no difference, morally speaking. The two

> stimulate each other's desire; their inclinations meet, but their object is not human nature but sex, and each of them dishonours the human nature of the other. They make of humanity an instrument for the satisfaction of their lusts and inclinations, and dishonour it by placing it on a level with animal nature. Sexuality, therefore, exposes mankind to the danger of equality with the beasts.[13]

One may legitimately use the work of another person's hands with that person's consent. Why not the service of another person's "sexual attributes" too? Because these "attributes" are integral to one's body, and the body is part of one's self, one's personhood, which is one and indivisible. Therefore one cannot "surrender" a part of one's body to another without thereby surrendering oneself completely. And a human being is not allowed to do that: "the underlying moral principle is that man is not his own property and cannot do with his body what he will."[14]

If so, how can humans ever engage in sex without offending against the moral law and lowering themselves to the level of animals? Only in monogamous marriage, defined by Kant as "the union of two persons of different sexes for lifelong possession of each other's sexual attributes."[15] This possession, and the sexual inter-course it makes possible, are redeemed by the fact that each spouse has a right over the whole person of the other, and in this way the two become "a unity of will":

> If I have the right over the whole person, I have also the right over the part and so I have the right to use that person's *organa sexualia* for the satisfaction of sexual desire. But how am I to obtain these rights over the whole person? Only by giving that person the same rights over the whole of myself. This happens only in marriage. ... Thus sexuality leads to a union of human beings, and in that union alone its exercise is possible.[16]

What Kant does not explain is how this transfer of rights over the individual's person and body can take place if, as he maintains, the individual does not have such rights over his or her person and body in the first place.[17]

Marriage also has an important place in Roger Scruton's statement of the other major view of sex – the view that ties sex to love. According to Scruton, erotic love has an immanent need for an institutionalized framework that can give it social recognition and sustain and protect it. That is marriage, which must not be understood as a contract, but rather as an organic and intrinsically valuable institution that provides the bond of love with the "pious arrangement of the home". Of course, there is erotic love outside marriage. But, Scruton says,

> it is love, and not some other power, which requires the forms of marriage. In these forms the violence of love is ended, while its strength remains. The authority of an established institution protects and makes intelligible the power which seeks for it. The daily demand for love becomes a painless ritual, but in no way relinquishes its essential power; while the confused sad feeling of one who loves and is betrayed becomes intelligible as a violated right.[18]

Marriage: some critiques

While monogamous marriage has never lacked philosophical apologists, it has also had philosophical critics.

Some of them were quite radical – none more so, perhaps, than William Godwin. In his *Enquiry Concerning Political Justice* (1793), he advanced an act-utilitarian theory of morals, maintaining that we need not adhere to moral rules, but should rather arrive at moral decisions by weighing good and bad consequences of possible actions in each and every particular situation of choice. This was the

basis for a radical critique of an array of conventional rules and institutions, including the institution of marriage. Marriage, with the
commitments it involves, prevents us from judging every particular
situation, every person, every possible personal relationship on its
merits, and is therefore both irrational and morally unjustifiable. It
stifles independence of mind. It is based on the "absurd [expectation]
that the inclinations of two human beings should coincide through
any long period of time. To oblige them to act and live together, is to
subject them to some inevitable portion of thwarting, bickering and
unhappiness." And the need for a lifetime companion is an indication
of cowardice: "it flows from the desire of being loved and esteemed
for something that is not desert."[19] Therefore, Godwin concludes
that marriage ought to be abolished.

Others have not rejected marriage as such, but have pointed out
many flaws and injustices plaguing patriarchal marriage in general,
and the type of patriarchal marriage characteristic of modern
capitalist society in particular. On this subject, there has been much
overlap between nineteenth and early twentieth century feminist
and socialist thinkers: both have depicted the domination of men
and subjection of women within marriage, the injustice and exploitation it involves, and its various and far-reaching consequences in terms
of unhappiness, alienation, stifling of personality, and preventing one
half of humanity from making its full contribution to society and
culture.

Socialist critics of bourgeois marriage have argued that this institution is part and parcel of the economic and social structure of
capitalism, and have predicted the demise of both. Bourgeois
marriage is seen as deeply morally flawed in that it introduces
extrinsic, economic considerations into a relationship which in a
truly human society would be based solely on mutual sexual attraction and love. Morally speaking, bourgeois marriage is of a piece
with prostitution.

A classic statement of this position is provided in *The Origin of the
Family, Private Property and the State* by Friedrich Engels. According
to Engels, monogamy is a result of the concentration of wealth in the
hands of individual men, and the concern of these men that their
wealth should be transferred to their own progeny to the exclusion
of all others. Given the property and power relations in capitalism,
the position of women in this type of marriage is one of subjection;
indeed, they can be seen as a sort of property of their husbands.
However, although monogamy is brought about by specific economic
conditions, the disappearance of these economic conditions, i.e. the

demise of capitalist property and power relations, will not mean the end of monogamy. What will disappear is only its specifically capitalist variety: bourgeois marriage.

> Full freedom of marriage can therefore only be generally established when the abolition of capitalist production and of the property relations created by it has removed all the accompanying economic considerations which still exert such a powerful influence on the choice of a marriage partner. For then there will be no other motive left except mutual inclination. And as sexual love is by its nature exclusive – although at present this exclusiveness is fully realized only in the woman – the marriage based on sexual love is by its nature individual marriage. ... Then, according to all previous experience, the equality of women thereby achieved will tend infinitely more to make men really monogamous than to make women polyandrous.[20]

The claim that monogamous marriage in our society is one of the central institutions of capitalism, and could be seen as a type of private property, has been put forward and elaborated in John McMurtry's paper "Monogamy: A Critique." McMurtry characterizes monogamous marriage in terms of four principles it involves. It is a formal contractual relation defined, sanctioned and controlled by law. The number of partners is two and only two. There can be only one such relation at a time. Finally, a married person must not have sex outside marriage. These constitutive principles of marriage function as drastic restrictions on human sexual and other possibilities, inclinations, and needs, and McMurtry's critique of monogamous marriage is, for the most part, the spelling out of these restrictions and their deleterious effects.

State control of marriage does not so much promote as endanger the close, loving relationship between the spouses, since it detracts from their freedom in and responsibility for the relationship. The principle of monogamy is the most restrictive principle possible "for limiting extended social union and intimacy."[21] And the principle enjoining sexual exclusivity confines what may be "the most compelling natural force toward expanded intimate relations with others" within the narrowest scope possible.[22] Moreover, this exclusivity in various ways fosters insecurity, jealousy, and alienation in marriage:

It officially underwrites a literally totalitarian expectation of sexual confinement on the part of one's husband or wife: which expectation is, *ceteris paribus*, inevitably more subject to anxiety and disappointment than one less extreme in its demand and/or cultural-juridical backing. ... It requires so complete a sexual isolation of the marriage partners that should one violate the fidelity code the other is left alone and susceptible to a sense of fundamental deprivation and resentment. It stipulates such a strict restraint of sexual energies that there are habitual violations of the regulations, frequently if not always attended by willful deception and reciprocal suspicion about the occurence or quality of the extramarital relationship, anxiety and fear on both sides of permanent estrangement from partner and family, and overt and covert antagonism over the prohibited act in both offender (who feels 'trapped') and offended (who feels 'betrayed').[23]

All these restrictions that make up the institution of monogamous marriage as we know it are based on a single, fundamental principle of exclusion: the principle whereby the spouse has the right to exclude indefinitely all others from sexual access to his or her partner. Accordingly, McMurtry maintains that this type of marriage is "a state-regulated, indefinite, and exclusive ownership by two individuals of one another's sexual powers. Marriage is simply a form of private property."[24]

Now this last and most radical objection to the type of monogamous marriage characteristic of contemporary Western societies is clearly invalid, if taken literally (and McMurtry says nothing to suggest that it should be taken in some other way). As David Palmer points out in his defense of monogamous marriage against McMurtry's critique, the institution of private property involves several basic provisions. If a person owns X, then that person has the right to exclude others from access to X or its use. On the other hand, the owner also has the right to allow others access to X or its use. The owner has the right to use X in any way he or she wishes, to rent or sell it, and even to destroy it. Finally, X itself has no rights in relation to the owner. It is obvious that none of this applies to monogamous marriage. One does not have a legal right to prevent one's spouse from having sex with someone else. If he or she does, one can at most sue for divorce on that ground. One does not have a legal right to let others have sex with one's spouse, the way one can, say, give or lend others one's car. One cannot use one's spouse sexually in any way one fancies. Many legal systems in the Western world today acknowledge the possibility of marital abuse and rape and provide for its punishment. A spouse does not have a legal right to sell or let out the other spouse's sexual services. Finally, both spouses have rights against each other. Therefore, neither is owned by the other, and their marriage is a contractual relation – equal and fair or unequal and unfair, as the case may be – and not a type of private property.[25]

But if the crucial thesis of McMurtry's critique of monogamous marriage is plainly wrong, some of his other objections cannot be so easily dismissed. Even if sexual exclusivity in marriage is not a legally enforced set of rights and duties, it is still true that in the view of very many people monogamous marriage does impose such exclusivity. It does so since it involves reasonable, and indeed legitimate, expectations of sexual fidelity backed up by morality and custom, and prohibits adultery. If so, it can still be claimed to generate jealousy and some other unpleasant and unwholesome feelings and attitudes pointed out by McMurtry.

This brings up two further subjects to be discussed in this chapter: adultery and jealousy.

Adultery

Adultery can be defined as extramarital sex: sex a married person has with someone other than his or her spouse. What is wrong with it, morally speaking?

The most obvious answer would be that adultery is wrong because it hurts the feelings of the unadulterous spouse: it inflicts pain or suffering on him or her. But this, it might be said, is not an argument against adultery as such; it is rather an argument against committing it in a tactless and indiscreet way. The pain and suffering are not caused by adultery itself, but by the unadulterous spouse's knowledge of it. If the adulterous spouse can only go about it with a modicum of sense and discretion, the other spouse need never know.

This, however, is not a very helpful reply. It suggests that all will be well if the adulterer avoids one moral wrong by committing another, not obviously less serious: that he or she avoid causing pain or suffering by resorting to deception. This deception may be outright lying. But even if it is not that, it will be deception nevertheless. For it will involve not telling in a context in which the other spouse has reasonable and legitimate expectations of being told, and is almost certain to construe the silence as implying that there is nothing to tell. This, indeed, is another standard moral argument against adultery: that it involves deception. And deception is, surely, morally wrong. So is promise-breaking. And it can also be argued that adultery is wrong because it is a breach of promise: the promise of sexual exclusivity, made at the time of contracting the marriage. Now although all promise-breaking (except in cases of trivial promises) is morally wrong, just how wrong it is in any particular case will depend on the circumstances of the case. One is the importance of the promise to the promisee: the more important it is held to be, the worse its breach. Another is the nature of the context: to break a promise in the context of a personal relationship is worse than to break a promise made to a stranger. Now in these terms, the breach of promise involved in adultery is very wrong indeed.

Adultery is often called "cheating on one's spouse," and cheating is morally wrong too. To be sure, cheating is often taken to be a type of deception or promise-breaking. If that is all there is to it, then we do not have an additional moral objection to adultery. But cheating can be conceived in a different way, so that it does not reduce either to deception or to the breaking of a promise. Bernard Gert offers such an account. He argues that although cheating often involves deception, it need not do so. Think of a boss playing golf with an employee, and openly cheating at it. It often seems to be a case of breaking a promise (usually an implicit one), but need not be that either – one can cheat at solitaire. Cheating is best defined as the violation of publicly known rules of an activity that has been joined freely and that has built-in goals, for the purpose of attaining those goals, when such violation does not entail a penalty specified by the rules. Now marriage in our society is a practice whose built-in goal is "exclusive possession of a sexual partner". "Possession" is not to be taken literally, but in a weaker sense of "access". Of course, Gert adds, "marriage is supposed to be much more than this, and often is, but exclusive sexual activity is central to it." It follows that in our society (and any other society with such an understanding of marriage) adultery is cheating; for it "involves gaining the goal of marriage, an exclusive sexual partner, without abiding by the standards of that practice, i.e. being an exclusive sexual partner."[26]

A similar argument, in a more clearly Kantian vein, is offered by Michael J. Wreen. He, too, defines marriage in terms of commitment to sexual exclusivity. The commitment amounts to the adoption of a policy of such exclusivity. Adultery is a violation of that policy, and implies the adoption of a policy contradictory to that of sexual exclusivity. This contradiction between policies is what makes adultery wrong. This objection, Wreen adds, "holds even if the spouse of an adulterer knows of and condones his/her spouse's adulterous behavior. The fact that they are married is sufficient for such behavior to be wrong."[27]

This last remark seems to me quite implausible. The wrongness of adultery is found in the fact that it contradicts a policy to which the adulterer committed himself or herself. But surely one can normally be absolved of one's commitment by the beneficiary of that commitment. If one has been so absolved, and if one's adulterous behavior does not undermine the very rule of sexual exclusivity of married people (either because it is not a matter of common knowledge, or because it is, but it is also clear that it is known to and accepted by the other spouse), how can the mere fact that it is not in accord with a commitment no longer binding make it wrong?

Therefore we should reject this piece of Kantian rule-worship, and limit the scope of Wreen's argument to those more typical cases where such knowledge and consent are lacking. Still, Wreen's remark is helpful in that it suggests a general response to all the arguments for the immorality of adultery mentioned so far. Each of these arguments assumes the rule of sexual exclusivity as a constitutive rule of marriage. But should this assumption be granted?

To ask this is to ask what is marriage. Does the concept of marriage, or the concept of marriage in our society, necessarily involve a rule of sexual exclusivity? Moreover, one might want to broaden this question, and ask instead: Does this concept involve *any* commitment with regard to sex?

David Palmer takes up these questions in a slightly different context, in the course of his response to McMurtry's critique of monogamous marriage. On Palmer's account, marriage is a relationship, usually of some duration, between two (or more) humans. It usually involves: (1) a sexual relationship; (2) the expectation of procreation; (3) some expectations or agreements concerning physical, psychological, or material support; (4) a ceremony whereby society recognizes the creation of the union. However, none of these elements is a necessary condition of marriage. If they are jointly sufficient for marriage, that is probably on the strength of the last one. But to say this is to say that marriage is what society recognizes as marriage, and thereby admit that we do not have a definition of marriage at all.[28]

Thus, some societies recognize common law marriage, i.e. marriage that has not been contracted by means of some ceremonial proceeding. People can live separately, neither extend nor expect any mutual physical, psychological, or material support, and still be married. For any of a number of reasons, there might be no expectation of procreation; that would not make it impossible for people to get or stay married.[29] Most importantly, two persons who, for whatever reason, are not going to have sexual relations of any sort with one another, will have no difficulty getting or staying married.[30] The concept of marriage in general, and in our society in particular, does not entail that the spouses will have sexual relations, nor that they must be able or willing to have them. Actually, as Richard Wasserstrom points out, the only thing that can be safely said of marriage and sex is that marriage is incompatible with a *prohibition* of sexual relations between the spouses. The only positive implication marriage has regarding sex is that they are *allowed* to have sex with one another.[31]

The principle of sexual exclusivity is therefore *not* a necessary component of the institution of marriage in general, nor of the institution of monogamous marriage as it exists in our society. Moreover, throughout the better part of this century – roughly, since the end of World War One – there have been couples in Western societies who opted for "open marriage": marriage that explicitly repeals the sexual exclusivity clause characteristic of traditional marriage. In the late 1920s, Bertrand Russell argued for such marriage; that was one of the reasons for the subsequent notoriety of his views on marriage and sex. Russell noted that sexual attraction between spouses was liable to weaken or even completely disappear with time. In such cases easily accessible divorce might be the obvious solution, if no children were involved. If there were children to be considered, however, divorce might not be the best solution. "... Where a marriage is fruitful and both parties to it are reasonable and decent, the expectation ought to be that it will be lifelong, but not that it will exclude other sex relations."[32] Another argument was based on the significance and value marital companionship has quite independently of sex. It can

> produce so deep a tie between a man and a woman that they will feel something infinitely precious in their companionship, even after sexual passion has decayed, and even if either or both feels sexual passion for someone else. This mellowing of marriage has been prevented by jealousy, but

jealousy, though it is an instinctive emotion, is one which can be controlled if it is recognised as bad ... A companionship which has lasted for many years and through many deeply felt events has a richness of content which cannot belong to the first days of love, however delightful these may be. And any person who appreciates what time can do to enhance values will not lightly throw away such companionship for the sake of new love.[33]

Whatever its pros and cons, open marriage is marriage; couples who define their relationship in these terms consider themselves, and are considered by most others, as married for all intents and purposes. Now if a marriage is an open one, i.e. if the spouses have agreed that their relationship does not rule out sex with others, none of the moral arguments against adultery discussed so far applies. Extramarital sex need not cause hard feelings, pain, or suffering. It need not lead the adulterous spouse to lie or deceive by not telling. It will not be a breach of promise, nor cheating, nor, finally, the adoption of a policy contradictory to one to which the spouse is already committed.

If so, then the conclusion must be that adultery is not morally wrong as such. It is wrong only in so far as it inflicts pain or suffering on the other spouse, or leads one to lie or otherwise deceive one's spouse, or constitutes cheating, or breach of promise or commitment. And when it does, it is the pain or suffering inflicted, or deception, or promise-breaking, etc. that is wrong, and not the fact of extramarital sex in itself.

There is, however, one more argument to consider, more complex and interesting than those discussed so far. It is also an argument from deception; but it brings up a kind of deception embedded in sexual experience itself, rather than in whatever one might say or imply by saying nothing about it. In our society, it might be maintained, sex is not simply a source of a certain kind of pleasure, which might be experienced with another person without necessarily having and conveying any deeply personal and important feelings about that person such as affection and love. Our society understands sex as bound up with such feelings; therefore sex in our society expresses, and is normally taken to express, such feelings. Furthermore, one can have such feelings only for one other person at a time. Accordingly, as Richard Wasserstrom puts it, it can be argued that

extramarital sex will almost always involve deception of a deeper sort. If the adulterous spouse does not in fact have the appropriate feelings of affection for the extramarital partner, then the adulterous spouse is deceiving that person about the presence of such feelings. If, on the other hand, the adulterous spouse does have the corresponding feelings for the extramarital partner but not toward the non-participating spouse, the adulterous spouse is very probably deceiving the nonparticipating spouse about the presence of such feelings toward that spouse. ... Thus extramarital sex involves deception of this sort and is for that reason immoral even if no deception vis-a-vis the occurence of the act of adultery takes place.[34]

If valid, this argument shows not only the immorality of adultery, but also the immorality of having sex with more than one person at a certain time in one's life. This may be thought either a flaw or an advantage. But is the argument valid?

It claims two vital connections: between sex and deep personal feelings such as affection and love, and between these feelings and exclusivity. And, as Wasserstrom goes on to argue, both these connections can be questioned. And both can be questioned at two levels: the level of fact, and that of value.

One might ask if people in our society, as a matter of fact, understand sex as necessarily expressive of deep personal feelings of affection and love. No doubt that is a traditional understanding of sex, and one still shared by many. But it is not shared by all. If we take a look at the history of the views and attitudes on sex in the West, we shall often find an undercurrent of a different, hedonist view: a view that refuses to subordinate sex either to procreation or to love, and asserts the legitimacy of sex for the fun of it, without any extrinsic saving grace. In the course of the so-called sexual revolution of the sixties, this view came to be accepted by a great many young people. There have been further changes in sexual attitudes since that time, but this view of sex is certainly still held by many, not necessarily as the only way they can conceive of sex, but as a part of their overall understanding of it. Anything more specific on the subject – e.g. what is the relative spread and influence of the two views of sex, or how they correlate with various aspects of social structure – could be said only on the basis of sociological research. But there is no need to be more specific. It is enough to point out that the view of sex as necessarily expressive of deep personal feelings of affection or love does not enjoy a monopoly in our society. Since it does not, since it is not the sole available understanding of sex, the first of the two connections claimed by the argument – that between sex and affection or love – is undermined at the empirical level. It cannot be assumed in each case of adultery; every such case needs to be looked into in its own right in order to determine whether the assumed connection obtains, and whether, accordingly, the argument from a deeper sort of deception applies to it. There will surely be many cases in which a person can, and does, understand and experience sex as an integral part of a deep personal relationship with his or her spouse, but also, simultaneously, as a source of pleasure and nothing more, when engaged in with other persons. In such cases there need not and should not be any such deception.

Moreover, even if the view of sex assumed in the argument were, as a matter of fact, the only view available in our society, there would still be room for asking whether we *should* think of sex in this way, and in this way only. There are things to be said for sex with love – but there are also things that can be said for sex without love, casual sex, enjoyed for its own sake and understood as not entailing any further commitments. Most importantly, the two views are not mutually exclusive, if conceived not as sets of norms, applicable to all and sundry and at all times, but rather as articulating certain possibilities of sex, which can be realized at different times and with different persons.[35] If this is granted, as it surely should be, then the connection between sex and affection or love, and the argument from a deeper sort of deception predicated on it, are undermined at the level of norms and values.

The second step of this argument is no less problematic. Is it true that our feelings of deep affection or love are exclusive as claimed, i.e. always focused on one person only at a time? And if they are, is that necessary, or just a contingent state of affairs? If the latter, is it good that they should be so? Might it not be better if they could be expanded to include more than one person at a time?

Exclusivity seems to be unavoidable in love or any deeply personal, affectionate relationship. The concept of a personal relationship presupposes the distinction between personal and impersonal relationships; the concept of friendship presupposes the distinction between friends and mere acquaintances or complete strangers. One's deeply personal, private, intimate thoughts, feelings, hopes and projects are shared with some, and withheld from others; this, in part, helps define the first term in both distinctions. If somebody were completely open and willing to share everything with everybody, would that mean that that person had a personal relationship with everybody, that all comers were his or her friends, or would it rather show that that person actually had no personal relationships, no friends to speak of? Aristotle raises this question in his discussion of friendship, and answers that "those who have many friends and mix intimately with them all are thought to be no one's friend ..."[36] And he is surely right on this.

But all this shows is that in these matters there must be a *degree* of exclusivity, not that there has to be the *most extreme* exclusivity possible, i.e. that everybody except a single person must be excluded. Some exclusivity is entailed by such concepts as personal relationship, friendship, or love; but what degree of exclusivity it is going to be looks like an empirical question. It seems to be a question of each person's personal traits and preferences, and his or her resources and circumstances in general, or at a particular stage in life: psychological and physical resources one has to invest in such relationships, the amount of time one can afford to spend with others, etc. And, as a matter of fact, most people do have more than one personal relationship, more than one close friend. Some also love more than one person at a time. Others do not, but that may be due to their personality traits, or tastes and preferences, or their circumstances. Of course, at this point it may be said that there are different types of love, and that the kind of love that involves sex is an exception in this respect. But this claim still has to be established by a convincing argument.

Moreover, if a person can and does have deep personal feelings of affection or love for, and a sexual relationship with, more than one other person at a time, why is that not a good, rather than a bad thing? Of course, having such feelings and desires and acting on them may turn out to entail too great a cost for that person or for others – that is, turn out not to be good all things considered. But that does not show that the capacity for expanded feelings and experiences of this sort is not a good thing *in itself*.[37]

One reason for accepting that human beings can feel the kind of affection or love that involves sex for more than one person at a time, and that this is something to be appreciated rather than deplored and suppressed, is that it might make us less prone to jealousy. But then, if this view were accepted, would there still be room for the feeling of jealousy at all?

Jealousy

Jealousy is a fairly common feeling among spouses and lovers. In some cases it becomes so strong that it takes over the whole relationship, with far-reaching unpleasant, if not harmful consequences for both sides. This might suggest the conclusion drawn by Roger Scruton: "Because jealousy is one of the greatest of psychical catastrophes, involving the possible ruin of both partners, [sexual morality] must forestall and eliminate jealousy. It is in the deepest human interest, therefore, that we form the habit of fidelity."[38]

But even if one agrees with Scruton that jealousy ought to be forestalled or contained, one need not agree with the proposed strategy. Instead of trying to live up to the expectations of the green-eyed monster in order not to wake it up, one might attempt to banish it by showing that its very existence is possible only on the basis of a misunderstanding. That, indeed, is the most popular argument against jealousy. As usually understood, jealousy presupposes a view of interpersonal relations in terms of possession and rights. But humans, including lovers and spouses, are persons, not things. Therefore the possessive attitude to one's lover or spouse, the expectations and claims of exclusivity and of rights to concern, affection, and love, which make up the background of jealous thoughts and feelings, are completely out of place.

One might build on this, as Richard Taylor has done, and claim that it is jealousy, rather than adultery, that constitutes true marital betrayal. The spouse has committed himself or herself to loving the other spouse. That, of course, means relating to the spouse as a person, not a thing. But to be jealous of him or her is to adopt an attitude of possessiveness, incompatible with relating to the other as a person and destructive of love.[39]

However, all this may be too quick. The usual account of jealousy in terms of possessiveness may not be the only account available, and it may be thought unattractive for the very reason Taylor finds it appealing: it presents all jealousy as based on a conceptual confusion, and therefore as irrational. Moreover, it makes it either futile or self-defeating. Affection and love are feelings, and thus not a matter of choice; accordingly, the rights a jealous person wants to enforce cannot be enforced. (One might wonder if the commitment to love one's spouse, often undertaken in the form of an explicit promise at wedding, makes sense at all. Since we cannot choose to have or not have certain feelings, a promise to have them is misconceived and void.[40]) On the other hand, if love could be controlled and exacted as a right, that would not satisfy the jealous person. For what such a person wants is genuine love, that is, love spontaneously felt and freely given.

An alternative account of jealousy is offered by Jerome Neu. He grants that there are cases that fit the popular account of jealousy as based on an understanding of affection and love in terms of exclusivity and rights. But jealousy is not always the unreasonable and futile or self-defeating desire to exact exclusive concern, affection, or love from the partner. In some cases it has the form of fear of loss of affection to a third party, a rival. "One need not think one has a right to someone else's love in order to fear its loss: all that is necessary is that one believe one has the love to begin with. ... For jealousy to exist all one needs is vulnerability, and we all have that in sufficient abundance."[41] In such cases, jealousy can be perfectly intelligible, and perhaps also justified.

Fearing loss of something valued is understandable. But why must A fear that B will stop loving him (completely, or as much as she does now), if she starts loving C? Such fear presupposes what might be termed the quantum view of love: the view that the amount of love any individual can feel and give is limited, so that whatever B gives to C will have to be taken away from A. Love is a zero-sum game.

Neu points out an interesting asymmetry: most people will not agree that this is true of *them*. They have no great difficulty imagining themselves loving someone, then meeting someone else, and coming to love the new person as well, while not loving the first person less than before. But they also, for some reason, find it difficult to think that others might be capable of expanding their love in this way. Otherwise they could never be jealous. A double standard is at work here: not the well-known male/female one, but rather one of the form I/others.

Obviously, if the quantum view of love is untenable, then all jealousy is irrational. But is that view completely wrong? Do we really reject it in our own case? If we believe we could simultaneously love strongly, and equally, two or three persons, do we believe the same of ten or twenty? It would seem not. If so, that means that although the quantum view of love is best discarded, there are still limits to the love we have to give. We can really love at most a relatively small number of persons. These limits have to do with contingent matters like time and psychical resources at our disposal. And as long as these do limit our possibilities, there is a background against which some jealousy may make sense after all. Whether it is a good or a bad thing is another question (and one that may not admit of a simple "Yes" or "No" answer).

8

PROSTITUTION

Positive morality

Prostitution is often defined simply as commercial or mercenary sex, sex for money. This short definition is not entirely accurate, however; for the word "sex" is not very specific. "Commercial sex" may refer to sexual intercourse performed for money; but it may also be taken to refer to such services catering to sexual needs of others and provided for money as sex shows, acting in pornographic movies, or sexual surrogacy. While prostitution is certainly the most widespread variety of commercial sex, it is not the only one. What distinguishes it from other types of commercial sex (or "sex work", as it is often called too) is that it grants the client direct sexual access. This may involve full-fledged sexual intercourse; but even if it does not, it differs from sex shows, for example, in that it normally provides sexual satisfaction to the client through direct physical contact of some sort.

Prostitution is one of the most contentious issues in sexual ethics. Its moral condemnation is one of the few traditional views on sex that have withstood the general liberalization of sexual morality in Western societies in recent decades. Today it is often supported by new arguments; but it tends to retain much of its traditional severity.

The morality of our society and that of most others today condemns prostitution in no uncertain terms. The facts of the condemnation and its various, sometimes quite serious and far-reaching consequences for those who practice it are well known and need not be recounted here. But what do these facts show? Surely not that prostitution *is* wrong, only that positive morality of this and many other societies *considers* it wrong. When discussing the morality of prostitution, as when discussing any other moral issue, we must distinguish between positive and critical morality. The former is the morality prevalent in a society and expressed in its public opinion, its laws, and the lives of its members. The latter is a set of moral principles, rules and values, together with the reasoning behind them, that an individual may adopt, not only to live by them, but also to apply them in judging critically the morality of any society, including his or her own.

To be sure, the importance, or even tenability of this distinction has been denied. There have been authors such as Emile Durkheim who maintained that whatever a society holds to be right or wrong *is* right or wrong in that society. But the flaws of this position, which may be termed moral positivism, are obvious and fatal. One is that it implies that all philosophers, religious teachers, writers and social reformers who set out to criticize and reform the moral outlook of their societies were not merely wrong – all of them may, and some of them must have been wrong – but completely misguided in what they were trying to do; for what they were trying to do logically cannot be done. There is no such thing as radical moral critique of one's society (or any other society, for that matter). Another unattractive implication of moral positivism is that the same practice can be both right (in one society) and wrong (in another). Prostitution would be a good example: both morally unobjectionable (in ancient Greece) *and* a moral abomination (in nineteenth-century England).

Another problem with positive morality is that it tends to reflect various conventional prejudices. In its judgment on prostitution, positive morality is clearly affected by standards of lifestyle and income that can have no possible moral relevance. As social historians of prostitution have remarked, "though it is a deviant or stigmatized occupation, the stigma attached to it depends on who is plying the trade. It varies significantly from the high-paid courtesan or call girl to the low-level prostitute, and generally the higher the fee the lesser the stigma."[1]

Finally, positive morality is often inconsistent. Prostitution is, again, a case in point. Historically, its condemnation has been bound up with the double standard: positive morality condemns the prostitute, but *not* the client, although both, equally and necessarily, take part in the condemned practice. Furthermore, many authors have pointed out that there is no morally significant difference between the common prostitute and the spouse in a marriage of convenience. This kind of marriage, said Friedrich Engels, for instance, "turns often enough into the crassest prostitution – sometimes of both partners, but far more commonly of the woman, who only differs from the ordinary courtesan in that she does not let out her body on piecework as a wage worker, but sells it once and for all into slavery."[2] The word "slavery" is too strong, and it may not be the spouse's body that is being sold, but otherwise the point is well taken. How can positive morality condemn mercenary sex in one case, but not in the other?

I am not saying that this inconsistency cannot be explained. It can, if we attend to the social meaning of marriage and prostitution.[3] Both can be called "sexual institutions," as both have to do with sex, both are institutional frameworks for satisfying sexual desire. But their social meaning is not the same. Throughout history, the most important social function of sex has been reproduction. Marriage has always been seen as the best institutional setup for procreating and socializing the offspring. Accordingly, marriage is the central, most respected and most strongly supported among the sexual institutions, while other such institutions, such as concubinage or wife exchange, are the less supported and respected the more they are removed from marriage. Prostitution is at the other end of this range, for in prostitution

> both parties use sex for an end not socially functional, the one for pleasure, the other for money. To tie intercourse to sheer physical pleasure is to divorce it both from reproduction and from the sentimental primary type of relation which it symbolizes. To tie it up to money ... does the same thing. ... On both sides the relationship is merely a means to a private end....[4]

Both money and pleasure may be very important to the individuals concerned but, as merely individual objectives, have no social significance. Therefore, society accords prostitution neither support nor respect. The traditional Western sexual morality considers sex as in itself morally problematic if not downright bad or sinful, and thus legitimate only as a means of procreation, and perhaps also of expression and reinforcement of emotions and attitudes usually associated with procreation. It is easy to see how Western society came to condemn and despise the practice of prostitution.

However, the inconsistency of condemning mercenary sex outside marriage but not within it still has not been explained. The missing part is the fact that society is concerned with practices and institutions, not with individuals; social morality judges primarily practices and institutions, and normally deals with individuals simply by subsuming them under the roles defined by practices and institutions. If it were otherwise, if social morality were interested in, and capable of, relating to the individual and his or her actions in their particularity and complexity, as serious and discerning moral thinking must do, it could not fail to condemn mercenary sex within marriage no less than outside it. For it does not consider marriage valuable in itself, but as the proper framework for procreation and the upbringing of offspring, and also, perhaps, as the framework that best sustains the emotions and attitudes helpful in the performance of these tasks. Therefore marital sex is not legitimate simply as marital, but as sex that serves the social purpose of marriage. When a person engages in sex within marriage, but fails to live up to this normative conception of the institution and has sex merely in order to secure economic benefits of the married state, that is no less mercenary than the sex sold on the street to all comers, and acordingly no less wrong from the point of view of the sexual morality to which society adheres on the level of rules and roles, practices and institutions. Society does not see this because it cannot be bothered to look into the life, actions and motives of the individual. But that is reason enough not to be guided by its pronouncements when seeking an answer to an important moral question.

Paternalism

Paternalism is interference with a person's liberty or autonomy justified by reasons of that person's own good, happiness, needs, interests, or values. Philosophical discussions of paternalism have often focused on paternalist legislation; for the most obvious, and often the most effective, kind of interference with an individual's liberty or autonomy is by means of law. But paternalistic arguments are sometimes brought up in debates about purely moral issues. It is sometimes argued that the wrongness of doing something follows from the fact that doing it has serious adverse effects on the good, happiness, etc. of the agent. This argument is then taken to call for the pressure of the moral sanction on the individuals concerned to get them to refrain from doing it. A popular way of arguing against prostitution is of this sort: it refers to such hazards of selling sex as (1) venereal and other diseases (including AIDS), (2) unpleasant, humiliating, even violent behavior of clients; (3) exploitation by madams and pimps; (4) the extremely low social status of prostitutes and the contempt and ostracism to which they are exposed.

The fact showing that these are, indeed, the hazards of prostitution are well known; are they not enough to show that prostitution is bad and to be avoided?

The basic flaw of arguments of this sort is that even if such claims are granted, they make only a prudential, not a moral case against prostitution.

Even when advanced under the heading of prudence, the paternalist argument is not a very good one. The first thing to note is that it is an argument from *occupational* hazards and thus, if valid, valid only against prostitution as an *occupation*. For in addition to the professional prostitute, whose sole livelihood comes from mercenary sex, there is also the amateur, who is usually gainfully employed or married and engages in prostitution for additional income. The latter – also known as the secret prostitute – need not at all suffer from (3) and (4), and stands a much lower chance of being exposed to (1) and (2). A reference to (3) is actually not even an argument against professional prostitution, but merely against a particular, by no means necessary way of practicing it. If a professional prostitute is likely to be exploited by a madam or pimp, that is a weighty reason for pursuing the trade on her own.

But it is more important to note that the crucial, although indirect cause of all these hazards of professional prostitution is the negative attitude of society, the condemnation of prostitution by its morality and its laws. But for that, the prostitute could enjoy much better medical protection, much more effective police protection from aggressive and abusive behavior of clients and legal protection from exploitation by pimps and madams, and her social status would be significantly different. Thus the paternalist argument takes for granted the conventional moral condemnation of prostitution, and merely gives an additional reason for not engaging in something that has already been established as wrong. But we can and should refuse to take that for granted, because we can and should refuse to submit to positive morality as the arbiter of moral issues. If we do so, and if a good case for morally condemning prostitution has still not been made out, as I hope to show here, then all these hazards should be seen in a different light. They should be taken as reasons for trying to disabuse society of the prejudice against prostitution and help change the law and social conditions in general in which prostitutes work, in order to reduce as much as possible, if not completely eliminate, such hazards.

However, there is one occupational hazard that has not been mentioned so far: one that cannot be blamed on unenlightened social morality, and would remain even if society were to treat prostitution as any other legitimate occupation. That is the danger to the sex life of the prostitute. As Lars O. Ericsson neatly puts it, "Can one have a well-functioning sexual life if sex is what one lives by?"[5]

One response to this particular paternalistic objection is to say, with David A.J. Richards, that perhaps one can. Richards claims that there is no evidence that prostitution makes it impossible for those who practice it to have loving relationships, and adds that "there is some evidence that prostitutes, as a class, are more sexually fulfilled than other American women."[6] The last claim is based on a study in which 175 prostitutes were systematically interviewed, and which showed that "they experienced orgasm and multiple orgasm more frequently in their personal, 'non-commercial' intercourse than did the normal woman (as defined by Kinsey norms)."[7] Another, safer response is to point out, as Ericsson does, that the question is an empirical one and that, since there is no conclusive evidence either way, we are not in a position to draw any conclusion.[8]

My preferred response is different. I would rather grant the empirical claim that a life of prostitution is liable to affect one's sex life adversely, and perhaps even wreck it, i.e. the minor premise of the argument, and then look a bit more closely into the major premise, the principle of paternalism. For there are two rather different versions of this principle. The weak version justifies interference with an individual's choice that is not fully voluntary, either because the individual is permanently incompetent or because the choice in question is a result of ignorance of some important facts or made under extreme psychological or social pressure. Otherwise the individual is considered the sole qualified judge of his or her own good, happiness, needs, interests, or values, and the choice is ultimately his or hers. Moreover, when a usually competent individual is prevented from acting on a choice that is either uninformed or made under extreme pressure, and is therefore not fully voluntary, that individual will, when the choice-impairing conditions no longer obtain, agree that the paternalist interference was appropriate and legitimate, and perhaps even be grateful for it.

Strong paternalism, on the other hand, *is* meant to protect the individual from his or her voluntary choices, and therefore will not be legitimized by retrospective consent of the individual paternalized. The assumption is not that the individual is normally the proper judge of his or her own good, happiness, etc., but rather that someone else knows better where the individual's true good, happiness, etc. lies, and therefore has the right to interfere in order to promote it, even though that means going against the individual's fully voluntary choice, which is judged to be merely "subjective" or "arbitrary."

Obviously, the weak version of paternalism does not conflict with personal liberty, but should rather be understood as its corollary; for it does not protect the individual from choices that express his or her considered preferences and settled values, but only against his or her "non-voluntary choices," choices the individual will subsequently disavow. Strong paternalism, on the other hand, is often seen as intellectual or moral arrogance by its supposed beneficiaries. It is essentially opposed to individual liberty, and cannot be accepted by anyone who takes liberty seriously.[9]

Accordingly, if the argument from the dangers to the prostitute's sex life is not to be made rather implausible from the start, it ought to be put forward in terms of weak rather than strong paternalism. When put in these terms, however, it is not really an argument against prostitution as an imprudent choice of occupation, but rather an argument against prostitution *if and when* it is taken up imprudently. It reminds us that persons permanently incompetent and those who have not reached the age of consent should not (be allowed to) take up the life of prostitution and thereby most likely seriously endanger and possibly even throw away the prospect of a good sex life. As for a competent adult, the only legitimate paternalist interference with the choice of such a person to work as a prostitute is to make sure that the choice is a free and informed one. These are no easy tasks, for prostitution has often involved minors, and has often been engaged in under extreme pressure of social and economic circumstances, without full understanding of its nature and hazards, and sometimes even as a result of fraud or coercion. But if an adult and sane person is fully apprised of the dangers of prostitution to the sex life of the prostitute and decides, without undue pressure of any sort, that the advantages of prostitution are worth it, then it is neither imprudent nor wrong for that person to embark on the line of work chosen.[10] In such a case, as John Stuart Mill put it, "neither one person, nor any number of persons, is warranted in saying to another human creature of ripe years that he shall not do with his life for his own benefit what he chooses to do with it."[11]

Things not for sale

In the view of many, by far the best argument against prostitution is brief and simple: some things are just not for sale, and sex is one of them.

It would be difficult not to go along with the first part of this argument. The belief that not everything can or should be bought and sold is extremely widespread, if not universal. The list of things not for sale is not exactly the same in all societies, but it seems that every society does have such a list, a list of "blocked exchanges."

The term is Michael Walzer's, and a discussion of such exchanges is an important part of his theory of justice. The central thesis of the theory is that there are several spheres of personal qualities and social goods, each autonomous, with its own criteria, procedures, and agents of distribution. Injustice occurs when this autonomy is violated, when the borders are crossed and a sphere of goods becomes dominated by another in that the goods of the former are no longer distributed in accordance with its own criteria and procedures, but in accordance with those of the other sphere.

The market is one such sphere – actually, the sphere with the strongest tendency to expand into, and dominate, other spheres of goods, at least in a modern capitalist society. But even this kind of society has an impressive list of things not for sale. The one Walzer offers as "the full set of blocked exchanges in the United States today," but which would be valid for any contemporary liberal and democratic society, includes the sale of human beings (slavery), political power and office, criminal justice, freedom of speech, various prizes and honors, love and friendship, and more.[12] This is, obviously, a mixed lot. In some cases, the very nature of a good rules out its being bought and sold (love, friendship); in others, that is precluded by the conventions that constitute it (prizes); in still others, the dominant conception of a certain sphere of social life prohibits its sale, as, for instance, our conception of the nature and purpose of the political process entails that political power and office must not be bought and sold. (To be sure, some of the things listed as a matter of fact are bought and sold. But that happens only on the black market, and the fact that the market is "black," and that those who buy and sell there do so in secret, goes to show both the illegitimacy and the secondary, parasitic character of such trans-actions.) There is, thus, no single criterion by reference to which one could explain why all these items appear on the list, and why no other does.

What of sex? It is not on the list; for sex, unlike love, can, as a matter of fact, be bought and sold, and there is no single, generally accepted conception of sex that prohibits its sale and purchase.

"People who believe that sexual intercourse is morally tied to love and marriage are likely to favor a ban on prostitution. ... Sex can be sold only when it is understood in terms of pleasure and not exclusively in terms of married love...."[13]

This is helpful, for it reminds us that the "Not for sale" argument is elliptic; the understanding of sex that is presupposed must be explicated before the argument can be assessed. But the remark is also inaccurate, since it conflates two views of sex that are both historically and theoretically different: the traditional view, which originated in religion, that sex is legitimate only within marriage and as a means to procreation, and the more modern, secular view that sex is valuable only when it expresses and enhances a loving relationship. Let me look briefly into these two views in order to see whether a commitment to either does, indeed, commit one to condemning prostitution.

The first views sex as something inferior, sinful and shameful, and accepts it only when, and in so far as, it serves an important extrinsic purpose which cannot be attained by any other means: procreation. Moreover, the only proper framework for bringing up children is marriage; therefore sex is permissible only within marriage. These two statements make up the core of the traditional Christian understanding of sex I have discussed in a previous chapter.[14] Do those committed to this understanding have to endorse the ban on prostitution?

At some level, they obviously must think ill of it. Their sexual ethics confines sex within the bounds of heterosexual, monogamous marriage, and rules out sexual relations between any possible partners except husband and wife. Moreover, it restricts the legitimate sexual relations between the spouses to those that are "by nature ordained" toward procreation, thus ruling out "artificial" birth control, masturbation, petting to orgasm, oral and anal sex. Prostitution or, more accurately, common prostitution, which is both non-marital and disconnected from procreation, would seem to be beyond the pale.

But then, even the legitimacy of marital and procreative sex is of a rather low order. As sex, it is intrinsically problematic; as marital and procreative, it is accepted as a necessary evil, an inevitable concession to fallen human nature. As Augustine says, a wise and pious person would prefer to beget children without experiencing any lust at all, if only it were possible.[15] Therefore, if it turns out that accepting sex within marriage and for the purpose of procreation is not concession enough, that human sexuality is so strong and unruly that it cannot be confined within these bounds and that attempts to so confine it may well prove harmful to the institution of marriage itself, the inevitable conclusion will be that further concession is in order. That is just the conclusion reached by many authors with regard to prostitution: it should be tolerated, for it provides a safety valve for a force that otherwise might subvert the institution of marriage and destroy all the chastity and decency this institution makes possible. My favorite quotation in this connection is from Bernard Mandeville. He, of course, sees this as but another instance of the general truth that private vices are often public benefits:

> If Courtezans and Strumpets were to be prosecuted with as much Rigour as some silly People would have it, what Locks or Bars would be sufficient to preserve the Honour of our Wives and Daughters? For 'tis not only that the Women in general would meet with far greater Temptations, and the Attempts to ensnare the Innocence of Virgins would seem more excusable to the sober part of Mankind than they do now: But some Men would grow outrageous, and Ravishing would become a common Crime. Where six or seven Thousand Sailors arrive at once, as it often happens at *Amsterdam*, that have seen none but their own Sex for many Months together, how is it to be supposed that honest Women should walk the Streets unmolested, if there were no Harlots to be had at reasonable Prices? ... There is a Necessity of sacrificing one part of Womankind to preserve the other, and prevent a Filthiness of a more heinous Nature.[16]

That prostitution makes an important contribution to the stability and the very survival of marriage has been pointed out not only by cynics like Mandeville, misanthropes like Arthur Schopenhauer,[17] or godless rationalists like William Lecky[18] and Bertrand Russell.[19] It was acknowledged as a fact, and as one that entails that prostitution ought to be tolerated rather than suppressed, by Augustine and Thomas Aquinas themselves.[20] Moreover, the complementary, indeed symbiotic relation between marriage and prostitution has been confirmed by sociological study of human sexual behavior. Sociological research shows that the majority of clients of prostitutes are married men who do not find complete sexual satisfaction within marriage, but are content to stay married, provided they can have extramarital commercial sex as well.[21] Accordingly, even if one adopts the most conservative and restrictive of the major views of sex, the view that ties sex to marriage and procreation, one need not, indeed should not condemn prostitution very harshly. One should rather adopt a tolerant attitude to it, knowing that it is twice removed from the ideal state of affairs, but that its demise is liable to bring about something much worse.

Another view which would seem to call for the condemnation of prostitution is the view of sex as essentially tied to love; for mercenary sex is normally as loveless as sex can ever get. The important thing to note is that whatever unfavorable judgment on prostitution is suggested by this view of sex, it will not be a judgment unfavorable to prostitution as such, but rather to prostitution as a type of loveless sex. It is the lovelessness, not the commercial nature of the practice that this view finds objectionable.

One response to this kind of objection would be to take on squarely the view of sex that generates it. One could take a critical look at the arguments advanced in support of the view that sex should always be bound up with love. One could bring out the difficulties of the linkage, the tensions between love and sex which seem to make a stable and fruitful combination of the two difficult, if not unlikely. One could even argue for the superiority of loveless, noncommital, plain sex over sex that is bound up with love.[22]

Another response would be to grant the validity of the sex with love view, but only as a personal ideal, not a universally binding moral standard. This is the tack taken by David A.J. Richards,[23] who points out that it would be signally misguided, indeed absurd, to try to enforce this particular ideal, based as it is "on the cultivation of spontaneous romantic feeling."[24] My preferred response to the rejection of prostitution from the point of view of sex with love is along these lines, but I would like to go a bit further. I would want to emphasize that it is possible to appreciate this ideal and at the same time not only grant that sex that falls short of it need not be wrong, but also allow that it can be positively good (without going as far as to claim that it is actually better than sex with love).

All this has to do with plain sex in general, rather than its mercenary variety in particular. That is due to the general character of this type of objection to prostitution: prostitution is seen as flawed not on account of its commercial nature, but rather because it has nothing to do with love. Accordingly, as far as this view of sex is concerned, by exonerating plain sex, one also exonerates its commercial variety.

Degradation of women

In this section and the next I deal with what might be termed feminist objections to prostitution. This should not be taken to suggest that these objections are put forward only by feminists, nor that they are shared by all feminists. Contemporary discussion of the rights and wrongs of prostitution is for the most part a debate between those who hold that the sale of sex is just another service, in itself as legitimate as any other and not to be interfered with as long as no coercion, exploitation, or fraud is involved, and those who deny this and claim that prostitution is essentially bound up with degradation or oppression of women. The particular concern for the role and status of women that motivates the latter position is clearly feminist; the former position can loosely be termed liberal. But there is a certain overlap: one of the currents of feminism is liberal feminism, and its adherents do not subscribe to the critique of prostitution advanced by feminists of other stripes, but rather think of it much as other liberals do, as morally unobjectionable in itself.[25]

One might want to take issue with the whole feminist approach to the question of prostitution as a question about women; after all, not all prostitutes are women. But this is not a promising tack; for, if not all, most of them are and always have been. So if prostitution involves either degradation or oppression, the great majority of those degraded or oppressed are women. But does it?

There is no denying that the belief that prostitution degrades those who practice it is very widespread. But this belief may be wrong. The question is: *Just why* should prostitution be considered degrading? There are four main answers: (1) because it is utterly impersonal; (2) because the prostitute is reduced to a mere means; (3) because of the intimate nature of the acts she performs for money; (4) because she actually sells her body, sells herself. Let me look into each of these claims in turn.

(1) Prostitution is degrading because the relation between the prostitute and her client is completely impersonal. The client does not even perceive, let alone engage the prostitute as the person she is; he has no interest, no time for any of her personal characteristics, but relates to her merely as a source of sexual satisfaction, nothing more than a sex object.

One possible response to this is that prostitution need not be impersonal. There is, of course, the streetwalker who sells sex to all comers (or almost). But there is also the prostitute with a limited number of steady clients, with whom she develops quite personal relationships. So if the objection is to the impersonal character of the relation, the most that can be said is that a certain kind of prostitution is degrading, not that prostitution as such is. I do not want to make much of this, though. For although in this, as in many other services, there is the option of personalized service, the other, impersonal variety is typical.

My difficulty with the argument is more basic: I cannot see why the impersonal nature of a social transaction or relation makes that transaction or relation degrading. After all, the personal relations we have with others – with our family, friends and acquaintances – are just a small part (although the most important part) of our social life. The other part includes the overwhelming majority of our social transactions and relations which are, and have to be, quite impersonal. One does not have a personal relationship with the newspaper vendor, the bus driver, the shop assistant, and all those numerous other people one interacts with in the course of a single day; and, as long as basic decencies of social intercourse (which are purely formal and impersonal) are observed, there is nothing wrong with that. There is nothing wrong in thinking of and relating to the newspaper vendor as just that and, as far as one is concerned, nothing more. That our social relations must for the most part be impersonal may be merely a consequence of the scarcity of resources we have to invest in them. But it is inescapable in any but the smallest and simplest, so-called face-to-face society.

It may be said that the selling and buying of newspapers and sex are quite different. While an impersonal attitude is unobjectionable in the former case, it is objectionable, because degrading, in the latter. But if this is the point, then the objection presupposes that sex ought to be personal; and that has yet to be established. It need not (always) be on three major views of sex: sex as bound up with procreation, sex as language, and sex as basically a source of a certain type of pleasure. It must always be on the sex with love view; but I hope to have shown in the preceding pages that the case against casual sex in general, and prostitution in particular, suggested by that view is not very strong.[26]

The next two points are suggested in the following remarks by Bertrand Russell:

> The intrusion of the economic motive into sex is always in a greater or lesser degree disastrous. Sexual relations should be a mutual delight, entered into solely from the sponta-

neous impulse of both parties. Where this is not the case, everything that is valuable is absent. To use another person in so intimate a manner is to be lacking in that respect for the human being as such, out of which all true morality must spring. ... Morality in sexual relations, when it is free from superstition, consists essentially of respect for the other person, and unwillingness to use that person solely as a means of personal gratification without regard to his or her desires. ... Prostitution sins against this principle....[27]

(2) Prostitution is said to degrade the prostitute because she is used as a means by the client. The client relates to the prostitute in a purely instrumental way: she is no more than a means to his sexual satisfaction. If so, is he not reducing her to a mere means, a thing, a sex object, and thereby degrading her?

If he were to rape her, that would indeed amount to treating her without regard to her desires, and thus to reducing, degrading her to a mere means. But as a customer rather than a rapist, he gets sexual satisfaction from her for a charge, on the basis of a mutual understanding, and she does her part of the bargain willingly. It is not true that he acts without regard for her desires. He does not satisfy her sexual desire; indeed, the prostitute does not expect him to do so. But he does satisfy the one desire she has with regard to him: the desire for money. Their transaction is not "a mutual delight, entered into solely from the spontaneous impulse of both parties," but rather a calculated exchange of goods of different order. But it does not offend against the principle of respect for human beings as such as long as it is free from coercion and fraud, and both sides get what they want.

Most of our social transactions and relations are impersonal, and most are instrumental. There is nothing wrong with either impersonal or instrumental way of relating to others as such. Just as the fact that A relates to B in a completely impersonal way is not tantamount to a violation of B's personhood, B's status as a person, so the fact that A relates to B in a purely instrumental way is not equivalent to A's reducing B to a mere means. In both cases B's informed and freely given consent absolves the relation of any such charge, and thereby also of the charge of degradation.

(3) Sex is an intimate, perhaps the most intimate part of our lives. Should it not therefore be off limits to commercial considerations and transactions? And is it not degrading to perform something so intimate as a sex act with a complete stranger and for money?

It is not. As Lars O. Ericsson points out,

> We are no more justified in devaluating a prostitute, who,
> for example, masturbates her customers, than we are in
> devaluating the assistant nurse, whose job it is to take care
> of the intimate hygiene of disabled patients. Both help to
> satisfy important human needs, and both get paid for doing
> so. That the harlot, in distinction to the nurse, intention-
> ally gives her client pleasure is of course nothing that
> should be held against her![28]

It might be objected that the analogy is not valid, for there is an
important asymmetry between pain and pleasure: the former has
significantly greater moral weight than the latter. While it may be
morally acceptable to cross the borders of intimacy in order to
relieve pain or suffering, which is what the nurse does, that does not
show that it is permissible to do so merely for the sake of giving
pleasure, which is what the prostitute provides. But if so, what are
we to say of a fairly good-looking woman who undergoes plastic
surgery and has her breasts enlarged (or made smaller, as the case
may be) in order to become even more attractive and make her sex
life richer and more pleasurable than it already is? Is she really
doing something degrading and morally wrong?

(4) Prostitution is degrading because what the prostitute sells is
not simply and innocuously a service, as it may appear to a superfi-
cial look. Actually, there is much truth in the old-fashioned way of
speaking of her as a woman who "sells herself." And if *that* is not
degrading, what is?

This point has been made in two different ways. David Archard
has argued that there is a sense in which the prostitute sells herself
because of the roles and attitudes involved in the transaction:

> Sexual pleasure is not ... an innocent commodity. Always
> implicated in such pleasure is the performance of roles,
> both willing and unwilling. These roles range from the
> possibly benign ones of doer and done-to, through superior
> and subordinate to abaser and abased. Thus, when a man
> buys 'sex' he also buys a sexual role from his partner, and
> this involves the prostitute in being something more than
> simply the neutral exchanger of some commodity.

More specifically,

if I buy (and you willingly sell) your allegiance, your obse-
quiousness, your flattery or your servility there is no easy
distinction to be made between you as 'seller' and the
'good' you choose to sell. Your whole person is implicated
in the exchange. So it is too with the sale of sex.[29]

However, commercial sex need not involve such things as obsequious-
ness, flattery, servility, or allegiance on the part of the prostitute. These
attitudes, and the "role" they might be thought to make up, are not
its constitutive parts; whether, when, and to what degree they characterize the transaction is an empirical question that admits of no
simple and general answer. Indeed, those who adhere to the sex with
love view often say that sex with prostitutes is an impoverished,
even sordid experience because of the impersonal, quick, mechan-
ical, blunt way in which the prostitute goes about her job.

Moreover, some services that have nothing to do with sex tend to
involve, and are expected to involve, some such attitudes on the part
of the person providing the service. Examples vary from one culture
to another; the waiter and the hairdresser come to mind in ours.
Now such attitudes are undoubtedly morally objectionable; but that
does not tell against any particular occupation in which they may be
manifested, but rather against the attitudes themselves, the individuals who, perhaps unthinkingly, come to adopt them, and the social
conventions that foster such attitudes.

Another way of trying to show that the prostitute sells herself,
rather than merely a service like any other, is by focusing on the
concept of self-identity. This is the tack taken by Carole Pateman.
She first points out that the service provided by the prostitute is
related in a much closer way to her body than is the case with any
other service, for sex and sexuality are constitutive of the body,
while the labor and skills hired out in other lines of work are not.
"Sexuality and the body are ... integrally connected to conceptions
of femininity and masculinity, and all these are constitutive of our
individuality, our sense of self-identity."[30] When sex becomes a
commodity, so do bodies and selves.

If so, what of our ethnic identity? When asked to say who they
are, do not people normally bring up their ethnic identity as one of
the most important things they need to mention? If it is granted
that one's ethnic identity is also constitutive of one's individuality,
one's sense of self-identity, what are we to say of a person who
creates an item of authentic folk art and then sells it, or of a singer
who gives a concert of folk music and charges for attendance? Are

they also selling themselves, and thus doing something degrading and wrong?

The likely response will be to refuse to grant our ethnic identity the same significance for our self-identity that is claimed for gender. Although people typically refer to their ethnic identity when explaining who they are, there are also many exceptions. There are persons who used to think of themselves in such terms, but have come to repudiate, not merely their particular ethnic affiliation, but the very idea that ethnicity should be part of one's sense of who one is. There are also persons who have always felt that way (perhaps because that is how they were brought up). They do not think of their own sense of self-identity as somehow incomplete, and neither should we. There are no analogous examples with regard to gender; we all think of ourselves as either men or women, and whatever particular conception one has of one's gender, the conception is closely connected with one's sexuality. Gender is much more basic than ethnicity, much more closely related to our sense of self-identity, than ethnicity or anything else that may be thought relevant.

Perhaps it is.[31] But if that is reason enough for saying that the prostitute sells her body and herself, and thus does something degrading and wrong, shall we not have to say the same of the wet nurse and the surrogate mother? Their bodies and gender are no less involved in what they do than the body and gender of the prostitute; and they charge a fee, just as the prostitute does. I do not know that anybody has argued that there is something degrading, or otherwise morally wrong, in what the wet nurse does, nor that what she does is selling her body or herself. Therefore I think she is a good counterexample to Pateman's argument.

The surrogate mother might be thought a less compelling one, for there has been considerable debate about the nature and moral standing of surrogacy. I do not need to go into all that, though.[32] The one objection to surrogacy relevant in the present context is that "it is inconsistent with human dignity that a woman should use her uterus for financial profit and treat it as an incubator for someone else's child."[33] However, we are not told just why it should be thought inconsistent with human dignity to do that. Indeed, it is not clear how it could be, if it is not inconsistent with human dignity that a woman should use her breasts for financial profit and treat them as a source of nourishment for someone else's child. And if it is not, why should it be inconsistent with human dignity that a woman should use her sex organs and skills for financial profit and treat them as a source of pleasure for someone else?

If what I have been saying is right, we still do not have an argument showing that prostitution is degrading in itself. This, of course, should not prevent us from attending to the degrading conditions in which prostitutes often have to ply their trade. As Janet Radcliffe Richards rightly says, "there is quite enough degradation in *surrounding circumstances* to account for women's being degraded, without having to resort to the idea that there is something bad about unsanctioned or commercially motivated sex."[34] Those circumstances are direct or indirect results of the condemnation of prostitution by conventional morality.

Oppression of women

The other main feminist objection to prostitution is that it exemplifies and helps maintain the oppression of women. This objection is much more often asserted than argued. It is frequently made by quoting the words of Simone de Beauvoir that the prostitute "sums up all the forms of feminine slavery at once."[35] But de Beauvoir's chapter on prostitution, although good as a description of some of its main types, is short on argument and does nothing to show that prostitution as such must be implicated in the oppression of women.

An argument intended to establish that with regard to our society has recently been offered by Laurie Shrage. She expressly rejects the idea of discussing commercial sex in a "cross-cultural" or "trans-historical" way, and grants that it need not be oppressive to women in every conceivable or, indeed, every existing society. What she does claim is that in our society prostitution epitomizes and perpetuates certain basic cultural assumptions about men, women and sex which provide justification for the oppression of women in many domains of their lives, and in this way harm both prostitutes and women in general.[36]

There are four such cultural assumptions, which need not be held consciously but may be implicit in daily behavior. A strong sex drive is a universal human trait. Sexual behavior defines one's social identity, makes one a particular "kind" of person: one is "a homosexual," "a prostitute," "a loose woman." Men are "naturally" dominant. In this connection, Shrage points out that the sex industry in our society caters almost exclusively to men, and "even the relatively small number of male prostitutes at work serve a predominantly male consumer group."[37] Finally, sexual contact pollutes and harms women.

The last claim is supported by a three-pronged argument. (1) In a woman, a history of sexual activity is not taken to suggest experience in a positive sense, expertise, high-quality sex. On the contrary, it is seen as a negative mark that marks off a certain kind of woman; women are valued for their "innocence". (2) That sex with men is damaging to women is implicit in the vulgar language used to describe the sex act: "a woman is 'fucked,' 'screwed,' 'banged,' 'had,' and so forth, and it is a man (a 'prick') who does it to her."[38] (3) The same assumption is implicit in "the metaphors we use" for the sex act. Here Shrage draws on Andrea Dworkin's book *Intercourse*,[39] which invokes images of physical assault and imperialist domination and describes women having sexual intercourse with men as being not only entered or penetrated, but also "split", "invaded", "occupied" and "colonized" by men.

These cultural assumptions define the meaning of prostitution in our society. By tolerating prostitution, our society implies its acceptance of these assumptions, which legitimize and perpetuate the oppression of women and their marginality in all the main areas of social life. As for prostitutes and their clients, whatever their personal views of sex, men and women, they imply by their actions that they accept these assumptions and the practice they justify.

Now this argument is unobjectionable as far as it goes; but it does not go as far as Shrage means it to. In order to assess its real scope, we should first note that she repeatedly speaks of "our" and "our society's" toleration of prostitution, and refers to this toleration as the main ground for the conclusion that the cultural assumptions prostitution is said to epitomize in our society are indeed generally accepted in it. But toleration and acceptance are not quite the same; indeed, toleration is normally defined as the putting up with something we *do not* accept. Moreover, prostitution is not tolerated at all. It is not tolerated legally: in the United States it is legal only in Nevada, and illegal in all other states, while in the United Kingdom and elsewhere in the West, even though it is not against the law as such, various activities practically inseparable from it are. Some of these restrictions are quite crippling; for instance, as Marilyn G. Haft rightly says, "to legalize prostitution while prohibiting solicitation makes as much sense as encouraging free elections but prohibiting campaigning."[40] It is certainly not tolerated morally; as I pointed out at the beginning of this chapter, the condemnation of prostitution is one of the prohibitions of the traditional sexual morality that are still with us. It is still widely held that prostitution is seriously morally wrong, and the prostitute is subjected to considerable moral pressure, including the ultimate moral sanction, ostracism from decent society. That the practice is still around is not for want of trying to suppress it, and therefore should not be taken as a sign that it is being tolerated.

Furthermore, not all the cultural assumptions prostitution in our society allegedly epitomizes and reinforces are really generally accepted. The first two – that human beings have a strong sex drive, and that one's sexual behavior defines one's social identity – probably are. The other two assumptions – that men are "naturally" dominant, and that sex with men harms women – are more important, for they make it possible to speak of oppression of women in this context. I am not so sure about the former; my impression is that at the very least it is no longer accepted quite as widely as it used to be a couple of decades ago. And I think it is clear that the latter is not generally accepted in our society today. The evidence Shrage brings up to show that it is is far from compelling.

(1) It is probably true that the fact that a woman has a history of sexual activity is not generally appreciated as an indicator of experience and expertise, analogously to other activities. But whatever the explanation is – and one is certainly needed – I do not think that entails the other half of Shrage's diagnosis, namely that women are valued for their "innocence". That particular way of valuing women and the whole "Madonna or harlot" outlook to which it belongs are well behind us as a society, although they characterize the sexual morality of some very traditional communities within our society. A society that has made its peace with non-marital sex in general and adolescent sex in particular to the extent that ours has could not possibly have persisted in valuing women for their "innocence."

(2) Shrage draws on Robert Baker's analysis of the language used to refer to men, women and sex. Baker's point of departure is the claim that the way we talk about something reflects our conception of it; he looks into the ways we talk about sex and gender in order to discover what our conceptions of these are. With regard to sexual intercourse, it turns out that the vulgar verbs used to refer to it such as "fuck", "screw", "lay", "have" etc. display an interesting asymmetry: they require an active construction when the subject is a man, and a passive one when the subject is a woman. This reveals that we conceive of male and female roles in sex in different ways: the male is active, the female passive. Some of these verbs – "fuck", "screw", "have" – are also used metaphorically to indicate deceiving, taking advantage of, harming someone. This shows that we conceive of the male sexual role as that of harming the person in the female

role, and of a person who plays the female sexual role as someone who is being harmed.[41]

This is both interesting and revealing, but what is revealed is not enough to support Shrage's case. Why is "the standard view of sexual intercourse"[42] revealed not in the standard, but in the vulgar, i.e. substandard way of talking about it? After all, everybody, at least occasionally, talks about it in the standard way, while only some use the vulgar language too. Baker justifies his focusing on the latter by pointing out that the verbs which belong to the former, and are not used in the sense of inflicting harm as well, "can take both females and males as subjects (in active constructions) and thus *do not pick out the female role*. This demonstrates that we conceive of sexual roles in such a way that only females are thought to be taken advantage of in intercourse."[43]

It seems to me that the "we" is quite problematic, and that all that these facts demonstrate is that some of us, namely those who speak of having sex with women as fucking or screwing them, also think of sex with them in these terms. Furthermore, the ways of talking about sex may be less fixed than Baker's analysis seems to suggest. According to Baker, sentences such as "Jane fucked Dick", "Jane screwed Dick" and "Jane laid Dick", if taken in the literal sense, are not sentences in English. But the usage seems to have changed since his article was first published (in the early seventies). I have heard native speakers of English make such sentences without a single (linguistic) eyebrow being raised. The asymmetry seems to have lost ground. So the import of the facts analyzed by Baker is much more limited than he and Shrage take it to be, and the facts themselves are less clear-cut and static too.

(3) Shrage's third argument for the claim that our society thinks of sex with men as polluting and harmful to women is the weakest. Images of physical assault and imperialist domination are certainly not "the metaphors we use for the act of sexual intercourse"; I do not know that anyone except Andrea Dworkin does. The most likely reason people do not is that it would be silly to do so.

What all this shows is that there is no good reason to believe that our society adheres to a single conception of heterosexual sex, the conception defined by the four cultural assumptions Shrage describes, claims to be epitomized in, and reinforced by, prostitution, and wants to ascribe to every single case of commercial sex in our society as its "political and social meaning," whatever the beliefs and values of the individuals concerned. Some members of our society think of heterosexual sex in terms of Shrage's four assumptions and some do not. Accordingly, there are in our society two rather different conceptions of prostitution, which in this context are best termed (a) prostitution as commercial screwing, and (b) prostitution as commercial sex *simpliciter*. What is their relative influence on the practice of prostitution in our society is a question for empirical research. Shrage rightly objects to the former for being implicated in the oppression of women in our society, and one need not be a feminist in order to agree. But that objection is not an objection to prostitution in our society as such.[44]

One final remark on feminist critique of prostitution: it is at odds with what those prostitutes who are getting organized in order to fight for their rights are saying about their work. There is, of course, no single understanding of the nature and moral status of prostitution that can be ascribed to prostitutes in general. But with the emergence of the international movement for prostitutes' rights in the last two decades, prostitutes now have a venue for articulating their position on the questions concerning their work and their lives. This development is especially significant in the light of the fact that, historically, those who have participated in the debates about prostitution and the way society and the law should deal with it, including both nineteenth-century and contemporary feminists, have usually taken a patronizing attitude to prostitutes. They have presumed to speak on their behalf, without making any sustained effort to enable them to speak for themselves.

Politically active prostitutes tend to resent this, as well as the view that their occupation is necessarily degrading and never freely chosen, and that their work and their lives are but examples of social pathology. According to the "Statement on Prostitution and Feminism" issued at the Second World Whores' Congress in 1986, "many prostitutes identify with feminist values such as independence, financial autonomy, sexual self-determination, personal strength and female bonding." However, "prostitutes reject support that requires them to leave prostitution; they object to being treated as symbols of oppression and demand recognition as workers. Due to feminist hesitation or refusal to accept prostitution as legitimate work and to accept prostitutes as working women, the majority of prostitutes have not identified as feminists...."[45] They also affirm "the right of all women to determine their own sexual behavior, including commercial exchange, without stigmatization or punishment."[46]

To be sure, none of this may count for much in the eyes of illiberal feminists; they are likely to dismiss such views of prostitutes as just another case of false consciousness.[47]

9

HOMOSEXUALITY

Homosexual, gay, queer

Another central issue in sexual morality with wide ramifications in political and legal philosophy is that of homosexual acts (sexual acts between persons of the same sex) and homosexuality (a relatively settled sexual preference for such acts). Before I begin discussing it, I should explain my decision to use the older term "homosexual", rather than the more recent, and possibly more popular, "gay".

Misgivings about the word "homosexual" have been based on three reasons. Linguistic purists dislike the combination of a Latin root with a Greek prefix. This kind of purism may safely be discounted as much too radical; if allowed across the board, it would result in a purge of our vocabulary much too sweeping to contemplate. Another objection is that the word refers only to same-sex sex acts, desires etc. between males, while leaving out lesbians. This worry is due to the mistaken belief that the prefix "homo-" is derived from the Latin word for man. Finally, some homosexuals reject the term on the ground that it was coined by the psychiatric establishment, which until a couple of decades ago saw homosexuality as a sickness in need of cure. But although the word was indeed taken over by psychiatrists and deployed as a label for a pathological variety of sexual desire and behavior, its origins are quite different. It was introduced in two anonymous pamphlets published in German in 1869 by Karoly Maria Kertbeny, a publicist and a homosexual himself, arguing against a Prussian law that prohibited homosexual acts. Thus, as Wayne R. Dynes and Warren Johansson remark, the term "was not born under the aegis of pure science as one might suppose, but was the creation of a closeted advocate of homosexual rights. It is a curious irony today that some gay activists ... oppose [it] as a label imposed on them by the enemy."[1]

The word "gay", preferred by many homosexuals, has a serious drawback: it tends to be used both (a) in a wide sense, equivalent to that of 'homosexual", and also in at least two more specific senses. Sometimes it is used to refer to (b) a person who not only has homosexual desires, and acts on them, but is also aware of, and comfortable with, his or her sexual preference, or (c) a person who is, in addition, a supporter of the homosexual liberation movement.

Another alternative to "homosexual" is "queer". This was originally a term of abuse. In the early nineties some activists of the homosexual liberation movement decided that "gay" was not radical enough, and adopted "queer" as more appropriate, because strongly emphasizing the "otherness" of homosexuals.[2] But although this term has its uses in a certain type of homosexual political activism, it is much too loaded, indeed deliberately provocative, to present an attractive alternative to "homosexual" in most other contexts.

What's wrong with homosexual sex?

Before the twentieth century, Western philosophy for the most part tended to ignore the subject of homosexual sex acts, except for an occasional remark in passing that they are immoral because unnatural, supported by some perfunctory argument. An early example is Plato's remark in *The Laws* that homosexual sex acts (or, more accurately, sex acts between men and youths) ought to be prohibited since they are not natural, as can be seen from the fact that animals do not commit them.[3] Another example is Kant, who adduces homosexual acts as one of the crimes of flesh against nature (other such crimes being masturbation and zoophilia). Homosexual sex is "contrary to the ends of humanity; for the end of humanity in respect of sexuality is to preserve the species without debasing the person...."[4] Kant simply takes it for granted that the end of human sexuality is procreation, as if this claim were not in need of some sort of support. One important exception in this respect is Bentham's discussion of the subject, written in the 1780s but published only in this century. Bentham's conclusion is that the traditional moral condemnation and legal prohibition of homosexual sex are not based on good grounds, but on sheer prejudice. But the essay is remarkable for historical, rather than philosophical reasons; for the arguments against homosexual sex Bentham has to tackle, although advanced by serious philosophers such as Voltaire or Montesquieu, are quite puerile.[5]

The traditional moral condemnation of same-sex sexual acts was, of course, based on the procreation view of sex. Those who adopt this view must think ill of homosexual sex; it is non-procreative, and therefore unnatural and immoral. It is condemned as an abomination in the Old Testament, and as unnatural in the New.[6] Both Augustine and Thomas Aquinas are emphatic on this. Even if all nations committed the sins of the men of Sodom, says the former, "they should all alike be held guilty by God's law which did not make men so that they should use each other thus. The friendship which should be between God and us is violated when that nature – whose author He is – is polluted by so perverted a lust."[7] The latter makes the same point, and draws out its moral and legal implications. Since homosexual sex is not merely against the human law but, being unnatural, offends against the law of God, it is worse than adultery, incest, or rape.[8] In explaining just how bad it is, Thomas compares it to the crime of homicide: "... The inordinate emission of semen is incompatible with the natural good; namely, the preservation of the species. Hence, after the sin of homicide whereby a human nature already in existence is destroyed, this type of sin appears to take next place, for by it the generation of human nature is precluded."[9] The Protestant reformers adopted the same view. For Luther homosexual sex was a vice of "unparalleled enormity", a perversion that comes from the devil.[10] It is only in this century that some Protestant churches and denominations modified this stand. The Catholic Church, however, has not done so, at least as far as homosexual behavior is concerned. The "Declaration on Some Questions of Sexual Ethics", issued in 1976 by the Sacred Congregation for the Doctrine of the Faith and approved by Pope Paul VI, distinguishes between persons whose homosexuality is neither innate nor incurable, and those who are innately and incurably homosexual. The latter cannot reasonably be blamed for their feelings and desires. But they too can and should be condemned if they *act* on those desires: "homosexual acts are disordered by their very nature and can never be approved."[11] I need not discuss this stand on homosexual sex in its own right. It stands or falls with the procreation view of sex and sexual perversion, and I have pointed out the difficulties of that view in earlier chapters.[12]

While on the traditional procreation view homosexual sex is judged immoral because unnatural, perverted, more recent moral accounts of sexual perversion imply that it is neither a perversion, nor morally unacceptable, nor bad as sex. Homosexual intercourse need be neither non-reciprocal, nor asymmetrical, nor non-complementary

(Sara Ann Ketchum). And it need not jeopardize any of the basic human goods (Donald Levy).[13]

It is a moot point whether the new natural law school of Catholic philosophy follows the tradition in seeing homosexual sex as perverted. But even if it does, it does not seem to make much of it. It rejects such sex as unequivocally as the traditional Catholic sexual ethics, but the argument for the rejection is no longer made in terms of the purpose or function of sex. Sexual ethics of writers such as Germain Grisez or John M. Finnis is rather based on a conception of marriage as a basic human good. It is a complex good, constituted by the distinct but inseparable goods of friendship (or conjugal love) and procreation. Marriage, thus conceived, helps define the concept of a marital act: it is an act of genital intercourse between husband and wife. In such an act they consummate, experience, and express their marriage as a unity of the two goods of friendship and procreation. That is the point of such acts and the source of their moral value. Non-marital sex – whether sex between spouses not in accord with this definition of marital sex, or sex between persons not married to one another – cannot actualize the good of marriage nor, indeed, any other good *common* to the participants. Such sex is accordingly pointless, devoid of all value. It is also morally unacceptable.

The latter claim, of course, does not follow from the former; it is supported by two complementary arguments. If the sexual partners seek to express feelings of affection, friendship, or love for one another in their sexual intercourse, but that intercourse is not marital in the relevant sense, their efforts are illusory and disintegrating. If they have sex solely for the fun of it, no illusions are involved, but what they do is still morally flawed because it is disintegrating. As Finnis explains, heterosexual genital intercourse unites the spouses biologically, since it is "the behavior which, as behavior, is suitable for generation". By uniting the spouses biologically, it also unites them personally, and they become two in one flesh:

> ...Reproduction is one function and so, in respect of that function, the spouses are indeed one reality, and their sexual union therefore can *actualize* and allow them to *experience* their *real common good* – *their marriage* with two goods, parenthood and friendship ... But the common good of friends who are not and cannot be married (for example, man and man, man and boy, woman and woman) has nothing to do with

their having children by each other, and their reproductive organs cannot make them a biological (and therefore personal) unit. So their sexual acts together cannot do what they may hope and imagine. Because their activation of one or even each of their reproductive organs cannot be an actualizing and experiencing of the *marital* good – as marital intercourse ... can, even between spouses who *happen* to be sterile – it can do no more than provide each partner with an individual gratification. For want of a *common good* that could be actualized and experienced *by and in this bodily union*, that conduct involves the partners in treating their bodies as instruments to be used in the service of their consciously experiencing selves; their choice to engage in such conduct thus dis-integrates each of them precisely as acting persons.[14]

One might think that the entertaining of illusions may be unwise, but need not be *morally* flawed. But the particular type of illusion said to plague homosexual and other non-marital sex stands condemned by an ethical theory that asserts that marriage, in the sense defined, is a basic human good, and maintains, as one of its moral principles, that "one may never *intend* to destroy, damage, impede, or violate any basic human good, or prefer an illusory instantiation of a basic human good to a real instantiation of that or some other human good."[15]

The point about disintegration is spelled out by Grisez: when one chooses to engage in a sex act solely for the pleasure of it,

the body becomes an instrument used and the conscious self its user. In most cases, using one's body as an instrument is not problematic. This is done when one works and plays, and also when one communicates, using the tongue to speak, the finger to point, the genitals to engage in marital intercourse. In such cases the body functions as part of oneself, serving the whole and sharing its resulting benefits. By contrast, in choosing to masturbate, one does not choose to act for a goal which fulfills oneself as a unified, bodily person. The only immediate goal is satisfaction for the conscious self; and so the body, not being part of the whole for whose sake the act is done, serves only as an extrinsic instrument. Thus, in choosing to masturbate one chooses to alienate one's body from one's conscious subjectivity.[16]

In this respect, all non-marital sexual acts, from masturbation to casual homosexual or heterosexual sex, to sex acts between spouses other than and independent of genital intercourse, are morally on a par. And a homosexual couple who believe that their sex acts embody and express their feelings of affection, friendship, or love for one another are to be condemned on two counts: because those acts are but illusory instantiations of the basic human good of marriage, and because they are masturbatory and involve alienation of the body and disintegration of personality.[17]

This raises more questions than can be addressed here. For instance, one may have doubts about the placing of genital sexual intercourse between sterile spouses on the right side of the moral divide on the grounds that it is "the behavior which, *as behavior*, is suitable for generation". I will focus on the main point about non-marital sex in general and homosexual sex in particular. In view of what I have said in this book so far, it is obvious that my main reservation concerns the moral rejection of pleasure sought and experienced for its sake, and not as part of a larger, more complex activity involving the whole of one's personality. I fail to see anything wrong, from a moral point of view, with pursuing and experiencing the pleasure of tasty food, for example, solely for its sake and not for the purposes of nutrition, health, or sociability. The same applies to the pleasures of sex. I am not saying that such pleasures are *morally* valuable, only that they are, in themselves, good in a non-moral sense *and* morally innocent, that is, not in need of moral justification in terms of their contribution to some larger, more complex pursuit. I am not making this claim about *all* pleasures; Aristotle was right to point out that "there are pleasures that are actually base and objects of reproach."[18] But while we can readily see why, say, the pleasures of a sadist are indeed morally flawed in themselves, that is not at all obvious with regard to those of a sexual hedonist.

The new natural law argument against non-marital sex in general, and homosexual sex in particular, can be rejected even by those who share the school's negative moral stance on pleasure for its sake. They will insist that sex acts should be part of a larger relationship that involves the whole personality of the partners, and should embody and express their common good. Now friendship or mutual love of two persons is certainly a highly valuable human good. When two men, or two women, have sex they feel embodies and expresses their friendship or love, just why are they deluding themselves? Sex acts need not express friendship or love; but surely they *can* do so. The objection is that in such a case sex acts cannot really embody and express a *common* good. But the friendship or love of two homosexuals is indeed a good common to them in the minimal sense of belonging to both or being shared by both. It is also common to them in the deeper sense of being a relationship that is internal to the personality of each one of them: constitutive of, rather than accidental to, who each one of them is. To assert at this point that their bodily union does not embody a real common good because it is not a marital act as defined by the new natural law, that is, "has nothing to do with their having children by each other", is to beg the question at issue.[19]

Other main views of sex imply no difference between homosexual and heterosexual sex in terms of moral or any other value. If sex is basically a source of a certain type of pleasure produced by contact with another person's body, it need not make any difference, either morally or in terms of good sex, whether the other person is of the same sex as the agent or not. If sex is a type of body language, communication by means of it may be successful whether the persons communicating are of the same sex or of different sexes. If human sex is defined by "individualizing intentionality" of desire that naturally evolves into intimacy and love, such desire and love can be either heterosexual or homosexual.

Roger Scruton explicitly grants the last point. But he does not leave it at that; for his philosophy of sex aims to provide not only an account of the basic phenomena of human sexuality, but also a basis for most of the traditional sexual morality, including the condemnation of homosexuality.[20] Thus he concedes that homosexual sex is not perverted, but offers two arguments in an attempt to show that it is nevertheless morally flawed. One refers to the phenomenon of the extinguishing of sexual arousal and desire in a certain kind of situation. In an earlier chapter we saw how he uses this type of argument in support of his claim about "individualizing intentionality" of human sexual arousal and desire: if one thinks one is being touched by one's lover, but then discovers that the hand belongs to someone else, the discovery will immediately put paid to one's arousal and desire.[21] In his discussion of homosexuality, Scruton recounts an event in Casanova's life. Casanova feels sexual desire for a person in woman's clothes whom he assumes to be a woman, but the desire is extinguished when he comes to believe that the person is actually a man.[22] This is supposed to show the moral import of gender and a morally significant difference between heterosexual and homosexual experience. But the argument cannot show that, for two reasons. For one thing, it works both ways. We readily understand what happened in Casanova's case since we know that Casanova was a heterosexual. But a homosexual would undergo the same change of feeling upon discovering that his or her partner was actually of the *opposite* sex. Moreover, as Edward Johnson remarks, one's sexual arousal and desire can be extinguished by all sorts of discoveries about one's partner, and it is not at all clear that this kind of thing has any moral implications.[23]

Scruton seems to accord greater weight to his second argument. As he sees it, the world we live in is one deeply divided by sex and gender. In a sexual context, one can understand another person of the same gender in a way and to a degree that are never possible with a person of the other gender:

> The homosexual unites with an individual who does not lie beyond the divide which separates the world of men from the world of women. Hence the homosexual has a peculiar inner familiarity with what his partner feels. His discovery of his partner's sexual nature is the discovery of what he knows. ... In the heterosexual act ... I move out *from* my body *towards* the other, whose flesh is unknown to me; while in the homosexual act I remain locked within my body, narcissistically contemplating in the other an excitement that is the mirror of my own.[24]

Thus heterosexual sex involves a kind of mystery, adventure, risk, and therefore also a kind of maturity, that are neither required nor possible in homosexual sex. Therefore heterosexual sex is morally superior, and homosexual sex morally flawed.

This argument, too, fails to convince. First, the final move is a *non sequitur*. Even if we grant that heterosexual sex exhibits certain virtues not to be found in homosexual sex, and is therefore more valuable, all that follows is that homosexual sex is less valuable, not that it is devoid of all value and stands morally *condemned*. Here, as elsewhere in his philosophy of sex, Scruton is much too quick to condemn something he can at most depict as falling short of his sexual ideal.[25] Second, as Martha Nussbaum has pointed out, one might deploy the same line of argument to show the moral superiority of sex with people on the other side of some other divide deep enough to restrict one's understanding of the other and generate a degree of mystery: certainly the divide of race, and perhaps those of culture and social class too.[26]

The first of these points needs to be made again as part of the response to a popular argument against homosexual sex: the argument that such sex is morally worthless or worse, because it tends to be impersonal and promiscuous. This argument, first of all, needs to be qualified: if valid, it is valid only with regard to male homosexuals. Lesbians, by and large, do not seem to be given to promiscuity and impersonal sex any more than heterosexual women. Very many male homosexuals, on the other hand, do tend to engage in sex that is utterly impersonal, if not anonymous, with a great many partners, picked up in environments such as homosexual bars or bathhouses that are geared to this kind of sexual interaction.[27] Now it could be said that this tendency of many homosexuals to shy away from establishing relatively permanent sexual and emotional relationships and to adopt a promiscuous lifestyle instead is a result of the conventional moral condemnation of homosexuality and all manner of prejudice and discrimination against homosexuals that are still quite widespread in our society and many others. But although the conventional rejection of homosexuality and homosexuals does contribute to their tendency to promiscuity and impersonal sex, it is not its only cause. As the following quotation from Frederick Suppe shows, the picture is actually rather complex:

> While many homosexuals avoid entangling lover relationships out of fear that such relationships will expose them as homosexuals, and thus make them more liable to societal prejudice and discrimination, many homosexuals who are 'out of the closet', to an extent that having a lover will not increase their vulnerability, prefer to engage in promiscuous sexual behavior. ... Many homosexuals combine promiscuous anonymous sex with a stable nonexclusive lover relationship, and many other homosexuals prefer to have a nonsexual, close-binding, affectional relationship while confining their sexual activity to anonymous promiscuous sex.[28]

Another response to this argument might be to say that it still needs to be shown, rather than assumed, that promiscuity is wrong. In the heyday of the "sexual revolution" and the gay liberation movement in the sixties and seventies, one might even have been tempted to add that there is something to be said for it;[29] after the onset of AIDS, one may want to be more cautious about this matter. But it is still true, and of decisive importance, that even if a comparison of promiscuous and impersonal sex with a more mainstream sexual lifestyle clearly favors the latter, we still have only a prudential objection to the former, not a reason to say that it is *morally wrong*.

Discrimination against homosexuals

Due primarily to the influence of the procreation view of sex, the history of homosexuals in the West has for the most part been one of persecution and discrimination. The ultimate authority for legislation against homosexuality was the Bible, which prescribed capital punishment for homosexual intercourse between men.[30] When Christianity became the state religion in the Roman Empire, its rejection of homosexual sex was written into state law; male homosexual intercourse became a very serious offense, and eventually a capital crime. (Then and in subsequent times, legislators and law enforcement agencies have not shown much interest in lesbianism.) The extreme harshness of the law can be explained, in part, by the assimilation of homosexual sex to heresy. Deliberately nonprocreative sexual behavior was seen as tantamount to rebellion against God's express commandments concerning sex; both heresy and sexual deviance were thought to be inspired by the devil. Moreover, when discussing the provisions against homosexual sex, legal scholars resorted to the story of Sodom and Gomorrah,[31] which was taken to show that God wanted "the sin of the Sodomites" to be extirpated, and would bring disaster on a community which failed to do so:

> ...In the sixth century the Emperor Justinian proclaimed that unchecked homosexual activity provoked the wrath of God to visit earthquakes on districts where it was rampant – the superstitious echo of the Sodom legend. A millennium later folk accretions had increased the number of sodomy-caused disasters to a roster of six: earthquakes, floods, famines, plagues, Saracen incursions, and large field mice.[32]

Mitigation of the laws prohibiting homosexual sex and their ultimate repeal in numerous jurisdictions were brought about by the enlightenment critique of the old regime and subsequent movement for legal and social reform. In the wake of the French Revolution, France introduced a new criminal code that no longer provided for punishments for offenses against religion and morality which caused no harm either to individuals or to society as a whole. Homosexual intercourse between consenting adults in private was one of them. The Napoleonic code, enacted in 1810, adopted the same approach. Many countries in Europe have followed suit since: some, such as Italy and Spain, did so in early nineteenth century, while some others, such as Germany, decided to decriminalize homosexuality only recently. In 1986, the European Court of Human Rights ruled that laws prohibiting homosexual sex violated the right to privacy protected by the European Convention on Human Rights.

The developments in common law jurisdictions have been somewhat different. As late as in 1828 the law of England reaffirmed that "every Person convicted of the abominable crime of Buggery committed either with Mankind or with any Animal shall suffer death as a Felon."[33] In legal parlance, "buggery" refers to anal sex between men or between a man and a woman, as well as to sex with animals. The other legal term relevant in this context, "sodomy", has even wider reference: it includes *any* homosexual sex, as well as zoophilia. But in practice "buggery" and "sodomy" laws have very rarely been applied to anyone except male homosexuals or zoophiles.[34] In 1861 England and Wales replaced capital punishment by imprisonment from ten years to life as the penalty for buggery. In 1885 other types of male homosexual activity, termed "gross indecency", were made punishable too. Change came only in 1967, when homosexual acts between consenting adults in private were decriminalized, in accordance with the recommendations of the Committee on Homosexual Offenses and Prostitution that had been appointed by Parliament in 1954 and chaired by Sir John Wolfenden.[35] Homosexual acts were subsequently decriminalized in Scotland, Northern Ireland, Canada, New Zealand, all states and territories of Australia except Tasmania, and more than half of the United States.

In the United States, a crucial test for sodomy laws came in 1986, with *Bowers v. Hardwick*. A male homosexual, Michael Hardwick, brought suit in the Federal District Court challenging the constitutionality of the sodomy law of the State of Georgia, under which adults engaging in sodomy in private could be punished with up to twenty years in prison. The case reached the United States Supreme Court. The court upheld the validity of the sodomy statute of Georgia (and other states that still had such laws). Hardwick had argued that such laws were unconstitutional: they infringed the right to privacy, and were based on nothing more than the conventional moral condemnation of homosexuality. The court construed Hardwick's argument from privacy as claiming a "fundamental right of homosexuals to engage in sodomy", and ruled that the Federal Constitution conferred no such right. The cases in which the right to privacy had been upheld involved contraception, abortion, procreation, child rearing and education, marriage, or family relationships. However,

> none of the rights announced in those cases bears any resemblance to the claimed constitutional right of homosexuals to engage in acts of sodomy ... No connection between family, marriage, or procreation on the one hand and homosexual activity on the other has been demonstrated ... Moreover, any claim that these cases nevertheless stand for the proposition that any kind of private sexual conduct between consenting adults is constitutionally insulated from state prosecution is unsupportable.[36]

As for Hardwick's argument that sodomy laws lacked any rational basis and were based only on the presumed view of the majority about the moral status of homosexual sex, the court found that that view did provide adequate ground for such laws.

The flaws of this ruling, adopted by a majority of five to four, were pointed out in Justice Harry A. Blackmun's dissenting opinion. The ruling misconstrues the issue, which is not about a right of homosexuals to commit sodomy, but rather about "the most comprehensive of rights and the right most valued by civilized men, namely, the right to be let alone."[37] The rights of privacy upheld in cases preceding *Bowers v. Hardwick* concerning procreation, marriage, and the family are not based on considerations of common interest regarding these matters; they acknowledge that a certain sphere of an individual's life is private, i.e. beyond the reach of law. Because of their intimate character and their centrality in human life, sexual activities performed in private belong to the protected realm of privacy if anything does. And this realm ought to be protected whatever the views and feelings of the majority may be; that is just the point of having the right of privacy (and any individual right whatever, for that matter).

The enforcement and, indeed, the very existence of sodomy laws is blatantly discriminatory against homosexuals. These laws present the exclusively homosexual male with the choice between abiding by the law, which means renouncing any sexual activity involving others, and engaging in behavior prohibited by law, which means conducting his sexual life covertly, dissociated from his other, socially and legally acceptable pursuits, from all other aspects of his identity, while under constant threat of being found out and made to pay a high social and legal price. The first choice amounts to an immense sacrifice. It is not a realistic option for the overwhelming majority, and tends to affect those who do manage it in various adverse and, indeed, unhealthy ways. Commenting on the requirement of traditional morality that sex be confined to marriage and that those who are not married should abstain, Freud wrote:

> The position sanctioned by every authority, that sexual abstinence is not harmful and not difficult to maintain, has also obtained a good deal of support from physicians. It may be said that the task of mastering such a mighty impulse as the sexual instinct is one which may well absorb all the energies of a human being. Mastery through sublimation, diverting the sexual energy away from its sexual goal to higher cultural aims, succeeds with a minority, and with them only intermittently ... Of the others, most become neurotic or otherwise come to grief. Experience shows that the majority of those who compose our society are constitutionally unfit for the task of abstinence.[38]

The context of these remarks is heterosexual, but they apply with equal force to the demand that homosexuals should renounce sex with others.

The second choice, that of maintaining a closeted sexual identity, also amounts to a major sacrifice, and tends to affect the individual in various unwholesome ways. Indeed, some of the ills bound up with it are well known; for they are often adduced, with a circularity that is both logically and morally vicious, as reasons for the moral and legal prohibition of homosexuality.

To be sure, in many jurisdictions sodomy laws are virtually never enforced. Therefore it might be objected that, at least as far as those jurisdictions are concerned, the above criticism does not apply. For all *practical* purposes, male homosexuals are just as free to pursue their sexual interests as anyone else. This, however, is too quick. First, unenforced sodomy laws tend to have *indirect* adverse effects on homosexuals. Even where, as a result of nonenforcement of these laws for quite some time, the public at large is no longer aware of their existence, judges know that they are still on the books. That tends to affect their decisions in cases where the homosexuality of one of the parties is brought up as relevant, such as some child custody cases. That is so because sodomy laws as such, i.e. independently of any attempt at their enforcement, convey society's moral and legal condemnation of "sodomy" and those who engage in it. This brings us to the second point: such laws are morally flawed independently of whatever direct or indirect harmful consequences they may have. For the message they convey is one of moral condemnation. But this condemnation is based on no good moral reason; it is an expression of collective sexual distaste masquerading as a moral judgment. Furthermore, as Richard D. Mohr puts it,

> when a state has unenforced sodomy laws on its books – not by oversight but even after the failure of law reform has drawn attention to their existence, and yet no attempt is made to enforce them though their frequent violation is a secret to no one – then insult is their main purpose. If the law is virtually never enforced, the law exists not out of concern with the *actions* of gay people, but with their *status*.... Unenforced sodomy laws are the chief systematic way that society as a whole tells gays they are scum.[39]

Sodomy laws are the most drastic type of discrimination against homosexuals.[40] There are other types of legal and social discrimination. The main areas of this discrimination have been employment, housing, and military service. Homosexuals are often refused employment not because they are not qualified for the job, but because they are homosexuals. They are denied accommodation not because there is reason to believe they will not be paying the rent in time or keeping the property in good order, but because they are homosexuals. They are refused admission into armed forces, or discharged before completing their term of service, not because they are not good enough as soldiers, but because they are homosexuals. The restriction of legal marriage to heterosexual couples is discriminatory too.

The issue of homosexual marriage is best discussed in a separate section. Before looking into other main areas of discrimination against homosexuals, it is important to distinguish two types of discrimination: by state and state-funded agencies, and by private individuals and corporations.

The state often denies homosexuals employment in its intelligence agencies and in diplomacy. This policy is justified by the "security risk" argument: homosexuals are liable to be blackmailed into divulging state secrets and otherwise harming national security. This justification is flawed for both formal and empirical reasons. It is clearly circular: if there were no policy of firing employees discovered to be homosexuals, they could not be blackmailed with the threat of disclosure. And, as Richard D. Mohr points out, "the government has never come up with even a single instance of a gay American soldier, sailor, or spy who was successfully blackmailed. The only example the government ever uses is an Austrian closet-case from the First World War."[41]

Another job often considered to be off limits to homosexuals is that of schoolteacher. Homosexuals are said to be unacceptable because they are liable to get sexually involved with their pupils, or to exert undesirable influence on them. The first concern seems to be based on nothing more solid than a popular stereotype about homosexuals.[42] As for the second, the question to ask is: Just what sort of undesirable influence? It is highly unlikely that the presence of a homosexual teacher could somehow make a pupil who would otherwise develop as a heterosexual develop into a homosexual instead. As for those pupils who are predisposed to evolve into homosexuals, it would seem that the presence of a teacher who is open about his or her homosexuality no more and no less than others are about their heterosexuality might rather exert a beneficial influence. For it might show by example that a homosexual, just as a heterosexual, can lead a normal life, and help countervail the destructive effect prejudices against homosexuality and homosexuals are bound to have on the young person.

There is thus no justification for the "homosexuals need not apply" provision in hiring schoolteachers, and it should no longer be imposed. Of course, the attaining of equality of homosexuals in the field of education would also require changes in the curriculum. Just what would need to be done in this respect is too large a question to be discussed here. What can safely be said is that heterosexuality should no longer be presented as the only healthy or socially acceptable sexual orientation, and that pupils should be provided some basic information about homosexuality too.[43]

In some countries homosexuals are excluded from the armed forces. One of them is the United States, where this issue has been much debated in the last two decades or so. The grounds for this exclusion usually offered by the military is that homosexual officers and soldiers would be making sexual advances to heterosexual officers and soldiers. That would turn the armed forces into yet another arena of sexual pursuits and tensions, which would be bad for morale. With the opening of armed forces to women, this argument lost any force it may have had. Another argument is that heterosexual soldiers and officers find homosexual sex morally unacceptable, or disgusting, or both, and therefore should not be required to live, train, and fight along with homosexuals. In response to this one might, first, point out that the factual claim is mere armchair psychology, and needs to be supported by research findings before it can be taken seriously. Second, even if the military were to come up with studies supporting the claim about the way heterosexual soldiers and officers tend to feel about homosexual sex and the prospect of integrating homosexuals, the argument would still be a bad one. In the absence of any attempt at showing that homosexual sex is indeed immoral, it can be based either on an admittedly parochial religious cum moral view of homosexuality, or on something that passes for positive morality but is actually prejudice or, finally, on mere collective distaste. And none of these is a good reason for discrimination. In practical terms, if it indeed turns out that (a significant number of) heterosexual soldiers and officers feel that they cannot live and work with homosexuals, the armed forces should undertake to disabuse them of their prejudice, and require them to keep their sexual likes and dislikes in check.

In 1993, United States military softened its opposition to homosexuals and adopted the policy popularly known as "Don't ask, don't tell". It no longer asks its personnel whether they are homosexuals, but discharges those who say they are. This policy does not do away with discrimination; instead, it substitutes one type of discrimination for another. Homosexuals are no longer excluded from military service, they are merely forced to stay in the closet if they want to be allowed to serve. But this latter – admittedly less harsh – type of discrimination is based on nothing more solid than the former. It expresses and enjoins systematic hypocrisy. It is morally objectionable because it conveys a message of groundless contempt, and is incompatible with dignity and self-respect of homosexuals.

In none of the cases I have reviewed has discrimination against homosexuals been justified by logically cogent and morally respectable reasons. It is therefore unjust, and should be stopped. But even if it were, there would remain a wide area in which homosexuals would still be less than equal: that of discrimination by private individuals and corporations. A private employer would still be able to refuse employment to an applicant who is fully qualified for the job for the sole reason that he or she is a homosexual. A landlord would still be able to refuse housing to a person who is otherwise quite suitable for the sole reason that he or she is a homosexual. When challenged to defend their actions, they might refuse to be drawn into a philosophical discussion about homosexual sex and justice, and assert their freedom of association and contract instead. In a free society, they might say, an individual, unlike the state or a state-funded agency, is surely free to associate or do business with whomever he or she chooses.

This is a difficult issue, on which those who consider liberty a paramount moral and political value will be found on both sides of the debate. Some will argue that while the state must not discriminate against homosexuals (for reasons such as those discussed above), it must also tolerate discrimination by private individuals or corporations. The liberal state has no business imposing liberal moral and political views on its citizens. Liberty worth the name is liberty accorded to adherents of parochial religious and moral views too, and even to those who will not be disabused of their prejudices. This position is well stated in Andrew Sullivan's recent book on homosexuality:

> For many people in Western societies, and most others, the sexual and emotional entanglement of two people of the same gender is a moral enormity. They find such behavior abhorrent, even threatening; and while, in a liberal society, they may be content to leave such people alone, they draw the line at being told they cannot avoid their company in the workplace or in renting housing to them. Anti-discrimination statutes that force them to do so are an affront to these people, and a flagrant violation, from their point of view, of the moral neutrality of the liberal state. ... This is not to say ... that much of the reaction does not spring from bigotry, or that the religious arguments used to condemn homosexuality are convincing: it does; and they're not. But it is to say that liberalism has always asserted that liberty is for bigots too.[44]

On the other hand, it has been argued that the existing legislation against discrimination by state *or* private agencies on racial, ethnic, or religious grounds should be broadened to include discrimination on the grounds of sexual preference. One argument is that as long as it is not so broadened, private discrimination against homosexuals taking place in many societies has the effect of denying or restricting their access to some of the fundamental rights virtually no one proposes to deny them. If a person is liable to be fired or to have housing contract discontinued if the employer or landlord finds out that he or she is a homosexual, that is often reason enough not to press charges after one has been victimized, since a trial would bring exposure. Thus freedom of association and contract of those who cannot stand homosexuals indirectly deprives homosexuals of equal protection of the law. The same hazard is often reason enough not to divulge one's homosexuality by voicing moral and political views on the subject or engaging in political activity that seeks to promote homosexual causes. In this way freedom of association and contract of those who cannot stand homosexuals indirectly curtails the freedom of speech, freedom of assembly, and freedom of political association of homosexuals.[45]

There is another and, in my view, more convincing argument for extending to homosexuals the same kind of legal protection against discrimination that is accorded to people of different race, ethnicity, or religion. Both religion and sexual orientation are matters of central importance to a person's life, and paradigmatically private matters too. If these two characteristics of religion are reason enough for passing laws against discrimination on religious grounds by state *or* private agencies, why are they not reason enough for passing laws against discrimination on the grounds of sexual preference by state *or* private agencies too? Unless a morally significant difference between the two cases can be demonstrated, it seems that sheer consistency calls for equal treatment.[46]

I will not pursue this issue further, as that would entail raising some basic questions of theory of rights, and that is well beyond the scope of this book. I am content to conclude this section on a circumspect note. Arguments for legally prohibiting both state *and* private discrimination against homosexuals in employment and housing may or may not be found ultimately convincing. But even if they are not, it will surely be granted that state discrimination against them is unjust, and therefore morally inadmissible too, and should be made against the law wherever that has not been done so far.

Homosexual marriage

Even the states that have advanced the most along the path to full equality of homosexuals are still, with very few exceptions, facing one major issue: that of recognizing homosexual marriage. In the United Sates, in particular, this has been one of the main issues in

127

the debate about the place and status of homosexuals in society in the last two decades or so.

One might fail to see why this particular issue should be thought so important. For one thing, some radical homosexual activists have drawn on the feminist and socialist critique of patriarchal marriage in general, and the type of such marriage typical of modern capitalist society in particular,[47] and argued that homosexuals have nothing to gain, and are likely to lose, by being admitted into an institution flawed beyond repair.[48] But this view can be convincing only in the context of homosexual cultural separatism; and separatism is by no means the sole, or even dominant, position among homosexuals. Those who hope for integration of homosexuals into mainstream society, rather than their separation from it, cannot afford to ignore an institution that has a major role in so many aspects of social life, nor reconcile themselves to the fact that this institution excludes homosexuals. Moreover, this rejection of the institution of marriage disregards the fact that marriage in our society is undergoing considerable change, and that the change is for the most part of the sort its critics should find welcome.[49]

It might be argued that marriage is important because of the array of specific rights and benefits associated with it: rights to support and alimony, the right to act on behalf of the incapacitated spouse, visitation rights in hospital or prison, the right not to testify against one's spouse, immigration rights for the nonresident spouse, the right to adopt children, inheritance rights, taxation and insurance advantages. But in many jurisdictions today a couple – heterosexual *or* homosexual – can secure many of these rights and benefits even though they cannot marry, either by making certain special legal arrangements, or by entering into legally recognized domestic partnership. In some Scandinavian countries, the rights of such partnership include almost all rights associated with marriage, with the significant exception of adoption. In other countries, however, some of these rights are still available only through marriage. Now if the issue of homosexual marriage boiled down to one of equality of these specific rights and benefits, it might not matter whether the state recognized homosexual marriage, or made it possible for homosexual couples to attain virtually all the rights and benefits of marriage by means of other legal arrangements. But most homosexuals seem to feel that there is more to it, and with good reason. In the words of William N. Eskridge, Jr., very many homosexual couples, do not want to be just another pair of friends or lovers, nor do they want to be domestic partners whose relation can end at the drop of a termination statement. ... Gay and lesbian partners want a level of commitment that domestic partnership does not provide. More deeply, [they] desire a link to the larger historical community, something marriage provides and the just-concocted domestic partnership does not.[50]

And when society denies their relationship the recognition and support it gives to the same relationship between heterosexual partners, they are quite reasonable in reading that as a declaration of inequality, exclusion, and contempt.

Of course, supporters of the *status quo* will reject this conclusion, for they will reject the wording that leads to it. The two relationships are *not* the same; accordingly, discrimination against homosexuals in marriage law is not arbitrary and invidious, but rather reasonable and justified. When pressed to explain just why homosexuals should not be able to marry one another, they tend to come up with some or all of the following: (1) the meaning of the word "marriage"; (2) the history of the institution of marriage; (3) the state interest in procreation; (4) the welfare of children; (5) the threat that homosexual marriage would pose to heterosexual marriage. Let me look into each of these arguments.

(1) "Marriage" means a certain kind of relationship between a man and a woman; "homosexual marriage" is impossible by definition.

In order to assess this argument, we must first ask just what kind of definition is being assumed: a definition reporting the way the word is used in ordinary language, or a technical legal one? If it is the former, it must be conceded that dictionaries do tend to define marriage in heterosexual terms. But this is not enough to settle the semantic question, let alone the substantive one, once and for all. Since marriage is a legal institution, the definition of its primary sense in ordinary language is informed by the legal definition of marriage. Now legal definitions too are couched in heterosexual terms. But that could be changed; indeed, the point at issue is whether it should be. If it is, ordinary usage will follow suit without much delay. So will dictionaries: they will no longer define marriage as a certain kind of relationship between two persons of different sexes, but as a certain kind of relationship between two persons, period.

(2) Throughout history, marriage has always been a heterosexual

institution; homosexual marriage is unheard-of. Therefore marriage should remain heterosexual.

This argument is flawed for two reasons. One is logical: even if the historical claim were true, it could not generate the normative conclusion. The fact that a certain arrangement has always been of a certain kind is no conclusive argument for the claim that it must remain that way. It is easy to see why. As Bentham puts it in his *Handbook of Political Fallacies*, "if the lack of a precedent presents a conclusive objection against the particular measure in question, so it would against any other measure that ever was proposed. This includes every measure that has ever been adopted, and so every institution which exists at the present time."[51]

Moreover, it is not true that homosexual marriage has no historical precedent. Actually, history of both Western and non-Western societies provides examples of same-sex quasi-marital unions and same-sex marriage proper.[52]

(3) The state has a legitimate interest in procreation. Therefore it legitimately may, and indeed should, recognize and support the type of union that makes for procreation, and withhold recognition and support from the type of union that is non-procreative.

This, too, can be challenged on two levels. Does the legal institution of marriage as we know it bear out this line of argument? And does legal exclusion of homosexuals as a matter of fact make a significant contribution to procreation? The answer to both questions is negative. If the state were to structure the institution of marriage with a view to procreation and nothing else, it would make marriage impossible for all couples that cannot or will not procreate: not only homosexual couples, but also heterosexual couples that cannot have children because of sterility or some other deficiency, those too old to have children, and those that could, but for whatever reason decide not to have children. Of course, the institution of marriage as we know it recognizes that there is more to marriage than procreation. Indeed, the example of couples too old to have children was used as early as Augustine's treatise *The Good of Marriage* as a *reductio ad absurdum* of the claim that there is not.[53]

Nor are we told just how the exclusion of homosexuals from the institution of marriage promotes procreation. Does it somehow motivate heterosexual spouses to procreate more than they otherwise would? Would legal recognition of homosexual marriage get them to procreate less than they do now? On the other hand, many homosexual couples do raise children: either children from previous marriage, or children they have by artificial insemination or surrogacy.

Allowing homosexual marriage would enable them to bring up children in more favorable conditions, and stimulate other homosexual couples to raise children. To be sure, there are bisexuals too; the current law of marriage may lead some of them to contract heterosexual marriage and have children within it. But can *this* trifling contribution to procreation carry the social, moral, and legal weight of the refusal of the right to marry to homosexuals?

(4) Allowing homosexual marriage would be bad for children. Children raised in such marriages would have just one, rather than two role models to look up to and learn from.

This argument assumes that each family must provide two role models, male and female, if children are to develop as they should and to be properly socialized. Some feminist writers have questioned this assumption.[54] But I need not go into this highly contentious issue here. For the need for the two sex roles can be granted for the sake of argument, and then taken to its logical conclusion. That would mean ruling out single-parent families whenever possible. The law would not permit artificial insemination of, or adoption by, single parents. Moreover, it would no longer allow divorce to couples with underage children. Would anyone seriously advocate that?

(5) Legalizing homosexual marriage would pose a threat to heterosexual marriage. John M. Finnis argues that homosexual orientation, being non-procreative, is in itself hostile to, and a standing denial of, the "self-understanding" of those who hold that sex and marriage are properly bound up with procreation. Any public recognition of homosexuality, and legal recognition of homosexual marriage in particular, would itself be hostile to, and amount to a standing denial of, this self-understanding. It would be "an active threat to the stability of existing and future marriages" based on this self-understanding.[55]

It is difficult to see, however, how homosexual sex could be hostile to heterosexual sex understood in terms of the procreation view, and how it could represent its standing denial. Those engaging in homosexual sex need not, and normally do not, have any critical or disparaging thoughts of heterosexual sex in general, and heterosexual sex bound up with procreation in particular, let alone feel and express any hostility to it. Their belief that their type of sex is valuable and legitimate implies nothing about the disvalue of heterosexual procreative sex. It implies only what must surely be granted: that the latter is not the *sole* valuable and legitimate type of sex.[56]

Nor is it clear why public recognition of homosexual sex and homosexual marriage should present a threat to the stability of heterosexual marriages. If the stability of such marriages did, as a matter of sociological fact, depend on the unquestioned monopoly of the procreation view of sex and marriage in the public realm, that would indeed raise interesting moral and legal questions. But we have no good reason to believe that it does.

None of the usual arguments in favor of the exclusion of homosexuals from the institution of marriage is convincing. The institution should therefore be changed: homosexuals should be admitted on an equal footing. As long as they are not, the state will be engaging in arbitrary and invidious discrimination that testifies to unthinking conservatism, prejudice, or both.[57]

10

PEDOPHILIA

Pederasty, ephebophilia, pedophilia

While debates on a number of questions about sexual morality can sometimes arouse strong feelings, the issue discussed in this chapter almost invariably does, and the feelings aroused are usually very strong indeed. It is understandable why that should be so. It is less clear why contemporary philosophers who have written on sexuality and sexual morality have tended to neglect the subject.

The discussion must be prefaced by a few words of clarification. Most instances of pedophilia that have recently received much media attention in some European countries, the United States, and Australia, have been cases of pedophilia within the family or in a child-care or educational institution. Many have involved physical or psychological abuse of the minor. Here, however, I focus on pedophilia as such. For if we are to be in a good position to understand and judge cases of pedophilia compounded by child abuse or violation of a relationship of parental responsibility, care, trust, or authority, we must first come to an understanding of pedophilia not aggravated by additional wrongdoing: pedophilia in itself.

Another clarification concerns terminology. We need to distinguish between "pederasty", "ephebophilia", and "pedophilia", as well as between the wide and narrow senses of the last term.

"Pederasty" refers to the sexual attraction of an adult male to boys and sex between an adult male and a boy in his mid-teens. It has been the characteristic form of male homosexuality in many societies; its best known type, of course, is the "love of boys" among the ancient Greeks. What is distinctive about pederasty is best described in contrast to the dominant type of male homosexuality in modern Western societies, in which both sides are adults. As Warren Johansson points out:

The aesthetic emphasis in pederasty, then and now, was on the ephemeral, androgynous quality of the youth that is lost the moment he crosses the developmental threshold of manhood – the negative event to which the Greek poets devote no little attention. The transient "bloom" (*anthos*) of the adolescent is a union of male and female beauties ... The pederast ... is normally repelled by adult males and has no wish to be the object of their sexual attention. It is solely the charm of the youth in his mid-teens that attracts and captivates him.[1]

"Ephebophilia", too, is a variety of male homosexuality. But unlike pederasts, ephebophiles are attracted to post-pubertal, sexually mature youths. An ephebophile finds sexually attractive the very thing that puts off a pederast: the fully developed, vigorous maleness of adolescence.[2]

Both pederasty and ephebophilia are varieties of pedophilia in the wide sense of the term, which is sexual attraction to, and sex with, minors (of the same or different sex). To be sure, ephebophilia would not count as pedophilia, if there were a single age of consent – the age at which consent to sex with another is recognized in law – for both males and females and for heterosexual and homosexual sex alike, *and* if it were to be set at the end of puberty. But that is often not the case: in Western societies today it tends to be fifteen or sixteen for heterosexual sex, but significantly higher (up to twenty-one) for homosexual sex among males.

In the narrow sense, "pedophilia" refers only to sexual attraction of adults to pre-pubescent and pubescent children and sex with them. When the term is used in this sense, ephebophilia is not included as one of its varieties, but rather distinguished from it, the end of puberty providing the line of demarcation.

What's wrong with pedophilia?

In our type of society, pedophile sex is considered both a grave moral offense and a crime deserving serious punishment. In purely moral contexts, it tends to be condemned as a sexual perversion. I will not discuss this particular point here, as I have argued in an earlier chapter that the concept of sexual perversion is quite unhelpful and is best discarded altogether.[3] There are two further arguments against pedophilia that constitute the standard rationale behind both its moral condemnation and legal proscription: first, sex with minors is wrong because it is non-consensual; second, it is harmful to them. But however straightforward and even obvious this rationale might seem, it bears looking into. Indeed, both arguments have been questioned.

Before discussing them, however, a few words may be in order on the way pedophilia tends to be conceived by the general public. The pedophile is often envisaged as "a dirty old man", a stranger to his victims, who forces himself on children and has a full-fledged sexual intercourse with them, thus putting them through a frightening and painful experience and inflicting serious long-term psychological damage on them. This popular notion explains why pedophiles are colloquially called child molesters, and why pedophilia seems to be "the most hated of all the sexual variations."[4] But, for the most part, it is not borne out by the known facts. What is true is that most pedophiles are men. But the majority are young or middle-aged. More often than not, they are not strangers; they are more likely to be family, lodgers, neighbors, or other adults from the immediate social environment of the minor. Nor is it true that pedophiles typically use force, or engage in full-fledged sexual intercourse. Summarizing the findings of a number of studies, Peter Righton writes that "the most characteristic paedophile activities are cuddling, caressing and genital fondling," and that "when full intercourse takes place, it occurs most commonly when the child is well into adolescence ..."[5] Finally, the harmful effects of pedophilia on the minor's sexual, emotional, and general personality development are still a matter of research and debate, rather than of well-established fact.[6]

To point out the inaccuracies and simplifications involved in the popular notion of pedophilia does nothing to show that its conventional condemnation is not justified. It merely helps clear the ground for a more rational discussion of the subject. Most importantly, it suggests that it may not be very fruitful to discuss pedophilia in its wider sense of sex with minors. Both the issue of harm and that of consent may well prove more tractable if we start by distinguishing between sex with pre-pubescent and pubescent children (pedophilia in the narrow sense) and sex with adolescents who have not yet reached the age of consent.

Not much needs to be said about the latter. In Western societies today, the age of consent for heterosexual sex is generally set at fifteen or sixteen, i.e. at the end of puberty or shortly thereafter. Adolescents are both legally and morally allowed to have sex with others – be it with other adolescents or with adults. The assumption is that adolescents are, by and large, physically and psychologically mature enough to be allowed to make their own decisions concerning sex. This assumption is surely quite sensible.

However, quite a few jurisdictions do not grant the same right to adolescent males with regard to homosexual sex, or homosexual sex with adults.[7] Ephebophilia is thus still out of bounds legally, and from the point of view of conventional morality as well. The rationale behind the legal prohibition appears to be the rejection of homosexuality on moral or prudential grounds, together with the psychological claim that sex between a male adolescent and a man makes it more likely that the adolescent will come to adopt homosexuality as his permanent sexual orientation. Whether this claim is true is very much a moot point; but even if it were, the argument would not be convincing. I hope to have shown in the preceding chapter that we have no good reason to think homosexuality morally illegitimate.[8] If it is rejected on prudential, rather than moral grounds, the argument displays the type of circularity we have already encountered while discussing prostitution: a prohibition of behavior that deviates from conventional sexual preference is justified by the harmfulness of such behavior – although the harm is, for the most part, caused by the very prohibition at issue.[9]

There seems to be no compelling reason for the age of consent for males, or male homosexuals, to be higher than that set for everybody else. The laws that make it several years higher are but another example of invidious discrimination against homosexuals, and should be changed. If and when they are, we will no longer have occasion to use the term "pedophilia" in its current, wide sense.

This leaves us with pedophilia in the narrow sense of sexual attraction of adults to pre-pubescent and pubescent children and sex with them. In the rest of this chapter I discuss only pedophilia in this sense, or pedophilia proper.

It clearly presents a much more controversial issue. The best way to approach it is by looking into the arguments of its defenders. I will leave aside discussions limited to the "Greek love" of boys,[10] and focus on two apologies of pedophilia in general, i.e. of its male *and* female, heterosexual *and* homosexual varieties: Tom O'Carroll's book *Paedophilia: The Radical Case*, and Robert Ehman's paper "Adult–Child Sex".[11]

Both O'Carroll and Ehman point out that pre-pubescent children are not asexual creatures. The idea that they are and their consequent exclusion from all discourse about, and experience of, sex, are not mandated by their nature and thus universal, but rather a comparatively recent development. Both authors draw on the well-known (and controversial) thesis first advanced by Philippe Aries that the understanding of children as sexually innocent was brought about by the far-reaching change in the Western conception of childhood that took place in the seventeenth and eighteenth centuries. According to Aries, in earlier periods, children were in many respects part of the same social world as adults: they wore the same type of clothes, played the same games, worked together with adults – and were not sheltered from manifestations of adult sexuality, nor denied sexual interests and activities of their own. By the end of the eighteenth century, however, the "discovery of childhood" was completed. Children came to be thought of as having a distinctive nature of their own, a set of characteristics significantly unlike those of adults that enjoined their systematic exclusion from many areas of adult experience and activity. In particular, they came to be considered innocent of sexual knowledge, interest, or desire, and in need of protection from all manifestations of adult sexuality.[12]

As O'Carroll and Ehman see it, our own unwillingness to acknowledge the facts of child sexuality shows that we still subscribe to this view of childhood, which considers all sexual contact between an adult and a child as molestation and defilement of the innocent and defenseless child.[13] It also suggests a suspicion of sex in general. In the words of Robert Ehman, "there is, of course, a remnant of sexual puritanism in this reaction toward adult-child sex, since unless there were something morally problematic and impure about sex, how could it corrupt the child? The attitude toward adult-child sex is the last unquestioned bastion of sexual puritanism."[14]

But the facts of child sexuality cannot be denied. They have been pointed out by Freud and some of his followers, and described in some detail in a number of empirical studies of human sexuality, including those by Alfred C. Kinsey and associates. These studies show that from a very early age, children of both sexes tend to engage in sex play and are capable of various types of sexual experience, including orgasm.[15] Not only do children enjoy such experiences; they also need them for their normal sexual development.[16]

Defenders of pedophilia argue that the harms widely believed to be typically inflicted on children by sexual contact with adults are by no means an established fact. Research that has been done on the subject has serious limitations, and its findings do not support the popular view in a clear and compelling way. For one thing, much research is based on clinical or legal data. But such data cannot be representative of the entire relevant child population; they relate only to children who were troubled, distressed, or harmed by their encounters with pedophiles, while leaving out those who were not. Furthermore, researches do not always differentiate clearly enough, if at all, between instances where the adult employed force or exerted pressure and those where that was not the case. Nor do they separate consistently enough, if at all, the harm caused by the sexual encounter or relationship itself, from that caused by the response of parents and others to such an encounter or relationship, and the harm attendant on the legal proceedings against the adult in which the child is made to play a part.

Both O'Carroll and Ehman are extremely suspicious of the over-whelming majority of research; indeed, each finds only one study of the effects of pedophilia on children reliable enough. O'Carroll singles out Lindy Burton's book *Vulnerable Children* – a study of children, mostly girls, most of whom had sexual encounters with adults before the age of ten.[17] Burton's general conclusion is that the experience "does not appear to have an excessively unsettling effect on the child's personality development ..."[18] Ehman's preferred research is that of Marvis Tsai and associates, who studied the effects of childhood sexual contacts with adults on psychosexual functioning in adult women.[19] On the basis of that study Ehman draws the following conclusions concerning the issue of harm:

> The two main causes, according to Tsai et al., of adult psycho-sexual problems on the part of sexually molested children are the negative feelings of the children toward their adult partner and their feeling of responsibility for, and guilt from, the violation of a social norm. There is nothing in the study to indicate that there would be a negative impact apart from an aversion to the adult and a violation of a norm. For this reason, the study does not provide the least evidence in favor of a norm prohibiting sexual contact between a child and adult when the child is not averse. On the contrary, the fact that the negative impact of the perceived violation of the norm is a large contributor to the harmful effects of adult–child sex is an argument *against* the norm.[20]

Not only authors who set out to defend pedophilia, such as O'Carroll or Ehman, but also some of those who define their task solely in terms of scientific research, have reached conclusions of this sort. Thus Kenneth Plummer writes that in cases of the child's willing participation in sexual contact with an adult "studies point to the experience being without trauma and frequently mutually pleasurable ... unless, and this is an important proviso, it is 'discovered' by the family or the community. When this happens, it appears that the child can become shocked by the engulfing anger and outrage of the adult ..."[21] Graham E. Powell and A.J. Chalkley offer a critical review of over forty studies of the impact on children of their sexual contacts with adults. Having emphasized the methodological limitations of the research done so far, which make interpretation of data difficult and any conclusion reached "somewhat muted", they say that the evidence does not bear out the popular belief that pedophile attention has long-term and wholly harmful effects on the child. Specifically, they point out that children who were disturbed after sexual contact with adults tended to be those who were disturbed beforehand, and that incidents of such contact do not seem to have long-term negative effects on the development of children.[22]

The other standard argument for the immorality of pedophilia is that from consent: children are incapable of valid consent to sex with adults, and such sex is therefore impermissible.[23] But Ehman claims that the argument over consent adds nothing to that of harm. Why, he asks, should a child's incapacity to give valid consent to *sex* with an adult be grounds enough for a prohibition of such sex, when we do not insist on such consent with regard to many other sorts of acts? The only reply seems to be that sex with adults is harmful to children. We are thus taken back a full circle to the argument from harm, which has been shown to be unconvincing.[24]

O'Carroll adopts a similar line. Children are said to be lacking knowledge and understanding of the various aspects and ramifications of sex; therefore they are considered incapable of giving valid consent to sex with adults. But then, do all adults really have that sort of knowledge and understanding?

> ...Even adults, in embarking on a sexual encounter or relationship, cannot be sure 'where it will all end'; nor do most people enter adulthood with a fixed idea as to the activities, and people, that might turn them on – the scope for experiment and discovery is a lifelong one. ... The usual mistake is to believe that sexual activity, especially for children, is so alarming and dangerous that participants need to have an absolute, total awareness of every conceivable ramification of taking part before they can be said to give valid consent. What there most definitely needs to be, is the child's *willingness* to take part in the activity in question ... But there is no

need whatever for the child to know 'the consequences' of engaging in harmless sex play, simply because it is exactly that: harmless.[25]

Since "the vast majority of sexual acts between children and adults are not aggressively imposed, any more than those between adults,"[26] in many cases the child is indeed willing. When it is, adult–child sex should be neither prevented nor condemned. The current moral rejection and legal prohibition of all sexual contact between children and adults is part and parcel of an unjustified, undiscerning and oppressive paternalism towards children. Children should have rights too, including the right to make their own sexual choices. The age of consent laws should be abolished, and the issues relating to sex between adults and children should for the most part be dealt with by means of civil, rather than criminal law.[27]

In assessing these arguments in defense of pedophilia, a good starting point are the remarks of Marilyn Frye in response to Ehman's discussion of the question of harm:

> ...I would have more questions: How was it for [the child]?
> Not: Did this, or is it likely to, result in lifelong psycho-
> sexual dysfunction? but: Was it nice? Did she have fun?
> Was it not soured by ambivalence, confusion, pain, feelings
> of powerlessness, anxiety about displeasing a partner on
> whom she is emotionally and materially dependent ... ?
> And if it is not good, can she, will she, would she dare,
> make this clear to him? ... An experience can be horrible
> without precipitating bedwetting or causing 'maladjust-
> ment'. Are we to say it is harmless if it is merely wretched
> but does not demonstrably cause behavior that parents or
> clinical psychologists identify as 'problematic'?[28]

Frye is making two separate but related points. If we are operating with a notion of harm that focuses on consequences and accordingly entails a distinction between harm and hurt, we need to look into the question of hurt too. An experience may not be bad in the sense of being harmful, and still be very bad indeed in that it hurts; that is, it may be bad in itself. And whether it is likely to be much more difficult to know than whether it has bad consequences, because of an important asymmetry of the situation in which it takes place.

This asymmetry is significant for the question of consent, or whatever type of a child's willingness to participate in a sex act with an adult Ehman and O'Carroll propose to substitute for full-fledged consent. It is true that the consent of some adults to sex might be thought flawed because of their insufficient knowledge of relevant facts and poor appreciation of various ramifications of their decisions and actions. But this is surely not reason enough for discarding the requirement of valid consent altogether. For in the case of adults this flaw is normally contingent, in that the adult could attain to more specific knowledge and better comprehension of such matters, if he or she made an effort to do so. The position of a child is importantly different. Owing to the child's limited experience and limited psychological resources, both cognitive and emotional, its knowledge and understanding of self and the world is inevitably limited too. Because of that, a child does not merely *happen to have*, but *cannot help having* a very limited comprehension of the physical, psychological, and social aspects of sex. Accordingly, *all* children are at a considerable and *inescapable* disadvantage on this count.

This is compounded by the fact that pedophiles and children involved with them tend to attach significantly different meaning to their actions and experiences. As Sandor Ferenczi pointed out in a lecture given in 1932, adult–child sexual contact is liable to generate much misunderstanding because of a fundamental difference between adult erotic experience and that of children. The former is characterized by sexual passion, whereas the latter usually amounts to nothing more than playfulness, tenderness, and affection. What often happens is that the adult "mistakes the child's playfulness for wishes of a sexually mature person," and then acts on the basis of this misperception.[29] This warning has been echoed by more recent research on children who willingly participate in sexual contact with adults. What such a child typically looks for in its relation with the adult is sympathy and affection, rather than sexual gratification. The actions which the adult interprets as sexually suggestive or even provocative are not meant as such by the child, but are rather expressions of curiosity or playfulness. Thus the whole interaction takes on sexual import for the adult, but not for the child.[30]

For consent to be morally (and legally) valid, it must be informed and given freely. In view of the asymmetry of knowledge and comprehension, compounded by the difference of meaning the interaction has for the adult and the child, it can be maintained that the willing child is not reasonably informed, and therefore its willingness cannot legitimize an adult's sexual involvement with it. It is also not free enough. David Finkelhor explains the child's lack of freedom by the fact that "adults control all kinds of resources that are essential to [children] – food, money, freedom, etc. In this sense, the child is exactly like the prisoner who volunteers to be a research subject. The child has no freedom in which to consider the choice."[31] It seems to me that the main cause of the child's predicament should be sought elsewhere: in the far-reaching asymmetry of physical and psychological maturity and power, as well as the consequent social standing, between a child and an adult. Because of this asymmetry and of the way it is acknowledged and reinforced in the course of bringing up children, a child tends to see an adult as something of an authority figure merely by virtue of being adult. It tends to defer to adults, and often finds it very difficult to assert itself against an adult, to say no to an adult's requests and advances. Therefore it can be maintained that a child's willingness to go along is not free enough to license an adult's sexual involvement with it.

To be sure, not every sexual involvement among adults takes place on an equal footing. An adult's consent to sex may be morally (and perhaps also legally) invalid, or flawed, because it is extorted by a threat, or procured by a coercive or exploitative offer, against a background of significant power inequality. But again, while only *some* adults are in a position of gross inequality in relation to others, *all* children are in a position of greatly unequal power in relation to adults.

Some defenders of pedophilia reject the argument over the asymmetry of power between adults and children sexually involved with them. They argue that the initial imbalance of power is redressed by the fact that "any minor has the potential power to send an adult partner to jail for half of his or her life."[32] This defense fails for two reasons. First, it is clearly not true of all adult–child sex: in some cases the child is much too young to even conceive, let alone carry out, such a feat. Second, to the extent that this particular "potential power" indeed exists, it is conferred by the very laws the apologists of pedophilia seek to abolish.

It seems to me, then, that although it must be granted that the harmfulness of pedophilia is still very much a moot point, other arguments against it are valid. They provide sufficient ground for both its moral condemnation and legal prohibition.

Of course, to say this is not to underwrite all current legal provisions relating to pedophilia, including the harsh punishments meted out to pedophiles in some jurisdictions. The existing legal arrangements surely leave something to be desired in terms of the interests and rights of both adults and children concerned.

This conclusion should not be mistaken for a throwback to the conception of childhood as innocent of all sexual knowledge and interest. That conception is at odds with reality. It generates a set of misguided attitudes and practices: the withholding from children of information about human sexuality, suppression of their sexual feelings and behavior, hindering of their sexual development. The arguments grounding the condemnation of pedophilia refer to the far-reaching asymmetry of knowledge, understanding, maturity, and power between adults and children. These arguments do not apply to sexual involvement of children with their peers. Therefore the rejection of pedophilia does not entail the rejection of sexual contacts of children with their peers too.[33] On the contrary, it is fully compatible with a generous conception of sexual education for children and a permissive attitude to their sexual play, exploration, and pleasure.

11

SEXUAL HARASSMENT
AND RAPE

Sexual harassment

"Sexual harassment" is a comparatively recent term, but the behavior it refers to is not. It includes an array of familiar situations: a boss or overseer using his status and power to get an employee to accept his sexual advances; a university teacher doing the same to a student; a superior or peer at a workplace or university engaging in unwelcome and, more often than not, offensive speech or physical conduct that relates to the sexuality of an employee or student. Conduct of this sort seems to have been part and parcel of modern economy and higher education ever since its emergence. Some of its specific varieties were thought serious enough to warrant moral condemnation, and possibly legal redress too; others were tolerated, or even ignored, being considered an embarrassing or unpleasant, but inevitable facet of integrated economy and education.

All these varieties of speech and conduct were first identified as varieties of *one legally unacceptable type of behavior* in the United States in the mid-seventies as a result of efforts of feminist legal scholars and political activists. The term itself was introduced into legal parlance at that time, and soon entered everyday discourse too. And social scientists began to study the practice as a highly topical social issue.

Much of the research so far is characterized by a great variety of techniques and samples used. Moreover, it has not been conducted on the basis of a standard, generally accepted definition of the practice. This makes it very difficult, and often impossible, to make all the comparisons and generalizations one would wish. But it is safe to say that research has shown sexual harassment to be widespread.

One of the most important early studies of sexual harassment in the workplace was carried out in 1981, with follow-up in 1988, by the United States Merit Systems Protection Board. The second study tended to confirm the main findings of the first. Sexual harassment was defined broadly, as "unwanted sexual attention"; the population studied were federal government employees. Approximately 42 percent of women and 15 percent of men reported that they had been sexually harassed at some point over the preceding two years.[1] Another early study, done at Cornell University, looked into the experience of working women in general. It defined sexual harassment as "any repeated or unwanted sexual comments, looks, suggestions, or physical contact you find objectionable or offensive and causes you discomfort on your job." This kind of behavior by male supervisors was perceived as a serious problem by 92 percent of respondents; 70 percent said they had personally experienced it; 56 percent reported having been harassed physically.[2]

Another area of concern is higher education. Here, too, sexual harassment appears to be widespread. The pioneering study carried out in 1979/80 by the National Advisory Council on Women's Educational Programs did not attempt to gauge the dimensions of the practice nationwide. But it used its findings to make some suggestions on policy and to offer a definition of academic sexual harassment as "the use of authority to emphasize the sexuality or sexual identity of a student in a manner which prevents or impairs the student's full enjoyment of educational benefits, climate, or opportunities."[3] It also distinguished five types of such harassment: generalized sexist remarks or behaviors; inappropriate and offensive, but sanction-free sexual advances; solicitation of sex or sex-linked behavior by promise of rewards; coercion of sexual activity by threats of punishment; and sexual assaults. When subsequently a number of colleges and universities looked into sexual harassment on their campuses, it turned out that at least some types were present in significant dimensions. A review of the research carried out in the eighties states that sexual harassment "exists as a common occurence in our universities. While reported frequencies vary, it is suggested that 30 percent may be a reliable estimate."[4]

It will be readily granted that much of what can be brought under the heading of sexual harassment is morally wrong. But there is considerable disagreement concerning its legal standing: Should sexual harassment be against the law? And, if so, what should be its legal definition, and just how should it be applied in the courts?

According to the current law in the United States and a number of other countries, sexual harassment is indeed legally unacceptable, and one can seek legal redress after having been subjected to it. In the United States, such harassment in the workplace offends against

Title VII, Section 703(a) of the Civil Rights Act of 1964, which makes it unlawful for an employer to refuse to hire or to discharge an individual, or to discriminate against an individual with respect to compensation, terms, conditions, or privileges of employment, because of the individual's race, color, religion, sex, or national origin. Sexual harassment in education is made unlawful by Title IX of the Education Amendments (1972), which states that no educational program or activity that receives federal funding shall exclude an individual from participating in it, or deny an individual its benefits, or otherwise discriminate against an individual, on the basis of sex. Sexual harassment is thus defined as a type of discrimination on the basis of sex.

American courts hearing sexual harassment cases also make use of the Equal Employment Opportunity Commission *Guidelines on Discrimination Because of Sex*, which explicate the notion of sexual harassment in the workplace in the following way:

> Unwelcome sexual advances, requests for sexual favors, and other verbal or physical conduct of a sexual nature constitute sexual harassment when (1) submission to such conduct is made either explicitly or implicitly a term or condition of an individual's employment, (2) submission to or rejection of such conduct by an individual is used as the basis for employment decisions affecting such individual, or (3) such conduct has the purpose or effect of unreasonably interfering with an individual's work performance or creating an intimidating, hostile, or offensive working environment.[5]

There are obvious differences between the type of harassment described under (1) and (2) and that described under (3). The first two types include sex-related threats or offers, and presuppose an asymmetry of status and power, while the third can also occur beween peers. The first two types involve (the prospect of) some tangible loss or benefit for the person harassed; the third may eventually bring about tangible loss too, but can be established even if it does not, provided it has inflicted emotional distress on the person harassed. These differences are summarized in the distinction between *quid pro quo* sexual harassment, which includes (1) and (2), and hostile environment harassment, which refers to (3).

One major concern in philosophical and legal discussions of sexual harassment has been the wide scope of the concept, which must include such apparently dissimilar things as extortion of sexual favors and display of *Playboy* or Page Three photographs in the workplace. Pointing this out, Ellen Frankel Paul writes that "sexual harassment is a notoriously ill-defined and almost infinitely expandable concept" liable to obfuscate conceptually and practically important distinctions.[6]

Attempts at giving a morally and legally illuminating account of sexual harassment (as defined in the Equal Employment Opportunity Commission Guidelines) have tended to focus on some important characteristic of (much of) such harassment and advance it as *the* reason for its moral condemnation and legal prohibition. The main such accounts have presented sexual harassment as morally and legally unacceptable because it is (1) a type of privacy-violating communication, (2) essentially coercive, (3) sexist, or (4) a type of discrimination on the basis of sex.

(1) Edmund Wall has argued that sexual harassment should be understood as a type of wrongful communication. It is wrongful because it refers to sexual matters *and* does so without obtaining the consent of the person concerned to receive such communication, thus violating that person's privacy rights. More specifically, X engages in sexual harassment of Y when the following conditions are met:

> (1) X does not attempt to obtain Y's consent to communicate to Y, X's or someone else's alleged sexual interest in Y. (2) X communicates to Y, X's or someone else's alleged sexual interest in Y. X's motive for communicating this is some perceived benefit that he or she expects to obtain through the communication. (3) Y does not consent to discuss with X, X's or someone else's alleged sexual interest in Y. (4) Y feels emotionally distressed because X did not attempt to obtain Y's consent to this discussion and/or because Y objects to what Y takes to be the offensive content of X's sexual comments.[7]

This characterization does not succeed in capturing what makes sexual harassment wrong in either of its two varieties. In *quid pro quo* type of harassment, it is not the infringement of privacy, but rather the *quid pro quo* suggested that is so wrong. A person may happen to be very open about sex in general and her own sexual preferences too and thus not be distressed or offended when others make non-consensual references to such matters. Or she may happen to be a very self-confident, sturdy person who is not easily distressed or offended by what others say to her on any subject. If such a person were threatened with dismissal by her employer, or with being failed in a course by her teacher, if she would not have sex with him, she might well be worried and perhaps even distressed by the prospect of being fired or failed. But she would not be distressed by the *sex-related contents* of the message. In such a case Wall's condition (4) would not be met, and he would have to give it a clean bill of health. Wall actually accepts this implication of his view,[8] but it seems to me that we should not.

On the other hand, Wall's account does not even speak to the hostile environment type of sexual harassment. For such harassment need not express anyone's alleged sexual interest in the person harassed.[9] If we are not willing to reduce the concept of sexual harassment and restrict the relevant legal provisions to the *quid pro quo* type, we must reject Wall's analysis.

(2) On another view, advanced by Nancy Tuana, sexual harassment is wrong because it is inherently coercive.

Tuana's writings on the subject discuss sexual harassment in higher education, but what she has to say should apply, *mutatis mutandis*, to such harassment at work too. She grants that at least some cases of hostile environment harassment do not involve coercion, but focuses for the most part on the *quid pro quo* type. Her discussion of sex-related threats displays the complexity of the practice and the insidious character of some of its varieties: such a threat may be implicit or unintended, but none the less coercive, and accordingly may count as sexual harassment.[10] Sex-related offers, on the other hand, would seem to resist such an interpretation. For, on what Tuana calls "the standard analysis of coercion", we distinguish between threats and offers by saying that threats make us do things against our will on pain of being harmed, while offers do not; accordingly, the former are, while the latter are not, coercive. The following remarks by Michael Bayles provide a good illustration of the standard analysis that is very much to the point:

> Assume there is a mediocre woman graduate student who would not receive an assistantship. Suppose the department chairman offers her one if she goes to bed with him, and she does so. In what sense has the graduate student acted against her will? She apparently preferred having an assistantship and sleeping with the chairman to not sleeping with him and not having an assistantship. So it would appear that she did what she wanted in the situation. [One might object] that the woman acted against her will in that

she would rather have had the assistantship and not slept with the chairman; that is, there was a consequence of her choice which she found undesirable. But the fact that a choice has an undesirable consequence does not make it against one's will. One may prefer to have clean teeth without having to brush them; nonetheless, one is not acting against one's will when one brushes them.[11]

Tuana concedes that cases of sex-related offers to students by teachers or to employees by employers that fit the above analysis would indeed be instances of non-coercive sexual harassment. But she argues that such an analysis is importantly incomplete: it disregards the context of many sex-related offers made by persons in a position of authority and thus misses a typical, but implicit, contextual type of coercion. In Bayles's example, the chair merely presents the graduate student with an option that, like many options, is a mixed blessing. She is free to accept or decline. If she declines, no harm is to befall her (not getting the assistantship does not amount to being harmed, since she has no claim to it). However, this does not take into account some things the student knows that are bound to affect her choice. Every department chair has the power to make a number of important decisions concerning a graduate student's career. Now that the chair has made his offer, the student also knows that he is not committed to making academic decisions solely on the basis of academic merit, and is not above abusing his position in order to get what he wants. Finally, she knows that her refusal may well offend, upset, or anger the chair and make him want to get back at her. It is therefore quite reasonable for her to fear that she will be harmed at some later time if she refuses the offer. The fear of such harm is what makes the offer coercive.[12]

As we shall see in the discussion of rape in the next section, Tuana is right in rejecting the standard analysis of coercion and its claim that offers can never be coercive. A coercive offer is an offer that, *qua* offer, expands the recipient's freedom in one respect, and at the same time, *qua* coercive, restricts her freedom in another respect. And Tuana undoubtedly provides an accurate depiction of many cases of sex-related offers made by teachers to students and by employers to employees. However, her account does not fit all such offers. Whether it does or not will depend on what kind of person the teacher or employer happens to be and the way he is perceived by the student or employee. He may indeed tend to take offense at rejections of his sexual advances, and may also be a vindictive type of person. Then again, he may not. If he is not, and if that aspect of his personality is correctly assessed by the student or employee, his offer will not be coercive in the way described by Tuana. It seems to me, though, that it would nonetheless be considered an instance of *quid pro quo* sexual harassment. If so, Tuana's argument fails to establish her claim that such harassment is inherently coercive.[13]

The next two theories of the nature of sexual harassment and the reasons for its moral condemnation and legal prohibition are advanced by feminist or, more accurately, radical feminist authors. Their common point of departure is the claim that there is more to sexual harassment than so many discrete acts of individuals towards other individuals; it should rather be understood as a deeply entrenched social practice. It is a practice characteristic of societies of considerable gender inequality, such as ours. Accordingly, it is also a practice that has much more to do with power, oppression, or exploitation, than with sex as such. One of these theories presents sexual harassment as inherently sexist; the other construes it as a type of sex discrimination.[14]

(3) Anita M. Superson objects to accounts of sexual harassment such as those discussed so far that their methodological individualism prevents them from grasping its social nature and recognizing that the harm it causes is primarily social, group harm. She defines such harassment as any verbal or physical behavior of a person belonging to the dominant sex directed at a person belonging to the subjugated sex that expresses and perpetuates the attitude that the latter person and/or members of that person's sex are inferior because of their sex, thereby causing harm to that person and/or members of that person's sex. In short, sexual harassment is any sexist speech or conduct.

In a society such as ours, of course, sexism is virtually always male sexism. Therefore each instance of sexual harassment is an attack on all women, and the harm it inflicts is inflicted on all women. That harm consists primarily in reinforcing sexist attitudes that women are, and ought to be, sex objects for men, and an array of stereotypes and prejudices complementing these attitudes. A woman might say or do to a man the same thing that, when said or done by a man to a woman, constitutes sexual harassment. But that would not amount to such harassment: the sexist message of female superiority and the reduction of men to sex objects for women would not be conveyed, because in this kind of society women are not considered superior and men are not reduced to sex objects for women.[15]

This last conclusion seems unattractive. If an employer were to say to an employee "I'll fire you if you won't have sex with me," it seems to me that this in itself should be enough to identify the threat as an instance of sexual harassment, and to judge it as morally wrong. We should not have to suspend judgment about the nature and moral status of the threat until we found out the gender of the persons involved. This is not to say that the contribution of the threat to the perpetuation of sexist attitudes in a sexist society is morally insignificant. Whenever it is made, such a contribution undoubtedly adds to the wrongness of the threat. But surely it is not the only, nor the main thing about such a threat that makes it morally wrong.

Superson's account of sexual harassment applies, and is meant to apply, only to sexist societies. She can imagine a society in which the sexist roles we are familiar with are reversed; in such a society, women could sexually harass men. But in a non-sexist society, according to her understanding of sexual harassment, such harassment logically could not take place. This, too, strikes me as implausible. In a non-sexist society, just as in ours, a supervisor or university teacher might use the authority and power that come with the position to try to pressure an employee or student into having sex with him or her. It seems to me that we should think of such a case as a clear and indeed paradigmatic instance of sexual harassment. If that is correct, that is another reason for rejecting Superson's account.

(4) An earlier and much more influential radical feminist theory of sexual harassment is advanced in the writings of Catherine A. MacKinnon.[16] MacKinnon focuses on sexual harassment in the workplace; her central claim is that "sexual harassment of women at work is sex discrimination in employment."[17]

Sexual harassment is a practice generated by mutual reinforcement of two types of inequality: that between men and women, and that between employers and employees. The gist of her analysis of such harassment is given in the following quote:

> Sexual harassment perpetuates the interlocked structure by which women have been kept sexually in thrall to men and at the bottom of the labor market. Two forces of American society converge: men's control over women's sexuality and capital's control over employees' work lives. Women historically have been required to exchange sexual services for material survival, in one form or another. Prostitution and marriage as well as sexual harassment in different ways institutionalize this arrangement.[18]

To be sure, women are sexually harassed outside the workplace too, while such harassment is not the only problem they must face at work. Still, it is legitimate, and indeed important, to focus on sexual harassment in the workplace. For

> work is critical to women's survival and independence. Sexual harassment exemplifies and promotes employment practices which disadvantage women in work ... and sexual practices which intimately degrade and objectify women. ... Sexual harassment at work undercuts woman's potential for social equality in two interpenetrated ways: by using her employment position to coerce her sexually, while using her sexual position to coerce her economically.[19]

The account of sexual harassment in the workplace as discrimination against women is exposed to the same objections I brought up against the understanding of such harassment in terms of sexism. It rules out the possibility of a woman sexually harassing a man at work in a society such as ours. "Were there no such thing as male supremacy, and were it not sexualized," MacKinnon says, "there would be no such injury as sexual harassment."[20] It also rules out any kind of sexual harassment in a society that, unlike ours, would no longer be plagued by considerable gender inequality and discrimination. But we can surely envisage both. Again, this is not to deny that in a society such as ours sexual harassment of women by men – which is incomparably more frequent than such harassment of men by women – is implicated in discrimination against women. Nor should it be taken to imply that this complicity is not important, morally speaking. It certainly adds to the wrongness of such harassment. But it is not its defining feature, nor its main moral flaw.

The claim that sexual harassment is a type of sex discrimination could be disconnected from the radical feminist analysis of our society as one of widespread inequality and oppression of women, and presented in a more abstract, gender-neutral form. It would then accommodate both sexual harassment of women by men and such harassment of men by women. But that would still not be a cogent account of the nature and wrongness of sexual harassment. I suspect that any plausibility this revised version of the discrimination account might have would stem from the ambiguity of the word "discrimination". "To discriminate" may mean either to distinguish (discriminate *between*), or to mark out for unfavorable treatment without a proper justification for doing so (discriminate *against*). While the former sense is neutral, the latter is morally loaded, as it implies unfair treatment. Now, in the wording of the Equal Employment Opportunity Commission Guidelines, sexual harassment consists in certain "unwelcome sexual advances, requests for sexual favors, and other verbal or physical conduct of a sexual nature". Obviously, anyone making sexual advances etc. will be making them in a discriminating way. A heterosexual man will be making such advances to women rather than men; a heterosexual woman will be making them to men rather than women; a homosexual man will be making them to men rather than women; a homosexual woman will be making them to women rather than men. That is, all such advances will be discriminating *between* men and women. They will be doing so *for better or worse*, that is, whether they turn out to be welcome or unwelcome. By virtue of that, however, they will not amount to discrimination *against* either sex. And it is the latter, morally objectionable, rather than the former, morally innocuous type of discrimination, that is relevant to the interpretation of sexual harassment as sex discrimination. Accordingly, this interpretation too is unsuccessful.[21]

If what I have been saying is right, sexual harassment is not wrong solely or primarily because it violates the privacy of the person harassed, nor because it is coercive, or sexist, or a type of discrimination on the basis of sex. If so, perhaps its wrongness should rather be explained simply, and exclusively, in terms of work- or study-related rights that are infringed by such harassment. In view of the significance of work and study in the lives of employees and students, respectively, it can be maintained that every employee or student has a right to fair treatment at work or in class. What happens when an employer or supervisor tells an employee that he will fire her, or refuse a deserved pay rise, if she will not have sex with him, is that the employee is not treated fairly. She is denied something she deserves *qua* an employee. The work-related reward that others get on merit is in her case arbitrarily made conditional on her sexual availability. The same holds, *mutatis mutandis*, when a teacher tells a student that he will fail her or give her a grade lower than deserved if she will not have sex with him. Again, what happens when an employee or student is subjected to unwelcome sex-related verbal or non-verbal conduct that unreasonably interferes with her work or study performance is that she is not treated fairly. The harassment makes it more difficult for her to perform adequately at work or in class than it is for others. This additional burden is imposed on her for reasons that have nothing to do with work or study, that is, arbitrarily.

If the wrongness of sexual harassment is explained along these lines, it can still be seen as discrimination, but not as discrimination on the basis of sex. By being unfairly denied equal opportunities at work or study, one is indeed discriminated against. However, one is not discriminated against as a *woman* or a *man*, but rather as an *individual* who happens to have attracted someone else's sexual interest (in *quid pro quo* and some cases of hostile environment harassment), or to be exposed to sex-related speech and conduct of others that is so disturbing as to interfere unreasonably with one's work or study performance (in other cases of hostile environment harassment). (In the latter type of case, of course, there is discriminatory effect, but not intent.)

When construed in this way, the concept of sexual harassment readily applies to such cases as that of Joseph Oncale, a heterosexual oil rig worker who had been subjected to sex-related taunting, touching and threats by his male, heterosexual coworkers. His sexual harassment suit was dismissed by a US federal appeals court on the ground that such harassment had to involve persons of different sex. But this decision was reversed in March 1998 by the Supreme Court, which ruled that the perpetrator and the victim can also be of the same sex.[22]

What if an employer or teacher does not threaten an employee or student, but rather makes a sex-related offer of an undeserved pay rise or course grade? Assuming that is not a threat masquerading as an offer, nor a coercive offer of the sort discussed by Nancy Tuana, it seems to present a problem for this understanding of sexual harassment. The employer or teacher is not unfairly imposing a burden on the employee or student, but only offering an option that can be declined without incurring a penalty. Such conduct is obviously wrong in that it amounts to abuse of power that comes with the position. But will it count as sexual harassment, if such harassment is interpreted in terms of a right to fair employment or study opportunities? The recipient of such an offer is surely not being harassed, since the law requires that whatever is to count as sexual harassment must be unwelcome to the person harassed, and such an offer may not be unwelcome to her.

This problem can be tackled in two ways. One is to grant that, unlike sexual threats, sexual offers should not in themselves be considered *quid pro quo* sexual harassment. Such offers may still amount to hostile environment harassment, when they are unwelcome to the recipient and persistent enough to cause unreasonable interference with her work or study performance. Alternatively, it might be argued that we need to take into account other employees or students. They could claim that this sort of sexual favoritism is unfair to *them*. It is unfair that they should have to earn job rewards or class grades in the usual way, by meeting the work- or study-related standards, while the recipient of the sexual offer gets them on grounds utterly irrelevant to those requirements. Moreover, when this sort of thing takes place at work, and the work-related benefits are distributed from a limited supply, sexual favoritism will adversely affect other employees' prospects. When it takes place at a university, it will tend to debase the currency of grades, and thus unfairly reduce the value of all the grades earned in the usual way. For these reasons, such sexual offers in the workplace or in class should count as *quid pro quo* sexual harassment after all. To be sure, calling them sexual *harassment* will perhaps sound strained. But this may not be a decisive objection. For "sexual harassment" is not an ordinary language term, but rather a technical, legal one; therefore its use need not always be constrained by ordinary usage.[23]

One final remark. The explanation of the wrongness of sexual harassment in terms of a right to fair treatment at work or in class readily applies to *quid pro quo* harassment and to the hostile environment harassment that amounts to unreasonable interference with work or study performance. But it can hardly apply to the other type of hostile environment sexual harassment (as defined by the Equal Employment Opportunity Commission Guidelines): the type that consists in unwelcome sex-related speech or conduct that creates "an intimidating, hostile, or offensive working [or studying] environment," but falls short of unreasonably interfering with work or study performance. Surely it is implausible to claim that people should have a *legal right* to a reassuring, friendly, inoffensive work or study environment.

This, however, may not be a disadvantage of the suggested account; for there are weighty reasons against including speech and conduct that does not go beyond creating an intimidating, hostile, or offensive environment in the legal ban on sexual harassment. Once that is done, the ban can be enforced only at the price of considerable curtailment of free speech.[24] And it can be argued that, generally, in a free society the law has no business preventing and penalizing mere offense to feelings.[25] Accordingly, the fact that the type of speech and conduct at issue cannot be construed as violating the right to fair treatment at work or study should rather suggest that such conduct ought not to count as sexual harassment. The hostile environment clause of the Guidelines should therefore be tightened by scrapping its second part, which refers to such conduct. Hostile environment sexual harassment should include only verbal or non-verbal conduct creating an environment that unreasonably interferes with work or study performance. Such a revision would restore the distinction between harmful and offensive but harmless behavior at work or in class, and make it possible to provide appropriate legal protection of the work- or study-related rights of employees and students, respectively, without unduly infringing personal liberty or freedom of speech of others.[26]

Rape

The subject of rape is similar to that of sexual harassment in that the debates about rape in the last two or three decades have been stimulated and, to a large extent, given focus and direction by feminist philosophy and legal theory. But unlike sexual harassment, the awareness of rape as a distinct phenomenon and a moral, legal, and political problem has a long history.

Until several decades ago, both the interpretation of rape and the laws pertaining to it were, by and large, informed by the traditional sexist view of relations between the sexes. On this view, the social and legal status of woman is essentially determined by her relations to her husband or, if she is unmarried, to her father or brother: her interests and rights are taken to be included in those of the man. The corresponding account of rape, seldom spelled out but operative none the less, finds the wrongness of rape not so much in the violation of the raped woman's rights as in the infringement of the man's rights. If the woman is unmarried, the father or brother is assumed to have an interest in her virginity, which is a condition of marrying her off. If she is married, the husband is held to have the right of exclusive sexual access to her.

This account helps understand the wide incidence of rape in war. In war, an almost exclusively male pursuit until quite recently, raping enemy women was but another way of hitting at the enemy himself. It also permeates much of the traditional rape law, starting with the usual definition of rape as something only a man can do, and only a woman can suffer, and as something a man does to a woman not his wife. It also helps explain such an apparently aberrant state of affairs as the virtual impossibility of a prostitute successfully suing for rape. As Keith Burgess-Jackson explains, according to the traditional view, "a prostitute 'belongs' to nobody, not a father and not a husband. By taking up this trade, she forfeits her entitlement to the law's protection. Materially, of course, she can be raped; but in reality the prosecution is likely to fail."[27]

But then, proving rape in a legal system based on the traditional sexist outlook was not easy for any woman. Both substantive laws and the laws of evidence and procedure were unfavorable to women, since they were predicated on the traditional view of male and female sexuality and sexual behavior as basically different: the former active, assertive, even aggressive, the latter initially passive and subsequently responsive to male initiative. Some pressure on the part of the man and some pretense of unwillingness on the part of the woman were accordingly considered normal preliminaries to sexual intercourse. This and some other sexist assumptions were given expression in the famous caution of Lord Chief Justice Matthew Hale that the charge of rape was one "easily to be made and hard to be proved, and harder to be defended by the party accused, tho' never so innocent."[28] Therefore the standards of proof of rape were made higher than those relating to other crimes. The definition of the crime usually required prosecution to show that the defendant had exerted actual force, and that the victim had offered physical resistance. The victim's testimony often had to be corroborated by evidence from other sources. The defense was usually allowed to bring in the victim's sexual past with a view to impugning the credibility of her claim that she had not consented. In some jurisdictions it was required that the rape be reported soon after the event, if it was to stand a good chance of being proven in court.

Although some remnants of the traditional approach to rape are still to be found in rape law, contemporary Western societies tend to see rape rather differently. Rape is no longer understood as a crime where the immediate victim is the woman raped, while the indirect, but principal victim is a man. The woman raped is recognized as *the* victim of rape. She has a right to bodily integrity; accordingly, she is the one who decides whether another may or may not touch her and engage her sexually. When another person does so without her consent, he violates her right to bodily integrity, and thereby also her personal autonomy, the ground of this and other basic rights. In legal parlance, he commits the crime of battery. Rape is thus understood as a type of battery. Morally speaking, it is a serious wrong because it is a serious violation of personhood. In the words of Carolyn M. Shafer and Marilyn Frye, the morally appropriate attitude upon encountering another person is one of respect: recognition of its domain, and deference to its rightful power of consent. ... To fail to defer to a person's rightful power of consent is to deny either the actual extent of its personhood or its actual personal identity. Either is flagrantly disrespectful, and thus grievously wrong. The closer the item is to the center of the domain of the person whose rightful power of consent over it is not recognized, the more violent is the attack upon that creature's personhood itself. To presume to wield an effective power of consent over the personal properties and/or the body of that creature, the center of its domain, is ipso facto to deny that there is a person there at all. The ultimate in disrespect is to exercise the power of consent over those properties and the body in action ... for it is precisely as a behaving body that the creature is a person and is a person that it is. The ultimate disrespect is, then, the exercise of the power of consent over another *person*. And this is exactly what rape is.[29]

This view of rape is reflected in many of the current rape law provisions. The reforms that have taken place in this area in the last couple of decades have introduced sex-neutral definitions of rape: it now tends to be seen as a crime where both the perpetrator and the victim may be either male or female. This is made possible by no longer defining it in terms of penetration of the female's sex organ by the male's. Because the word "rape" in common usage still carries the suggestion of something done by a man to a woman, some jurisdictions have replaced it by such terms as "sexual battery" or "sexual assault". In ever more jurisdictions, spouse rape is no longer ruled out by definition. Prostitutes are no longer fair game for rapists. Many jurisdictions have abolished the requirements of resistance by the victim, of evidence corroborating the victim's testimony, and of prompt reporting of the crime in rape suits. After all, there are no such requirements in cases of non-sexual battery, nor of robbery or murder, for instance. The admissibility of evidence concerning the victim's sexual past has been considerably restricted.

While this view of rape – which can be termed liberal – is clearly preferable to the traditional one, there is one point on which it might not be thought an improvement. The traditional view at least presented rape as a *sexual* crime. The liberal view, it might be objected, assimilates rape to battery, and thus fails to capture the sexual character of rape, the specifically sexual reason for holding it seriously morally wrong. In reply, it can be said that rape appears as a unique, and uniquely wrong, crime only against the background of a conception of sex that endows sex with a special moral significance: either the procreation view of sex or, alternatively, the view of sex as bound up with love. But if one subscribes to neither of these views, one may not think of rape as somehow unique; one may have no difficulty seeing it as, intrinsically, on a par with non-sexual battery. Without a certain theoretical background, it is not easy to show that rape is indeed special, that it is different from non-sexual battery in a morally important way. If it is claimed to be unique because in rape, unlike in cases of non-sexual battery, the assailant focuses on the sexual, and thus most private, areas of the victim's body, certain methods of torture that have the same focus provide a damaging counterexample. If it is said that rape, unlike both sexual torture and non-sexual battery, involves the sexual gratification of the perpetrator, one can point out in reply that more and more jurisdictions now define rape with no reference to either sexual gratification or sexual arousal of the rapist.[30]

The latter tendency is in line with the thesis, originally advanced in the pioneering feminist study of rape, Susan Brownmiller's book *Against Our Will*,[31] and subsequently adopted by many feminist and other authors, that rape has little, if anything, to do with sex, and everything to do with violence. But not every feminist account of rape concurs. And even when it does, a radical feminist understanding of rape differs from the liberal on every other main point.

Radical feminism rejects the methodological individualism of the liberal approach to rape: the tendency to see rape as but a discrete act of one individual upon another that offends against the moral and legal norms concerning sexual behavior. Rape can be truly understood only when interpreted in its social context, as a distinct social practice. When approached in this way, and when the fact that almost all perpetrators are men and almost all victims are women is given its proper weight, rape can be recognized as the extreme expression of the basic characteristics of all gender relations in our society. As an early radical feminist analysis of rape puts it, "the special wrongness of rape is due to, and is only an exaggeration of, the wrongness of our sexual interactions in general."[32] Rape is the most dramatic epitome of the inequality of men and women, and of the degradation and oppression of women by men. It is not a sporadic deviation, but a deeply entrenched social practice that both expresses and reinforces the inequality, degradation, and oppression of women.

One way in which rape sustains male domination is intimidation. In developing this point, several radical feminist authors, beginning with Susan Griffin, have argued that rape functions as a terrorist social practice. As Griffin puts it, "rape is a kind of terrorism which severely limits the freedom of women and makes women dependent on men. ... The threat of rape is used to deny women employment. ... The fear of rape keeps women off the streets at night. Keeps women at home. Keeps women passive and modest for fear that they be thought provocative."[33]

A good example of radical feminist analysis of rape can be found in the writings of Catherine A. MacKinnon. She argues that in the type of society we live in, sexuality is "a social construct of male power: defined by men, forced on women, and constitutive of the meaning of gender. ... Male and female are created through the erotization of dominance and submission. The man/woman difference and the dominance/submission dynamic define each other."[34] Sexuality is permeated through and through by gender inequality and male dominance of women. This is true not only of some, but of *all* sex: from "normal" intercourse to prostitution and pornography to sexual harassment and rape. MacKinnon invites us to compare the reports of rape victims with women's reports of sex and with the way pornography portrays sex, and claims that they all look very much alike. In view of this, it is difficult to sustain the usual distinctions between the normal and the pathological and between violence and sex. And rape must be acknowledged as "indigenous, not exceptional, to women's social condition."[35]

MacKinnon rejects the argument that rape is not really about sex but about violence, as it "fails to answer the rather obvious question, if it is violence not sex, why didn't he just hit her?"[36] The truth of the matter is that rape is inherently both. The argument merely "makes it possible for rape to be opposed by those who would save sexuality from the rapists while leaving the sexual fundamentals of male dominance intact".[37]

The liberal takes the presence or absence of consent as the difference between legitimate sexual intercourse and rape. That would be quite appropriate, if the social conditions in which a woman gives or refuses consent were those of equality of power and freedom of choice. But the actual conditions in which sex is negotiated in our society are not at all like that; the far-reaching gender inequality and the domination of women by men in all areas of social life vitiate any consent that may be given. Much too often, perhaps even typically, women engage in sex they do not want. They are made to do so in all kinds of ways, ranging from actual violence to various types of explicit or implicit coercion to economic considerations or psychological pressures and needs. MacKinnon's illustrations include having sex "as a means to male approval; male approval translates into nearly all social goods",[38] "acquiescence [to sex], the despairing response to hopelessly unequal odds",[39] coercion "by something other than battery, something like economics, maybe even something like love",[40] as well as the following: " ...We continue to stigmatize the women who claim rape as having experienced a deviant violation and allow the rest of us to go through life feeling violated but thinking we've never been raped, when there were a great many times when we, too, have had sex and didn't want it."[41]

In view of all this, the very idea of consent is no longer helpful nor, indeed, meaningful. Accordingly, MacKinnon proposes that "rape should be defined as sex by compulsion, of which physical force is one form. Lack of consent is redundant and should not be a separate element of the crime."[42] However, we are not told just what is to count as compulsion. In view of her examples quoted above, it seems to be a *very* wide notion – wide enough to imply that whenever a woman has sex with a man that she does not want for its own sake, but engages in it for some extrinsic reason, she is coerced, and therefore also raped.

The last conclusion is radical indeed; but it is by no means atypical of discussions of rape in radical feminist writings. To give just one additional example, let me quote from Robin Morgan's article "Theory and Practice: Pornography and Rape":

> ...Rape exists any time sexual intercourse occurs when it has not been initiated by the woman out of her own genuine affection and desire. ... Anything short of that is, in a radical feminist definition, rape. Because *the pressure is there*, and it need not be a knife blade against the throat; it's in his body language, his threat of sulking, his clenched or trembling hands, his self-deprecating humor or angry put-down or silent self-pity at being rejected. How many millions of times have women had sex 'willingly' with men they didn't want to have sex with? Even men they loved? How many times have women wished just to sleep instead or read or watch 'The Late Show'? It must be clear that, under this definition, most of the decently married bedrooms across America are settings for nightly rape.[43]

Now this kind of discourse may have its uses; but it seems to me that when rape is redefined in this way, nothing is gained and much is lost, if what we are hoping for is discerning moral judgment and appropriate legal regulation of human sexual behavior. By and large, sex that is not an expression of mutual sexual desire compares unfavorably, as sex, with sex that does embody mutual desire. But it is not at all clear that this comparison translates into *moral* terms without additional argument. And even if such argument could be provided and the translation accomplished, one central problem remains. When the notion of consent is discarded and cases as different as a woman forced to have sex by a knife at her throat, and a woman having sex she has not initiated and does not want for its own sake, but for any of the extrinsic reasons cited by MacKinnon or Morgan, are all lumped together under the heading of "rape", we still need to be told just *how wrong* rape is. I take it that MacKinnon, Morgan and other radical feminists do not mean to suggest that cases of the latter sort should be judged with the gravity appropriate in cases of the former sort, nor the other way around. (If they did, those critics who accuse them of either trivializing rape proper or wildly exaggerating the wrongness of "rape" would have a point.[44]) But they also fail to provide any criterion for the discrimination needed.

The obvious candidate for such a criterion is that of consent, which we are invited to dispense with. At this point, then, we need to look into the way the concept of consent is employed in the liberal conception of rape. It takes consent as the criterion of demarcation between sexual intercourse that does and intercourse that does not count as rape: rape is defined as nonconsensual sexual intercourse. Now in the most extreme case of rape a person is compelled into intercourse by the use of sheer physical force. When that is not the case, a person may be given a choice and may choose not to resist, or even "go along with it". Whether that choice amounts to consent, and thus rules out rape, will depend on just how it was brought about. It may not amount to consent, and even if the person concerned said "I consent" or something to that effect, that may not count as valid consent, if she was coerced and did not act voluntarily. But then again, it may. Whether it is valid or not will depend on just how involuntary it was, just how coerced she was into giving it. For while consent is an all-or-nothing concept, the concepts of voluntariness and coercion admit of degrees.

The relevant aspects of the complex relations between these three concepts can best be set out by means of a list of different backgrounds to sexual intercourse between M and W. What all the cases on the list have in common is that the intercourse was neither initiated nor engaged in by W out of sexual desire, but for an extrinsic reason, in response to a proposal made by M.

(1) M threatens to kill or inflict serious bodily injury on W if she will not have sex with him.

(2) M threatens to inflict grave economic harm on W if she will not have sex with him.

(3) M invites W to join him on a trip in the mountains, and deliberately gets them into a very dangerous situation which W cannot survive on her own wihout serious bodily injury, if at all. M offers to help if she will have sex with him.

(4) M comes across W (a stranger), who is in a very dangerous situation she cannot survive on her own without serious bodily injury, if at all, and offers to help if she will have sex with him.

(5) M offers to W, who is extremely poor and cannot pay for the desperately needed medical treatment of her child, to foot the bill if she will have sex with him.

(6) M, who is well-off, offers to pay W, who is not, if she will have sex with him.

(7) M, who is well-off, offers W, who is not, a long-term arrangement that involves his providing for her, and her having sex with him.

In cases (1) and (2) W's consent is secured by M's threat. All conditional threats of killing or inflicting serious bodily injury or grave economic harm are coercive to a degree which makes consent highly involuntary and therefore invalid in any moral or legal context. Accordingly, in both cases W was raped.

Unlike the first two, the remaining five are not cases of threats but of offers. According to the view mentioned in the preceding section as "the standard analysis of coercion", a threat faces us with the prospect of harm and makes us do something against our will, thereby reducing our freedom. An offer, on the other hand, presents us with a (comparatively) desirable prospect, thus adding to our options and expanding our freedom. Therefore offers, unlike threats, do not make us do things against our will and are not coercive. But according to another, more complex and more convincing view, advanced by Joel Feinberg, an offer can be coercive.[45] On that view, the offers made in cases (3), (4), and (5) would be considered coercive, although not in the same degree and with the same implications concerning the validity of consent given in response. They are offers in that they present the recipient with an option not otherwise available and thus expand her freedom overall. But they are at the same time coercive in that they reduce her freedom with regard to that particular option: she is coerced into choosing it, however unattractive it may be in itself, since the sole alternative under the circumstances (death or serious bodily injury in cases (3) and (4), death of the child in (5)) is utterly unacceptable. The voluntariness of her choice is thus significantly reduced. The question is whether she was coerced enough, whether the voluntariness of her choice was reduced significantly enough, for her consent to be made invalid, and for the sexual intercourse involved to qualify as rape.

In order to answer it, we must look into the circumstances of making the choice and consenting to the offer. In case (3) the circumstances that make the option bound up with refusal clearly unacceptable to W were themselves put in place by M; in cases (4) and (5), on the other hand, M exploits W's predicament for which he is in no way responsible. The difference is both morally and legally significant. In Feinberg's words, what we see at work in cases of the former type is "active coercion which both creates and exploits a situation of vulnerability;" the offer is "simply the climactic event in [a] whole episode created to undermine [the recipient's] freedom."[46] Coercive offers of the latter sort "enlarge [the recipient's] freedom *in the circumstances*, so that [her] consent *given those circumstances* may be voluntary enough to be valid (for some purposes)."[47] The purposes referred to are those of the criminal law. W's consent in case (3) was coerced, and thus involuntary, to the extent that it was rendered invalid, and therefore cannot rebut the charge of rape. W's consent in cases (4) and (5) was also coerced and thus not fully voluntary, but not in the same degree; it is therefore valid as far as the criminal law is concerned, and does rebut the charge of rape.

This, of course, does not mean that consent given in cases of the latter sort is in no way morally flawed nor, indeed, that it would be valid for all legal purposes. It is best described as an extreme case of exploited consent. M's conduct is morally abominable: he is exhibiting complete indifference to W's dire circumstances, and relates to them solely as an opportunity to be exploited in order to coerce her into doing something she would otherwise not do.[48] And W's consent, thus procured, although valid for the purposes of criminal law and sufficient to rebut the charge of rape against M, would not be considered voluntary enough and therefore valid for the purposes of the law of contract. If M were to do his part of the bargain first and W then reneged on her consent to have sex with him, M could not successfully sue for breach of contract.

As for cases (6) and (7), economic inequality is not enough by itself to make an offer coercive. If it were, most transactions between individuals in most societies that have existed or are likely to exist would have to be considered coerced, involuntary, and morally unacceptable, and the very notion of consent would indeed no longer make much sense. Thus all talk of "rape" in such cases strikes me as odd. And if what I say in my discussion of prostitution in chapter 8 is correct, exchanges of this sort need not be morally wrong at all.

Accounts of rape along these lines are challenged from the radical feminist point of view. One objection is that the line between cases that do and those that do not count as rape is arbitrary. "Why should it matter," asks Keith Burgess-Jackson, "whether the person who exploits another's vulnerability created it? The harm is the same; the choice confronting the vulnerable party is the same; in both cases the exploiter hopes the victim chooses one way rather than another. There seems no good reason for the distinction."[49] But it seems to me that we do have an important reason for making the distinction. What we are discussing is the moral and legal standing of an interaction between *two persons*. If we are to pass judgment on it, surely we must take a good look at the nature and degree of involvement of *both*. While W has hardly any choice in all three cases, the character and depth of the involvement of M is significantly different in case (3), on one hand, and in cases (4) and (5), on the other.

Another objection does not seek to undermine the distinction between first bringing about another's predicament and then exploiting it, and exploiting another's predicament for which one is in no way responsible, but rather questions the application of the distinction to the subject at hand. It connects with the thesis, mentioned above, that in a sexist society rape functions as a terrorist social practice. In "Men in Groups: Collective Responsibility for Rape" Larry May and Robert Strikwerda argue that in such a society all men, as a group, are responsible for the prevalence of rape and the ways in which it affects women. Moreover, this collective responsibility is distributive: not only the group itself, but each individual member too is responsible.[50] Building on this argument, Keith Burgess-Jackson maintains that in a society like ours, when a man makes a coercive offer to a woman with a view to getting her to have sex with him, he does not merely seek to exploit a predicament for which he bears no responsibility. He rather exploits a state of affairs for which he, too, is personally responsible. "... He is not like the bush pilot who happens upon a lost hiker. Rather, he has participated in, reinforces, and is a direct beneficiary of a regime in which women are induced by bush pilots to get lost in the wilderness."[51]

May and Strikwerda build up their case for distributive collective responsibility of men for rape by making a number of points; but ultimately it depends on the argument that in a society like ours, *every* man benefits from the practice of rape. The practice of rape imposes a kind of curfew on women, and thus provides men with a comparative advantage with regard to the freedom of movement. It also makes women dependent on men for protection when they move about.[52]

However, I find it difficult to appreciate these alleged benefits, at least in the kind of society we live in today. The freedom of movement is certainly a major benefit, but surely it need not be a *comparative* one. There is no reason why both men and women should not enjoy it, and when only men do, its value is not enhanced by the fact that women do not. And if a man has to provide protection to his wife, female friend, or daughter, whenever she needs to go to certain places at certain times, I should think that a burden rather than a benefit. This is not to deny that *some* men may value the benefits described by May and Strikwerda. But for the argument to work, *every* man would have to; and that is clearly not the case.[53]

12

CONCLUDING REMARKS

Positive morality and its pitfalls

In discussing the issues in sexual morality in preceding chapters I have occasionally referred to positive morality. But these references have not been supportive: I have insisted that we must always attend to the distinction between positive and critical morality, and that the discussion is conducted at the level of the latter and implies no commitment to the former. This stand on positive morality, fairly popular among moral philosophers (although by no means accepted by all of them), seems to be particularly appropriate in sexual ethics in view of the rather poor record of conventional sexual morality. This morality cannot provide helpful and reliable moral guidance. It differs in important respects from one particular society to another, as well as within the same society over time. If it were to be accepted as authoritative in moral questions, it would lead to a far-reaching moral relativism: the same practice – say, prostitution or homosexuality – would have to be *both* condemned and judged as morally innocuous, since it has been judged in one way in some societies or historical periods, and in a different way in others.

Even if we were to confine ourselves to our own society and our own times, positive morality would not be of much help. For sexual morality of the type of society we live in is plagued by inconsistencies; it tends to make moral distinctions where such distinctions should not be made, and not to make them where they surely ought to be made. It often appears to be bound up with stereotypes and outright prejudices. One or two examples should suffice. Prostitution tends to be morally condemned, and so does the prostitute – but not the client too, although his part in the transaction is no less essential. This, of course, is an instance of the application of the double standard: in a society that is still characterized by considerable gender inequality, the same act can be seen as seriously wrong when done by a woman, and as much less wrong, or as excusable, when done by a man. The same double standard seems to affect, albeit to a much lesser degree, the conventional attitude to adultery. The gravity of the conventional condemnation of prostitution varies with the prostitute's economic standing: the high class prostitute is judged less harshly than the streetwalker. On the other hand, positive morality sometimes appears oblivious to certain morally significant differences. Thus it subsumes all sex between adults and minors under the heading of pedophilia, "the most hated of all the sexual variations", although there is surely a great difference in most, if not all relevant respects, between a pre-pubescent child and a seventeen-year-old youth, and accordingly between pedophilia proper and ephebophilia. Pedophilia also provides a good example of a sexual practice whose conventional moral assessment is informed by a set of stereotypes for the most part belied by the facts. Another, albeit less drastic example of this is homosexuality: stereotypes and prejudices about homosexual sex and homosexuals are so familiar that I felt no need to discuss them in the chapter dealing with the subject. Interestingly enough, the conventional condemnation of homosexuality is sometimes propped up by the claim that homosexuals tend to be pedophiles. But this is not borne out by the facts either. Actually, there is some indication that homosexuals are somewhat less likely to seek sexual involvement with children than heterosexuals.[1]

It can safely be said that, in discussing the rights and wrongs of sexual behavior, we learn next to nothing from positive morality. It can, at best, serve as a convenient starting point for a discussion of some issues that is in no way constrained by its pronouncements and, indeed, quite likely to lead to the conclusion that many of these pronouncements cannot withstand critical scrutiny.

Morality and prudence, rules and ideals

In the preceding chapters – both in the first part, dealing with the main views of the nature and significance of human sexuality, and in the second part, discussing the issues in sexual morality – we repeatedly came across one or the other of two distinct, but somewhat similar confusions. One is the conflation of morality and prudence; the other is the confusion of rules and ideals.

Thus in the chapter on homosexuality I discussed Roger Scruton's attempt to justify the moral condemnation of homosexual sex by arguing that homosexual experience lacks the sort of mystery, risk, and adventure that enriches heterosexual sex. One of the flaws of this argument is that, if the factual claim is true, the argument can only show that if one has the choice, other things being equal, one should choose heterosexual rather than homosexual sex, or heterosexual rather than homosexual orientation, since it will provide a deeper, richer sexual experience. But to say this is to offer prudential advice, rather than to lay down a moral rule. We do not have a *moral* duty to make prudent choices and advance our own best interest as much as we possibly can. When we fail to do so, our choice and action may be judged unwise, but cannot properly be morally condemned. The same applies to another argument frequently brought up in discussions of the moral status of homosexual sex: that it is morally objectionable because it tends to be promiscuous and impersonal. To the extent that homosexual orientation does tend to promiscuity and impersonal sexual encounters, and the heterosexual orientation does not, the latter is indeed, by and large, more worthwhile than the former in this particular respect. But, again, it is more worthwhile in the prudential, rather than moral sense; there is, accordingly, room for regret that someone should prefer the former over the latter, but no call and no ground for moral condemnation.

In my discussion of prostitution I had occasion to look into paternalistic objections to mercenary sex: objections that point out the hazards of this line of work for the physical and psychological well-being, economic interests, and social standing of the prostitute. I also cited the objection that sex for money is as loveless as sex can ever get. The true import of the first criticism is that prostitution is not a very attractive or worthwhile line of work; that of the second, that sexual service that is paid for will, by and large, provide a much less satisfying and fulfilling experience than all or most alternative types of sexual encounter. That is, both objections are prudential rather than moral, and fail to accomplish the aim with which they are advanced, which is to generate moral condemnation of the practice.

Such confusion of prudence with morality at the level of particular arguments on issues in sexual morality is sometimes a symptom of the same confusion at a more basic level: that of the theory of the nature and value of sex. Peter A. Bertocci's attempt to support the traditional procreation view of sex by his thesis about an "inner progression of love" is a case in point. Bertocci argues that if human beings are to make the most of what sex has to offer, they ought to let sexual attraction and involvement develop into love, marriage, and family. That may or may not be true; but if it is, it gives us a counsel of prudence, not a precept of morality.

At this point it may be objected that I am assuming an overly narrow view of the nature and scope of morality, and relegating to the sphere of prudence considerations which a more comprehensive understanding of morality would recognize as genuinely moral. In addition to rights and duties, prescriptions and proscriptions, morality includes certain conceptions of the human good, certain ideals of human flourishing. Bertocci's account of a sexual relationship evolving beyond itself into something much more complex, lasting and fulfilling is one such conception or ideal. Roger Scruton's phenomenology of human sexuality offers another: the development of sexual desire, directed at another's body as the embodiment of the particular person he or she is, into the long-term commitment of intimacy, love, and marriage. Surely the significance of these portrayals of what is preeminently good for humans in the realm of sex is not only prudential, but also moral.

Now the question of the scope of morality is much too large to take up here; I will make only a few brief comments that have a direct bearing on the specific point at issue. Ideals of human life, or of a particular sphere or aspect of life, a particular type of activity, play a familiar and highly important role in our evaluation, deliberation, and action: they confer meaning on, and provide direction to, the lives, or the relevant activities, of those committed to them. But such ideals are many and varied; even if we adopt a wider conception of morality that leaves room for ideals, we will surely not consider all ideals as endowed with *moral* significance. We may agree that the ideal of self-effacing devotion to the poor, the sick, and the dying exemplified by Mother Theresa, or of solidarity with the dispossessed and oppressed and participation in their struggle for liberation and justice, are indeed moral ideals. (If we do, that is most likely because these ideals can be seen as extensions of certain moral duties.) But what of the ideal of withdrawing from the world into a life of asceticism and contemplation, or of a life of extreme luxury and sophisticated pleasures of both body and mind, or of power and glory for its own sake? Would we ascribe any distinctively moral significance and value to any of these?

The same question can be raised at the level of ideals of a more limited scope: those that relate to particular spheres or aspects of life, such as sexual ideals. Is it clear that either Bertocci's or Scruton's sexual ideals are *moral* ideals, that the value inherent in a life in accordance with either is *moral*, rather than merely prudential?

And if we are not sure, do we have a meta-ethical criterion to settle the question? It seems to me that the answer to both questions is negative. But these questions need not be settled here. For even if we were to agree that these sexual ideals do have moral significance, they would still be moral *ideals*, rather than accounts of moral rules, relating to human sexual behavior. These two types of moral considerations have different standing and play different roles in morality. Moral rules, requirements and prohibitions, rights and duties, constitute the basis of morality. They are not optional, but obligate everyone who finds himself or herself in the relevant circumstances. Compliance with moral rules, respect for moral rights, fulfillment of moral duties are required as a matter of course, and do not call for admiration or praise. But offenses against moral rules, violations of moral rights, failure to fulfill moral duties, bring about moral condemnation. Moral ideals, on the other hand, are not, and indeed – in view of their variety and, often, incompatibility – could not be prescribed for everybody; their acceptance is optional. A person who adopts such a moral ideal and lives up to it may be appreciated, admired, praised for it. But a person who does not is not properly subjected to moral condemnation on that account. Such a person may be said to be failing to realize something morally valuable, but not to be doing something morally wrong. Just where on the scale of moral considerations the line between rules and ideals is to be drawn is one of the major questions in moral philosophy. As Lon L. Fuller puts it:

> There are those who struggle to push it upward; others work to pull it down. Those whom we regard as being unpleasantly – or at least, inconveniently – moralistic are forever trying to inch the pointer upward so as to expand the area of duty. Instead of inviting us to join them in realizing a pattern of life they consider worthy of human nature, they try to bludgeon us into a belief we are duty bound to embrace the pattern. All of us have probably been subjected to some variation of this technique at one time or another. Too long an exposure to it may leave in the victim a lifelong distaste for the whole notion of moral duty.[2]

As we have seen, the accounts of sex offered by Bertocci and Scruton are vulnerable to this charge. Each presents his account as *the* ethics of human sexuality that generates an array of moral prescriptions and proscriptions and gives grounds for condemning those who do not comply, whereas he should be offering it as *a* moral ideal that singles out a valuable option with regard to sex, without entitling us to condemn those who are not attracted to it and choose to live their sexual lives differently.

Today the understanding of sex as ordained for procreation and the conception of sex as bound up with love are much less influential than they used to be. There is another view that should be mentioned at this point: the view that people should not engage in sex for any extrinsic reason, but only for its own sake, out of mutual sexual attraction. This view is much more in tune with some important social and cultural currents of the last decades, and exerts considerable influence. In the nineteenth and early twentieth century it was adopted by socialist and feminist authors as the basis of their critique of sexual mores and practices of capitalist society. In the foregoing chapters we saw how it was used to generate moral condemnation of prostitution and bourgeois marriage. When discussing rape, I took a critical look at the argument advanced by radical feminists today that all heterosexual sex that is not motivated by the woman's genuine sexual attraction to, and desire for, the man, is to be understood and condemned as rape.

I trust it will be readily granted that the portrayal of sex as something that is never bought or sold, nor indeed engaged in with any ulterior purpose, but only when two people are brought together by mutual sexual attraction, is very alluring. But again, it can plausibly be advanced only as a (moral or prudential?) ideal, not as an account of sex that can be laid down as a moral rule binding all and sundry and justifying moral condemnation of those who do not comply. Moreover, it is best advanced as a personal ideal, rather than an ideal that a society could hope to realize. Regrettable as it may be, the ideal society in which there is no need and no occasion for the use of sex as a means to an extrinsic purpose and in which people have sex only out of mutual attraction has no prospect of coming true in our world. For that would require a sort of sexual pre-established harmony in which every desire meets with a complementary desire, while no persons too unattractive to be sexually desired by others are around.

Sexual morality is not the only part of morality where we come across condemnation generated by a confusion of morality and prudence, or by a conflation of moral rules and moral ideals. But it does seem to be a sphere of morality where this tendency is very prominent. Why that should be so is more of a psychological and sociological than a philosophical question.

Is there a sexual morality?

The question whether there is a sexual morality can be understood in two different senses. In one sense, it is not much of a question: for obvious reasons, much of human sexual behavior is subject to moral judgment and in need of moral guidance and restraint. In another sense, it is a highly contentious question; it has been in the focus of discussion throughout the first part of the book, and has loomed large in the background of some of the arguments in the second part. It refers to sexual morality in the strict sense of a set of moral rules and considerations that give expression to the distinctive moral significance of sex and apply only in the sphere of sex.

If what I have been saying is correct, the answer to the question construed in the latter sense is negative. We have no reason to believe that there is only one morally acceptable aim or purpose of human sexual experience and behavior, whether prescribed by nature or enjoined by society. Nor do we have reason to believe that there is only one course of human sexual desire that is morally acceptable in virtue of being distinctively human. Sex has no special moral significance; it is morally neutral. No act is either morally good or bad, right or wrong, merely in virtue of being a sexual act. As we have seen in the preceding chapter, even rape need not be construed as an essentially *sexual* crime. Accordingly, there is neither need nor room for a set of moral considerations that apply only to sex and constitute sexual morality in the strict sense of the term. What does apply to choices, acts, and practices in the field of sex are the same moral rules and principles that apply in non-sexual matters. In sex, just as in non-sexual matters, we can hurt, harm, coerce, deceive, or exploit others, or default on our promises and commitments – and we are morally required not to do so. When we go against any of these requirements, the sexual nature of our conduct makes it neither more nor less wrong than it otherwise would be.

Thus adultery is not wrong as extramarital *sex*, but only when it involves breach of promise, or seriously hurts the feelings of the non-adulterous spouse, etc. Prostitution is not wrong as commercial *sex*, but if and when the prostitute is forced into this line of work by the lack of any real alternative. Pedophilia is not wrong as adult-child *sex*, but because even when the child is willingly participating, its willingness is extremely suspect in view of the radical asymmetries of maturity, knowledge, understanding, and power of children and adults. Sexual harassment is not wrong because it is *sexual*, but because it is *harassment*. Rape is not wrong as *sexual* battery, but as sexual *battery*.

This conclusion might be thought basically correct, but in need of qualification. Although sexual morality is not distinctive in the strong sense, it nevertheless differs from, say, political or business morality in an important way. Even though guided by moral considerations that apply elsewhere as well, moral deliberation and conduct in the sexual sphere must also acknowledge and be informed by the peculiar and morally relevant character of this particular sphere. Now this is surely plausible, if we can single out some such morally significant trait peculiar to human sexual relations. Just what is it about sex that makes it special in this weaker sense?

It might be argued that the particularly high degree of vulnerability brought about by intimacy provides the answer to this question. In her discussion of consent to sex Onora O'Neill emphasizes the intimacy of sexual relations:

> To treat another as a person in an intimate, and especially an intimate sexual, relationship requires far more [than refraining from coercion and deceit]. These further requirements reflect the intimacy rather than the specifically sexual character of a relationship. However, if sexual relationships cannot easily be merely relationships between consenting adults, further requirements for treating another as a person are likely to arise in any sexual relationship. Intimate bodies cannot easily have separate lives.[3]

Because intimacy involves both a certain type of knowledge about the other and certain desires that can be described only by reference to the desires of the other, O'Neill maintains that an intimate relationship is a relationship "where special possibilities for respecting and sharing (alternatively for disrespecting and frustrating) another's ends and desires develop. It is in intimate relationships that we are most able to treat others as persons – and most able to fail to do so."[4]

The claim that sexual morality is distinctive in some weaker, but nevertheless interesting sense cannot be established along these lines. For one thing, even if all sexual relationships are intimate, not only sexual relationships are. (Indeed, in the first sentence of the first quote O'Neill concedes as much.) Secondly, and more importantly, the argument trades on an ambiguity of the word "intimate", and assumes, instead of showing, that sexual encounters and relationships are intimate in the required sense. If "intimacy" in this context refers to mere physical intimacy then, obviously, all sexual encounters involving physical contact are indeed intimate. But if intimacy is understood as an involvement pointing beyond the particular sexual encounter, expanding into the future lives of the persons concerned, then it is simply not true that all sex between humans is intimate. Intimate bodies can and quite often do lead separate lives.[5]

These comments might be felt to provide an overly down-to-earth ending to a book on ethics and sex. But then, sex has often been the subject of exaggerated and moralistic claims. O'Neill's remark about the lives of intimate bodies is one example. Another is the claim of G.E.M. Anscombe that "there is no such thing as a casual, non-significant sexual act; everyone knows this."[6] Still another is Roger Scruton's assertion that "it is in the experience of sexual desire that we are most vividly conscious of the distinction between virtuous and vicious impulses, and most vividly aware that, in the choice between them, our happiness is at stake."[7] As an alternative to the approach to sex epitomized in such comments, the argument for what I consider a more realistic understanding of sex offered in this book may perhaps serve a useful purpose.

NOTES

1 INTRODUCTION

1 A. Schopenhauer, *The World as Will and Representation*, trans. E.F.J. Payne, New York, Dover Publications, 1966, vol. 2, pp. 532–3.
2 Ibid., p. 533.
3 To be sure, Schopenhauer knew nothing of Kant's most extended discussion of human sexuality, as Kant's *Lectures on Ethics* were first published only in 1924 (see I. Kant, *Lectures on Ethics*, trans. L. Infield, London, Methuen, 1930, pp. 162–71).
4 Epictetus, *The Discourses*, trans. P.E. Matheson, New York, Heritage Press, 1968, bk. II, ch. XVIII, pp. 115–16.
5 F. Nietzsche, *On the Genealogy of Morality*, ed. K. Ansell-Pearson, trans. C. Diethe, Cambridge, Cambridge University Press, 1994, pp. 80–1.
6 See in particular his "Philosophy in the Bedroom", in *The Complete Justine, Philosophy in the Bedroom, and Other Writings*, ed. and trans. R. Seaver and A. Wainhouse, New York, Grove Press, 1965, pp. 314–29.
7 A. Schopenhauer, "On Women", *Parerga and Paralipomena*, trans. E.F.J. Payne, Oxford, Oxford University Press, 1974, vol. 1.
8 R. Atkinson, *Sexual Morality*, London, Hutchinson, 1965.
9 J. Wilson, *Logic and Sexual Morality*, Harmondsworth, Penguin Books, 1965.
10 R. Baker and F. Elliston (eds), *Philosophy & Sex*, Prometheus Books, Buffalo, NY, 1975; second, expanded edition, 1984. Another important collection of contemporary writings is A. Soble (ed.), *Philosophy of Sex*, Littlefield, Adams & Co., 1980; third, revised edition 1997. D.P. Verene (ed.), *Sexual Love and Western Morality*, New York, Harper & Row, 1972; second, expanded edition, Boston, Jones & Bartlett, 1995, includes material from the Greeks to the twentieth century.
11 See A. Soble (ed.), *Sex, Love, and Friendship: Studies of the Society for the Philosophy of Sex and Love 1977–1992*, Amsterdam and Atlanta, GA, Rodopi, 1997.

2 SEX AND PROCREATION

1 I Corinthians vii, 1–3, 5–9 (RSV).

2 St. Augustine, *The City of God against the Pagans*, trans. P. Levine, Cambridge, MA, Harvard University Press, 1966, vol. IV, bk. XIV, ch. XVI, pp. 353–5.

3 Ibid., ch. XVIII, p. 363.

4 St. Thomas Aquinas, *Summa Contra Gentiles*, trans. V.J. Bourke, Notre Dame, Notre Dame University Press, 1975, bk. III, pt. II, ch. 122, p. 144.

5 See *infra*, p. 171

6 R. Baker and F. Elliston, "Introduction", P&S2, p. 13.

7 See J. Moulton, "Sex and Reference", P&S1.

8 Pope Paul VI, "Humanae Vitae", P&S2, sect. 9, pp. 170–1.

9 Ibid., sect. 12, p. 72.
   The inseparability thesis has been reasserted in the latest authoritative pronouncement of the Catholic church on the subject; see Pope John Paul II, *Letter to Families*, Vatican Libreria Editrice Vaticana, 1994, sect. 12, pp. 34–40.
   The thesis retains its crucial role in the sexual ethics developed in the new natural law school of Catholic philosophy. In the writings of its leading representatives, Germain Grisez and John M. Finnis, the emphasis is no longer on procreation as the natural and moral purpose of sex. They rather focus on marriage, conceived as a complex basic human good constituted by the two goods of friendship (or conjugal love) and procreation. Most of the moral work is now to be done by the concept of a marital act, defined as an inseparable unity of the two goods. As Finnis puts it, "sexual acts are not unitive in their significance unless they are marital (actualizing the all-level unity of marriage) and (since the common good of marriage has two aspects) they are not marital unless they have not only the generosity of acts of friendship but also the procreative significance, not necessarily of being intended to generate or capable in the circumstances of generating but at least of being, as human conduct, acts of the reproductive kind – actualizations, so far as the spouses then and there can, of the reproductive function in which they are biologically and thus personally one" (J.M. Finnis, "Law, Morality, and 'Sexual Orientation'", *Notre Dame Law Review*, 1993/4, vol. 69, p. 1067). Accordingly, the moral guidance offered remains the same as before. See ibid., pp. 1063–70; G. Grisez, *Living a Christian Life*, Quincy, IL, Franciscan Press, 1993, ch. 9, especially pp. 553–80, 633–56. See also *infra*, pp. 113–17.

10 On this see S. Smilansky, "Is There a Moral Obligation to Have Children?", *Journal of Applied Philosophy*, 1995, vol. 12. Smilansky reviews a wide range of arguments for and against such an obligation, and reaches the conclusion that "there is only rarely a strict obligation to have children, but more moderate, *inclining* moral considerations in favour of having children, have a place in our moral world" (p. 51).

11 See "Humanae Vitae", loc. cit.

12 Pope Paul VI, op.cit., sect. 11, p. 172. Cf. Pope John Paul II, op.cit., sect. 12, p. 35.

13 C. Cohen, "Sex, Birth Control, and Human Life", P&S2, p. 179.

14 Pope Paul VI, loc.cit.

15 C. Cohen, op.cit., pp. 193–5.

16 See G.E.M. Anscombe, "Contraception and Chastity", HS.
17 J. Teichman, "Intention and Sex", in C. Diamond and J. Teichman (eds), *Intention and Intentionality: Essays in Honour of G.E.M. Anscombe*, Brighton, Harvester Press, 1979, p. 157.
18 J. Fletcher, *Morals and Medicine*, Boston, Beacon Press, 1969, p. 95.
19 P.A. Bertocci, *The Human Venture in Sex, Love, and Marriage*, New York, Association Press, 1949, ch. 2.
20 Ibid., p. 47.
21 Ibid., p. 52.
22 Ibid., p. 48.
23 See *infra*, p. 33.
24 See *infra*, pp. 75–6.
25 See M. Missner, "Why Have Children?", *International Journal of Applied Philosophy*, 1987, vol. 3.

3 SEX AND LOVE

1 R. Scruton, *Sexual Desire: A Philosophical Investigation*, London, Weidenfeld & Nicolson, 1986. See also Scruton's essays "Analytical Philosophy and Emotion" and "Sexual Morality and the Liberal Consensus", both in *The Philosopher at Dover Beach*, Manchester, Carcanet, 1990.
2 R. Scruton, *Sexual Desire*, p. 14.
3 Ibid., pp. 20–1.
4 Ibid., pp. 73–4.
5 Ibid., p. 76.
6 Ibid., p. 87.
7 Ibid., pp. 90–1.
8 Ibid., p. 92.
9 Ibid., p. 32.
10 Ibid., p. 289. On Scruton's understanding of sexual perversion see *infra*, pp. 45–5.
11 R. Scruton, op. cit., p. 356.
12 Ibid., p. 339.
13 Ibid., p. 30.
14 Ibid., p. 90.
15 W.J. Earle, "Depersonalized Sex and Moral Perfection", HS, p. 68.
16 See J. Martin Stafford, "Love and Lust Revisited: Intentionality, Homosexuality and Moral Education", HS, pp. 179, 182.
17 See C.L. Stevenson, "Persuasive Definitions", *Facts and Values*, New Haven, Yale University Press, 1963.
18 See R. Scruton, op. cit., p. 20.
19 See *supra*, pp. 18–20.
20 R. Scruton, op. cit., p. 93.
21 Ibid., p. 3.
22 A. Goldman, "Plain Sex", HS, pp. 108–10, 119–20.
23 Ibid., p. 110.
24 D. Hume, *A Treatise of Human Nature*, ed. by L.A. Selby-Bigge, Oxford, Oxford University Press, 1960, bk. II, pt. II, sect. XI, p. 395.
25 H.A. Lesser, "Love and Lust", HS, p. 77.

in saying that the inclusion of the traditional sexual perversions, under the new name of paraphilias, in the mental disorders manual "is unwarranted, unscientific, and only serves to reinforce the suspicion that in the psychosexual arena, at least, psychiatry reduces to the codification of social mores masquerading as objective science" (F. Suppe, "The Diagnostic and Statistical Manual of the American Psychiatric Association: Classifying Sexual Disorders", in E.A. Shelp (ed.), *Sexuality and Medicine*, Dordrecht, D. Reidel, 1987, vol. 2, p. 132).

However, the current position of the American Psychiatric Association is significantly different: paraphilias are now said to be "characterized by recurrent, intense sexual urges, fantasies, or behaviors that involve unusual objects, activities, or situations and cause clinically significant distress or impairment in social, occupational, or other important areas of functioning" (*Diagnostic and Statistical Manual of Mental Disorders*, 4th ed., Washington, American Psychiatric Association, 1994, p. 493). That means that mere deviance from social norms is no longer enough and that a sexual inclination or behavior will be treated as paraphiliac only if it brings about distress or impairment of some important function in the agent. If it does not, an unusual sexual inclination or behavior will be considered just that, and nothing more.

7 MARRIAGE, ADULTERY, JEALOUSY

1 St. Augustine, "The Good of Marriage," trans. C.T. Wilcox, M.M., *Treatises on Marriage and Other Subjects*, ed. R.J. Deferrari, Washington, The Catholic University of America Press, 1969, ch. 3, pp. 13, 12.
2 Ibid., ch. 6, pp. 16–17.
3 St. Thomas Aquinas, *Summa Contra Gentiles*, trans. V.J. Bourke, Notre Dame, Notre Dame University Press, 1975, bk. III, pt. II, ch. 126, p. 155.
4 Ibid., ch. 122, pp. 144–5.
5 Ibid., ch. 123, p. 147.
6 G. Grisez, *Living a Christian Life*, Quincy, IL, Franciscan Press, 1993, p. 569. See ibid., pp. 553–84. See also *infra*, pp. 113–16, 129–32.
7 M. Luther, "The Natural Place of Women," in D.P. Verene (ed.), *Sexual Love and Western Morality*, 2nd ed., Boston, Jones & Bartlett, 1995, pp. 96–7.
8 D. Hume, "Of Polygamy and Divorces," *Essays Literary, Moral and Political*, London, George Routledge & Sons, s.a., p. 107.
9 Ibid., p. 109.
10 Ibid., p. 112.
11 Ibid., p. 113.
12 I. Kant, *Lectures on Ethics*, trans. L. Infield, London, Methuen, 1930, p. 163.
13 Ibid., p. 164.
14 Ibid., p. 166.
15 I. Kant, *The Metaphysics of Morals*, trans. and ed. M. Gregor, Cambridge, Cambridge University Press, 1996, p. 62.
16 I. Kant, *Lectures on Ethics*, p. 167.

26 For examples of this kind of reasoning and a detailed discussion of its structure, see J. Wilson, *Logic and Sexual Morality*, Harmondsworth, Penguin Books, 1965, pp. 59–74.
27 R. Vannoy, *Sex without Love: A Philosophical Exploration*, Buffalo, NY, Prometheus Books, 1980.

4 SEX AS LANGUAGE

1 J.P. Sartre, *Being and Nothingness*, trans. H.E. Barnes, London, Methuen, 1957, pt. III, ch. III, sect. I-II.
2 Ibid., pp. 390–1.
3 T. Nagel, "Sexual Perversion", POS3, p. 15.
4 H.P. Grice, "Meaning", *Philosophical Review*, 1957, vol. 66.
5 R. Solomon, "Sexual Paradigms", HS; "Sexual Perversion", P&S1.
6 R. Solomon, "Sexual Paradigms", p. 87.
7 Loc.cit.
8 R. Solomon, "Sexual Perversion", p. 276.
9 Loc.cit.
10 While Solomon maintains that love is not *best* expressed by sex, Russell Vannoy argues for the more radical view that sex cannot express love *at all*. See his "Can Sex Express Love?", SLF. For a critical response, see E. Johnson, "Lovesexpressed", ibid.
11 R. Solomon, "Sexual Perversion", p. 281.
12 H.T. Wilder, "The Language of Sex and the Sex of Language", SLF.
13 R. Solomon, "Sexual Paradigms", p. 88.
14 R. Solomon, "Sexual Perversion", pp. 280, 283.
15 H.T. Wilder, op.cit., p. 28.
16 R. Solomon, op. cit., p. 283.
17 J. Moulton, "Sexual Behavior: Another Position", HS, p. 97.
18 R. Solomon, op.cit., pp. 278–9.
19 Ibid., p. 282.
20 Ibid., p. 284.

5 THE PLEASURE OF SEX

1 See *supra*, p. 31.
2 A. Goldman, "Plain Sex", HS, p. 109.
3 Ibid., p. 104.
4 Ibid., p. 106.
5 J. Fortunata, "Masturbation and Women's Sexuality", POS1, p. 390.
6 St. Thomas Aquinas, *The Summa Theologica*, trans. by fathers of the English Dominican Province, London, Burns Oates & Washbourne, s.a., vol. 13, pt. II/ii, q. 154, art. 12, p. 160.
    Contemporary Catholic sexual ethics may not be committed to all the comparative judgments Thomas made in this connection, but it still considers masturbation morally wrong. The declaration on some questions of sexual morality issued in 1976 by the Sacred Congregation for the Doctrine of the Faith and approved by Pope Paul VI focuses on premarital sex, homosexuality, and masturbation. Masturbation is depicted as "the deliberate use of the sexual faculty outside of normal

conjugal relations [which] essentially contradicts its finality", and adjudged "a serious moral disorder". Its frequency is said to be "connected with innate human weakness deriving from original sin" ("Vatican Declaration on Some Questions of Sexual Ethics", in T.A. Mappes and J.S. Zembaty (eds), *Social Ethics*, 4th ed., New York, McGraw-Hill, 1992, pp. 200–1). See also G. Grisez, *Living a Christian Life*, Quincy, IL, Franciscan Press, 1993, pp. 646–51, 662–6, 669.

7 R. Scruton, *Sexual Desire*, London, Weidenfeld & Nicolson, 1986, pp. 345–6.
8 Ibid., p. 319.
9 See *supra*, p. 38.
10 A. Goldman, loc.cit.
11 A. Soble, *Sexual Investigations*, New York, New York University Press, 1996, p. 70.
12 G. Groddeck, *The Book of the It*, trans. V.M.E. Collins, New York, International Universities Press, 1976, p. 58.
13 For more on masturbation, see J. Fortunata, op.cit.; A. Soble, "Masturbation", HS; *Sexual Investigations*, ch. 2.
14 For a more detailed account of sexual desire, sexual arousal, and sexual satisfaction along similar lines see J.A. Shaffer, "Sexual Desire", SLF.
15 A. Soble, *Sexual Investigations*, p. 129.
16 Ibid., p. 134.
17 Ibid., p. 139.

6 SEXUAL PERVERSION

1 See *supra*, pp. 15–18.
2 On homosexuality, see *infra*, pp. 111–19; on pedophilia, see *infra*, pp. 134–43.
3 S. Ruddick, "Better Sex", P&S2, p. 287.
4 Ibid., p. 288.
5 Ibid., p. 287.
6 Ibid., p. 291.
7 R. Scruton, *Sexual Desire: A Philosophical Investigation*, London, Weidenfeld & Nicolson, 1986, p. 289.
8 Ibid., p. 292.
9 Ibid., p. 294.
10 See *supra*, pp. 29–30.
  Thomas Nagel's account in "Sexual Perversion", POS3, fails for the same reason: what it presents as perverted sex is merely non-ideal sex. To be sure, Nagel's ideal differs from that of Scruton's, both in content and, more importantly, in the type of evaluation involved. On Nagel's account, sex that combines embodiment and reflexive multi-leveled mutual recognition of arousal by arousal (see *supra*, pp. 34–5) is not a moral, but a morally neutral, purely sexual ideal.
11 R. Solomon, "Sex and Perversion", P&S1, p. 282.
12 R. Solomon, "Sexual Paradigms", HS, p. 90.
13 R. Solomon, "Sex and Perversion", pp. 284–5.
14 A. Goldman, "Plain Sex", HS, p. 121.
15 Ibid., p. 122.

16 S.A. Ketchum, "The Good, the Bad and the Perverted: Sexual Paradigms Revisited", POS1, p. 149.
17 Ibid., p. 152.
18 Ibid., p. 153.
19 D. Levy, "Perversion and the Unnatural as Moral Categories", POS1, p. 179.
20 Ibid., p. 186 n. 43.
21 See ibid., pp. 185–6, n. 42.
22 For a discussion of the sources of these inconsistencies and confusions, see James M. Humber, "Sexual Perversion and Human Nature", HS.
23 Marquis de Sade, *The Complete Justine, Philosophy in the Bedroom, and Other Writings*, ed. and trans. R. Seaver and A. Wainhouse, New York, Grove Press, 1965, pp. 320, 323.
24 See ibid., pp. 314–29.
  For another version of the view that sexual perversion is essentially sexual behavior markedly deviating from the prevailing sexual taste see J. Margolis, "Perversion", *Negativities: The Limits of Life*, Columbus, Charles E. Merrill, 1975. Margolis argues that "what is most intimately involved in sexual desire eludes every form of moral review, being not voluntary, and what *is* subject to review is often made such because of independent considerations, as in the cruelty of sadists or the invasion of privacy by voyeurs. So the restriction of sexual practice reflects the variable tastes of one society or another" (p. 121). The proper attitude to sexual perversion, thus understood, is tolerance (ibid., p. 128).
25 M. Slote, "Inapplicable Concepts and Sexual Perversion", P&S1, p. 263.
26 J.M. Humber, op.cit., p. 159.
27 For another discussion of sexual perversion that takes a different route but reaches the same conclusion, see G. Priest, "Sexual Perversion", *Australasian Journal of Philosophy*, 1997, vol. 75.
28 By discarding the idea of sexual perversion, philosophers would do what American psychiatrists have already done. Up to 1987, the *Diagnostic and Statistical Manual of Mental Disorders* issued by the American Psychiatric Association treated all traditional sexual perversions except homosexuality as mental disorders. To be sure, the old term "sexual deviations" had by then been replaced by the less loaded "Paraphilias", but they were described in the following way: "The Paraphilias are characterized by arousal in response to sexual objects that are not part of normative arousal-activity patterns and that in varying degrees may interfere with the capacity for reciprocal, affectionate sexual activity" (*Diagnostic and Statistical Manual of Mental Disorders*, 3rd ed. revised, Washington, American Psychiatric Association, 1987, p. ...). This understanding of paraphilias was at odds with the definition of mental disorders in the same manual which expressly ruled out deviance from social norms as ground for diagnosing mental disorder and required the suffering or increased risk of suffering some harm to the agent for such a diagnosis (ibid., p. xxii). And it showed that the core idea was still that of deviation from some norm of convention, morality or prevailing sexual taste. Frederick Suppe was therefore ...

17 For an attempt at salvaging a part of Kant's account of sex and marriage, see B. Herman, "Could it Be Worth Thinking about Kant on Sex and Marriage?", in L.M. Antony and C. Witt (eds), *A Mind of One's Own: Feminist Essays on Reason and Objectivity*, Boulder, Westview Press, 1993.

18 R. Scruton, *The Meaning of Conservatism*, 2nd ed., London, Macmillan, 1984, pp. 161–2. See Scruton's *Sexual Desire*, London, Weidenfeld & Nicolson, 1986, pp. 356–61.

19 W. Godwin, *An Enquiry Concerning Political Justice*, ed. M. Philip, London, William Pickering, 1993, bk. VIII, ch. VI, p. 453.

20 F. Engels, *The Origin of the Family, Private Property and the State*, trans. A. West, Harmondsworth, Penguin Books, 1985, p. 113.

21 J. McMurtry, "Monogamy: A Critique", P&S2, p. 109.

22 Ibid., p. 110.

23 Ibid., pp. 111–12.

24 Ibid., p. 113.

25 D. Palmer, "The Consolation of the Wedded," P&S2, pp. 126–7.

26 B. Gert, *Morality: A New Justification of the Moral Rules*, New York, Oxford University Press, 1988, p. 134.

27 M. J. Wreen, "What's Really Wrong with Adultery," *International Journal of Applied Philosophy*, 1986, vol. 3, p. 46.

28 D. Palmer, op. cit., pp. 119–20.

29 Therefore Hume's definition of marriage, quoted above (p. 72), is wrong.

30 Therefore Kant's definition of marriage, cited above (p. 73), is wrong too.

31 R. Wasserstrom, "Is Adultery Immoral?", P&S2, p. 103.

32 B. Russell, *Marriage and Morals*, London, George Allen & Unwin, 1976, p. 95. Another way of dealing with the problem might be the conceptual, legal, and practical separation of the two institutions, marriage and family; see J. Margolis and C. Margolis, "The Separation of Marriage and Family", in M. Vetterling-Braggin, F.A. Elliston, and J. English (eds), *Feminism and Philosophy*, Totowa, NJ, Rowman & Littlefield, 1977.

33 B. Russell, op. cit., pp. 95–6.

34 R. Wasserstrom, op. cit., pp. 98–9.

35 See *supra*, pp. 31–3.

36 Aristotle, *The Nicomachean Ethics*, trans. D. Ross, London, Oxford University Press, 1954, 1171a, p. 244.
   On the importance of privacy for personal relations, see J. Rachels, "Why Privacy Is Important," *Philosophy & Public Affairs*, 1974/5, vol. 4; J.H. Reiman, "Privacy, Intimacy, and Personhood," ibid., 1976/7, vol. 6.

37 For more on exclusivity, see A. Soble, *The Structure of Love*, New Haven, Yale University Press, 1990, ch. 9.

38 R. Scruton, *Sexual Desire*, p. 339.

39 See R. Taylor, *Having Love Affairs*, Buffalo, NY, Prometheus Books, 1982, pp. 143–6.

40 For attempts at salvaging the marriage promise, see S. Mendus, "Marital Faithfulness," *Philosophy*, 1984, vol. 59; J. Wilson, "Can One Promise to Love Another?", ibid., 1989, vol. 64.

41 .J. Neu, "Jealous Thoughts," in A. Oksenberg Rorty (ed.), *Explaining Emotions*, Berkeley, University of California Press, 1980, pp. 444–5.

8 PROSTITUTION

1 V. Bullough and B. Bullough, *Women and Prostitution: A Social History*, Buffalo, NY, Prometheus Books, 1987, p. 313.

2 F. Engels, *The Origin of the Family, Private Property and the State*, trans. A. West, Harmondsworth, Penguin Books, 1985, p. 102.
   The point was made as early as 1790; see M. Wollstonecraft, *Works*, ed. J. Todd and M. Butler, London, William Pickering, 1989, vol. 5, pp. 22, 129.

3 Here I am drawing on K. Davis, "The Sociology of Prostitution," in S. Dinitz, R.R. Dynes and A.C. Clare (eds), *Deviance*, 2nd ed., New York, Oxford University Press, 1975.

4 Ibid., p. 328.

5 L.O. Ericsson, "Charges against Prostitution: An Attempt at a Philosophical Assessment," *Ethics*, 1979/80, vol. 90, p. 357.

6 D.A.J. Richards, *Sex, Drugs, Death, and the Law: An Essay on Human Rights and Overcriminalization*, Totowa, NJ, Rowman & Littlefield, 1982, p. 113.

7 Ibid., p. 146 n. 251. The study referred to is described in W.B. Pomeroy, "Some Aspects of Prostitution," *Journal of Sex Research*, 1965, vol. 1.

8 L. O. Ericsson, loc.cit.

9 For an analysis of the two types of paternalism, see J. Feinberg, "Legal Paternalism," *Canadian Journal of Philosophy*, 1971, vol. 1.

10 Many authors who have written on prostitution as a "social evil" have claimed that it is virtually never a freely chosen occupation, since various social conditions (lack of education, poverty, unemployment) force innumerable women into it. This argument makes it possible for Mrs Warren (and many others) to condemn prostitution, while absolving the prostitute. But even if the empirical claim were true, it would not amount to an argument against prostitution, but only against the lack of alternatives to it.

11 J.S. Mill, *On Liberty*, ed. C.V. Shields, Indianapolis, Bobbs-Merrill, 1956, p. 93.
   It was clear to Mill that his rejection of paternalism applied in the case of prostitution just as in any other case, but the way he says that is somewhat demure; see ibid., pp. 120–2.

12 M. Walzer, *The Spheres of Justice*, New York, Basic Books, 1983, pp. 100–3.

13 Ibid., p. 103. (The parts of the quotation I have deleted refer to religious prostitution, which is not relevant here.)

14 *Supra*, ch.2.

15 See *Supra*, pp. 10–1.

16 B. Mandeville, *The Fable of the Bees*, ed. F.B. Kaye, Oxford, Oxford University Press, 1957, Remark (H.), vol. 1, pp. 95–6, 100.
   Mandeville discusses prostitution in detail in *A Modest Defence of Publick Stews: or, an Essay upon Whoring, As it is now practis'd in these*

Kingdoms, London, A. Moore, 1724 (published anonymously). The argument I have quoted from the *Fable* is elaborated on pp. ii-iii, xi-xii, 39–52.

17 See A. Schopenhauer, "On Women," *Parerga and Paralipomena*, trans. E.F.J. Payne, Oxford, Oxford University Press, 1974, vol. 1, p. 623.

18 See W.E.H. Lecky, *History of European Morals*, London, Longmans, Green & Co., 1869, vol. 2, pp. 299–300.

19 See B. Russell, *Marriage and Morals*, London, George Allen & Unwin, 1976, pp. 97–9.

20 See St. Thomas Aquinas, *The Summa Theologica*, trans. by fathers of the English Dominican Province, London, Burns Oates & Washbourne, s.a., vol. 9, pt. II/ii, q. 10, art. 11, pp. 142–3.

On the other hand, Luther discusses this argument and rejects it. He marshalls several counter-arguments: scriptural (Hebrews xiii, 4), empirical (toleration of prostitution tends to corrupt public morals), and the argument from the absolute character of the prohibitions enjoined by religious morality ("… We cannot do, permit, or tolerate anything against God. *Fiat iustitia et pereat mundus* …") (Martin Luther, "The Natural Place of Women," in D.P. Verene (ed.), *Sexual Love and Western Morality*, 2nd ed., Boston, Jones & Bartlett, 1995, pp. 100–1).

21 H. Benjamin and R.E.L. Masters, *Prostitution and Morality*, London, Souvenir Press, 1965, p. 201.

22 See *supra*, ch. 3.

23 D.A.J. Richards, op.cit., pp. 99–104.

24 Ibid., pp. 103–4.

25 See J.R. Richards, *The Sceptical Feminist: A Philosophical Enquiry*, Harmondsworth, Penguin Books, 1984, pp. 241–6.

26 See *supra*, pp. 26–33, 98.

27 B. Russell, op.cit., pp. 101–2.

28 L.O. Ericsson, op.cit., p. 342.

29 D. Archard, "Sex for Sale: The Morality of Prostitution," *Cogito*, 1989, vol. 3, pp. 49–50.

30 C. Pateman, "Defending Prostitution: Charges against Ericsson," *Ethics*, 1982/3, vol. 93, p. 562.

31 But see A. Appiah, "'But Would That still Be Me?': Notes on Gender, 'Race,' Ethnicity, as Sources of 'Identity'," *Journal of Philosophy*, 1990, vol. 87.

32 On the arguments for and against see *Report of the Committee of Inquiry into Human Fertilisation and Embryology*, London, HMSO, 1984, ch. 8; M. Warnock, "The Artificial Family," and M. Lockwood, "The Warnock Report: A Philosophical Appraisal," in M. Lockwood (ed.), *Moral Dilemmas in Modern Medicine*, Oxford, Oxford University Press, 1985.

33 *Report*, p. 45.

34 J.R. Richards, op.cit., p. 243.

35 S. de Beauvoir, *The Second Sex*, trans. and ed. H.M. Parshley, London, Pan Books, 1988, p. 569.

36 By "our society" Shrage most of the time seems to mean contemporary American society, but toward the end of the paper claims to have

discussed "the meaning of commercial sex in modern Western culture" (L. Shrage, "Should Feminists Oppose Prostitution?", HS p. 289).

37 Ibid., p. 282.

38 Ibid., p. 283.

39 A. Dworkin, *Intercourse*, New York, The Free Press, 1987.

40 M.G. Haft, "Hustling for Rights," *Civil Liberties Review*, 1973/4, vol. 1, p. 20; quoted in A.M. Jaggar, "Prostitution," POS1, p. 350.

41 See R. Baker, "'Pricks' and 'Chicks': A Plea for 'Persons'," P&S2.

42 Ibid., p. 262.

43 Ibid., p. 264.

44 In a more recent statement of her argument, Shrage appears to grant some of these points (see L. Shrage, *Moral Dilemmas of Feminism: Prostitution, Adultery, and Abortion*, New York, Routledge, 1994, pp. 135–6, 207 n. 22).

45 "Statement on Prostitution and Feminism," in G. Pheterson (ed.), *A Vindication of the Rights of Whores*, Seattle, Seal Press, 1989, p. 192.

46 Ibid., p. 194.

47 Feminists and activist prostitutes have occasionally collaborated in attempts to bring about change of laws relating to prostitution. But such collaboration has not taken place as a result of converging views on the nature and moral status of prostitution, but rather in spite of persisting differences in these views. See B.M. Hobson, *Uneasy Virtue: The Politics of Prostitution and the American Reform Tradition*, Chicago, University of Chicago Press, 1990, ch. 9.

9 HOMOSEXUALITY

1 W.R. Dynes and W. Johansson, "Homosexual (term)", in W.R. Dynes (ed.), *Encyclopedia of Homosexuality*, Chicago, St. James Press, 1990, vol. 1, p. 555.

2 See A. Sullivan, *Virtually Normal: An Argument about Homosexuality*, London, Picador, 1995, pp. 83–93.

3 Plato, *The Laws*, trans. A.E. Taylor, London, Dent, 1966, 836bc, p. 223.

   To be sure, both Plato and Socrates held that the relevant type of homosexual *desire*, properly controlled and denied physical consummation, had an important educational role. See K.J. Dover, *Greek Homosexuality*, London, Duckworth, 1978, pp. 153–68.

4 I. Kant, *Lectures on Ethics*, trans. L. Infield, London, Methuen, 1930. p. 170.

5 See J. Bentham, "An Essay on 'Paederasty'", P&S2.

6 See Lev. xviii, 22; xx, 13; Rom. i, 26–7; I Cor. vi, 9–10; I Timothy i, 9–10.

7 St. Augustine, *The Confessions*, trans. F.J. Sheed, London, Sheed & Ward, 1951, bk. III, ch. 8, p. 39.

8 See *supra*, p. 44.

9 St. Thomas Aquinas, *Summa Contra Gentiles*, trans. V.J. Bourke, bk. III, pt. II, ch. 122, p. 146.

10 M. Luther, "The Natural Place of Women", in D.P. Verene (ed.), *Sexual Love and Western Morality*, 2nd ed., Boston, Jones & Bartlett, 1995, p. 101.

11 "Vatican Declaration on Some Questions of Sexual Ethics", in T.A. Mappes and J.S. Zembaty (eds), *Social Ethics*, 4th ed., New York, McGraw-Hill, 1992, p. 200. See also *Letter to the Bishops of the Catholic Church on the Pastoral Care of Homosexual Persons*, London, Catholic Truth Society, 1986.

12 See *supra*, pp. 13–20, 51–3.

13 See *supra*, pp. 58–9, 61.

14 J.M. Finnis, "Law, Morality, and 'Sexual Orientation'", *Notre Dame Law Review*, 1993/4, vol. 69, pp. 1066–7.

15 Ibid., p. 1069.

16 G. Grisez, *Living a Christian Life*, Quincy, IL, Franciscan Press, 1993, p. 650.

17 See J.M. Finnis, op.cit., p. 1067; G. Grisez, op.cit., pp. 653–4.

18 Aristotle, *The Nicomachean Ethics*, trans. D. Ross, London, Oxford University Press, 1963, 1152b, p. 184.

19 For more on the new natural law and the issue of homosexuality, see S. Macedo, "Homosexuality and the Conservative Mind", *Georgetown Law Journal*, 1995/6, vol. 84; R.P. George and G.V. Bradley, "Marriage and the Liberal Imagination", ibid.; S. Macedo, "Reply to Critics", ibid.

  Finnis also offers an argument against legal recognition of homosexual marriage; see *infra*, pp. 131–2.

20 R. Scruton, *Sexual Desire*, London, Weidenfeld & Nicolson, 1986, p. 3.

21 See *supra*, pp. 22–3, 28.

22 R. Scruton, op.cit., p. 282.

23 E. Johnson, "Inscrutable Desires", HS, p. 57.

24 R. Scruton, op.cit., pp. 283, 310.

25 See *supra*, pp. 30–1.

26 M. Nussbaum, "Sex in the Head", *The New York Review of Books*, December 18, 1986, p. 51.

27 See J.A. Lee, "Impersonal Sex and Casual Sex", in W.R. Dynes (ed.), op.cit., vol. 1.

28 F. Suppe, "Curing Homosexuality", P&S2, p. 405.

29 See F. Elliston, "In Defense of Promiscuity", P&S1.

30 Lev. xx, 13.

31 Gen. xix, 1–29.

32 W.R. Dynes, "Myths and Fabrications", in W.R. Dynes (ed.), op.cit., vol. 2, p. 870.

33 Quoted in M. Ruse, *Homosexuality: A Philosophical Inquiry*, Oxford, Basil Blackwell, 1988, p. 238.

34 See W.R. Dynes, "Buggery", in W.R. Dynes (ed.), op.cit., vol. 1; W. Johansson, "Sodomy", ibid., vol. 2.

35 See *Report of the Committee on Homosexual Offences and Prostitution*, London, HMSO, 1957.

36 Justice B.R. White, "Majority Opinion in *Bowers v. Hardwick*", in T.A. Mappes and J.S. Zembaty (eds), op.cit., p. 233.

37 Justice H.A. Blackmun, "Dissenting Opinion in *Bowers v. Hardwick*", in T.A. Mappes and J.S. Zembaty (eds), op.cit., p. 236.

38 S. Freud, "'Civilized' Sexual Morality and Modern Nervousness", *Collected Papers*, trans. J. Riviere, vol. 2, London, Hogarth Press, 1956, p. 88.

39 R.D. Mohr, *Gays/Justice: A Study of Ethics, Society, and Law*, New York, Columbia University Press, 1988, pp. 59–60.
40 Another type of legal discrimination against homosexuals is the higher age of consent set for adolescents with regard to homosexual sex, or homosexual sex with adults; see *infra*, pp. 135–6.
41 R.D. Mohr, op.cit., p. 198.
42 See ibid., pp. 24–5.
43 See J.M. Stafford, *Homosexuality and Education*, Manchester, J.M. Stafford, 1988, ch. 4–5.
44 A. Sullivan, op.cit., pp. 161–2.
45 See R.D. Mohr, op.cit., pp. 162–81.
46 See ibid., pp. 188–91.
47 See *supra*, pp. 75–8.
48 See P.L. Ettelbrick, "Since When is Marriage a Path to Liberation?", *Out/Look: National Gay and Lesbian Quarterly*, no. 6, Fall 1989; N.D. Polikoff, "We Will Get What We Ask For: Why Legalizing Gay and Lesbian Marriage Will Not 'Dismantle the Legal Structure of Gender in Every Marriage'", *Virginia Law Review*, 1993, vol. 79.
49 For an account of the debate in homosexual circles about the pros and cons of homosexual marriage, see W.N. Eskridge, Jr., *The Case for Same-Sex Marriage*, New York, Free Press, 1996, ch. 3.
50 Ibid., p. 79.
51 J. Bentham, *The Handbook of Political Fallacies*, ed. H.A. Larrabee, New York, Harper Torchbooks, 1962, pp. 74–5.
52 See W. N. Eskridge, Jr., op.cit., ch. 2.
53 See *supra*, p. 69.
54 See A. Ferguson, "Androgyny as an Ideal for Human Development", and J. Trebilcot, "Two Forms of Androgynism", in M. Vetterling-Braggin, F.A. Elliston, and J. English (eds), *Feminism and Philosophy*, Totowa, NJ, Rowman & Littlefield, 1985.
55 J.M. Finnis, op.cit., pp. 1069–70.
56 See *supra*, pp. 13–20, 111–19.
57 For an argument for legal recognition of homosexual marriage along different lines, focusing on the nature and significance of the marital relationship, see R.D. Mohr, "The Case for Gay Marriage", HS.

A more extensive treatment of homosexuality than can be attempted here would also include some discussion of the legitimacy of "outing" (the publication of a person's homosexuality against the person's will) and the moral questions raised by the AIDS epidemic. On the former, see T.F. Murphy (ed.), *Gay Ethics: Controversies in Outing, Civil Rights, and Sexual Science*, New York, Haworth Press, 1994, pt. II: Outing and the Closet. On the latter, see R.D. Mohr, op.cit., ch. 8–10; C. Pierce and D. VanDeVeer (eds), *AIDS: Ethics and Public Policy*, Belmont, CA, Wadsworth, 1988; P. Illingworth, *AIDS and the Good Society*, London, Routledge, 1990.

10 PEDOPHILIA

1 W. Johansson, "Pederasty", in W.R. Dynes (ed.), *Encyclopedia of Homosexuality*, Chicago, St. James Press, 1990, vol. 2, p. 961.

2 See S. Donaldson, "Ephebophilia", in R.W. Dynes (ed.), op.cit., vol. 1.
3 See *supra*, ch. 6.
4 K. Plummer, "'The Paedophile's' Progress: A View from Below", in B. Taylor (ed.), *Perspectives on Paedophilia*, London, Batsford, 1981, p. 130.
5 P. Righton, "The Adult", in B. Taylor (ed.), op.cit., p. 27.
6 On the stereotypes of pedophilia see K. Plummer, "Pedophilia: Constructing a Sociological Baseline", in M. Cook and K. Howells (eds), *Adult Sexual Interest in Children*, London, Academic Press, 1981, pp. 224–8; P. Righton, op. cit.
7 To be sure, there are still some jurisdictions where *all* homosexual sex, or homosexual sex between males, is against the law; see *supra*, pp. 120–1.
8 See *supra*, pp. 111–119.
9 See *supra*, pp. 91–2.
10 Such as J.Z. Eglinton, *Greek Love*, London, Neville Spearman, 1971.
11 T. O'Carroll, *Paedophilia: The Radical Case*, London, Peter Owen, 1980; R. Ehman, "Adult-Child Sex", P&S2.
12 See P. Aries, *Centuries of Childhood: A Social History of Family Life*, trans. R. Baldick, New York, Vintage Books, 1962, in particular pt. I, ch. V: From Immodesty to Innocence. For a good account of the main problems plaguing the Aries thesis, see D. Archard, *Children: Rights and Childhood*, London, Routledge, 1993, ch. 2–3.
13 Roger Scruton has recently endorsed the idea of sexual innocence of children: "We desire that [sexual] initiation should not occur before the 'age of innocence' has expired, since we desire sexual expression to be withheld until it can exist as an interpersonal response. Our perception of the moral innocence of the child is therefore combined with a powerful interdiction: not to awaken in the child an interest in these things which are forbidden to him" (R. Scruton, *Sexual Desire: A Philosophical Investigation*, London, Weidenfeld & Nicolson, 1986, p. 297).
14 R. Ehman, op.cit., p. 433.
15 See A.C. Kinsey, W.B. Pomeroy, and C.E. Martin, *Sexual Behavior in the Human Male*, Philadelphia, W.B. Saunders, 1948, ch. 5; A.C. Kinsey, W.B. Pomeroy, C.E. Martin and P.H. Gebhard, *Sexual Behavior in the Human Female*, Philadelphia, W.B. Saunders, 1953, ch. 4.
16 See T. O'Carroll, op.cit., ch. 2 and 5.
17 L. Burton, *Vulnerable Children*, London, Routledge & Kegan Paul, 1967.
18 Quoted in T. O'Carroll, op.cit., p. 64.
19 M. Tsai, S. Feldman-Summers, and M. Edgar, "Childhood Molestation: Variables Related to Differential Impacts on Psychosexual Functioning in Adult Women", *Journal of Abnormal Psychology*, 1979, vol. 88.
20 R. Ehman, op.cit., pp. 435–6.
21 K. Plummer, op.cit., p. 227.
22 G.E. Powell and A.J. Chalkley, "The Effects of Paedophile Attention on the Child", in B. Taylor (ed.), op.cit.
23 See D. Finkelhor, "What's Wrong with Sex between Adults and Children?", *American Journal of Orthopsychiatry*, 1979, vol. 49.
24 R. Ehman, op.cit., pp. 439–41.
25 T. O'Carroll, op.cit., p. 153.

26 Ibid., p. 56.
27 For a detailed proposal of legal reform along these lines, see T. O'Carroll, op.cit., ch. 6. On children's rights in general, see D. Archard, op.cit., ch. 4–7.
28 M. Frye, "Critique", P&S2, pp. 450–1.
29 S. Ferenczi, "Sprachverwirrung zwischen den Erwachsenen und dem Kind (Die Sprache der Zaertlichkeit und der Leidenschaft)", *Bausteine zur Psychoanalyse*, 2. Aufl., Bd. III, Bern, Verlag Hans Huber, 1964, p. 518.
30 See e.g. M. Ingram, "Participating Victims: A Study of Sexual Offenses with Boys", in L.L. Constantine and F.M. Martinson (eds), *Children and Sex: New Findings, New Perspectives*, Boston, Little, Brown & Co., 1981.
31 D. Finkelhor, op.cit., p. 695.
32 P. Califia, "Man/Boy Love and the Lesbian/Gay Movement", in D. Tsang (ed.), *The Age Taboo: Gay Male Sexuality, Power and Consent*, Boston, Alyson Publications, 1981, p. 138.
33 Sexual interaction of children with other children who are *not* their sexual peers, i.e. between a pubescent and a pre-pubescent child, may well be a different matter, since such cases are liable to involve a significant degree of asymmetry of the sort that vitiates adult–child sex.

11 SEXUAL HARASSMENT AND RAPE

1 US Merit Systems Protection Board, *Sexual Harassment in the Federal Workplace: Is It a Problem?*, Washington, DC, US Government Printing Office, 1981; *Sexual Harassment in the Federal Government: An Update*, Washington, DC, US Government Printing Office, 1988.
2 J.C. Hughes and L. May, "Sexual Harassment", *Social Theory and Practice*, 1980, vol. 6, p. 250.
3 F.J. Till, *Sexual Harassment: A Report on the Sexual Harassment of Students*, Washington, DC, National Advisory Council of Women's Educational Programs, 1980, p. 7.
4 L.J. Rubin and S.B. Borgers, "Sexual Harassment in Universities During the 1980s", SH, p. 32.
5 Equal Employment Opportunity Commission, *Guidelines on Discrimination Because of Sex*, reprinted as Appendix I in B.W. Dziech and L. Weiner, *The Lecherous Professor: Sexual Harassment on Campus*, Boston, Beacon Press, 1984, pp. 189–90.
6 E. Frankel Paul, "Bared Buttocks and Federal Cases", SH, p. 153.
7 E. Wall, "The Definition of Sexual Harassment", SH, p. 73.
8 Ibid., p. 79.
9 See ibid., pp. 82–3.
10 N. Tuana, "Sexual Harassment in Academe: Issues of Power and Coercion", SH.
11 M. Bayles, "Coercive Offers and Public Benefits", *The Personalist*, 1974, vol. 55, pp. 142–3; quoted in N. Tuana, "Sexual Harassment: Offers and Coercion", *Journal of Social Philosophy*, 1988, vol. 19, p. 31.
12 N. Tuana, op.cit.
13 For another account of *quid pro quo* sexual harassment as essentially coercive, which fails for similar reasons, see L. May and J.C. Hughes, "Is Sexual Harassment Coercive?", SH.

14 Not all feminists subscribe to this approach to sexual harassment. For a review of some rather different feminist views, see L. LeMoncheck and M. Hajdin, *Sexual Harassment: A Debate*, Lanham, MD, Rowman & Littlefield, 1997, pp. 25–40.

15 A.M. Superson, "A Feminist Definition of Sexual Harassment", HS.

16 C.A. MacKinnon, *Sexual Harassment of Working Women*, New Haven, CN, Yale University Press, 1979; "Sexual Harassment: Its First Decade in Court", *Feminism Unmodified*, Cambridge, MA, Harvard University Press, 1987; *Only Words*, London, Harper/Collins, 1994, ch. II: Racial and Sexual Harassment.

17 C.A. MacKinnon, *Sexual Harassment of Working Women*, p. 4.

18 Ibid., pp. 174–5.

19 Ibid., p. 7.

20 C.A. MacKinnon, *Only Words*, p. 41.

21 For more on sexual harassment as discrimination on the basis of sex, see L. LeMoncheck and M. Hajdin, op.cit., pp. 121–40, 176–83.

22 Oncale vs. Sundowner Offshore Services, Inc., 118 S. Ct. 998 (1998).

23 See A. Altman, "Making Sense of Sexual Harassment Law", HS, pp. 425–7.

24 See L. LeMoncheck and M. Hajdin, op.cit., pp. 144–6.

25 See A. Ellis, "Offense and the Liberal Conception of the Law", *Philosophy & Public Affairs*, 1984, vol. 13.

26 See E. Frankel Paul, op.cit.

27 K. Burgess-Jackson, *Rape: A Philosophical Investigation*, Aldershot, Dartmouth Publishing Co., 1996, p. 46.

28 Quoted in S. Estrich, *Real Rape*, Cambridge, MA, Harvard University Press, 1987, p. 5.

29 C.M. Shafer and M. Frye, "Rape and Respect", in M. Vetterling-Braggin, F.A. Elliston, and J. English (eds), *Feminism and Philosophy*, Totowa, NJ, Rowman & Littlefield, 1985, pp. 339–40.

30 For a discussion of rape as no more and no less than battery, see M. Davis, "Setting Penalties: What Does Rape Deserve?", *Law and Philosophy*, 1984, Vol. 3.

31 S. Brownmiller, *Against Our Will: Men, Women and Rape*, New York, Simon and Schuster, 1975.

32 P. Foa, "What's Wrong with Rape", in M. Vetterling-Braggin, F.A. Elliston and J. English (eds), op.cit., p. 347.

33 S. Griffin, "Rape: The All-American Crime", in M. Vetterling-Braggin, F.A. Elliston and J. English (eds), op.cit., pp. 329, 331. See also S.R. Peterson, "Coercion and Rape: The State as a Male Protection Racket", ibid.; C. Card, "Rape as a Terrorist Institution", in R.G. Frey and Christopher W. Morris (eds), *Violence, Terrorism, and Justice*, Cambridge, Cambridge University Press, 1991.

34 C.A. MacKinnon, *Toward a Feminist Theory of the State*, Cambridge, MA, Harvard University Press, 1989, pp. 128, 113.

35 Ibid., p. 172.

36 Ibid., p. 134.

37 Ibid., p. 135.

38 Ibid., p. 147.

39 Ibid., p. 168.

40 C.A. MacKinnon, "Sex and Violence: A Perspective", *Feminism Unmodified*, p. 88.
41 Ibid., pp. 88–9.
42 C.A. MacKinnon, *Toward a Feminist Theory of the State*, p. 245.
43 R. Morgan, "Theory and Practice: Pornography and Rape", in L. Lederer (ed.), *Take Back the Night: Women on Pornography*, New York, William Morrow & Co., 1980, pp. 134–5.
44 See e.g. N. Gilbert, "Realities and Mythologies of Rape", *Society*, 1991/2, Vol. 29, No. 4, p. 10.
45 See J. Feinberg, *Harm to Self*, New York, Oxford University Press, 1986, ch. 24.
46 Ibid., pp. 248, 246.
47 Ibid., p. 246.
48 For more on procuring exploited consent to sex, see T.A. Mappes, "Sexual Morality and the Concept of Using Another Person", in T.A. Mappes and J.S. Zembaty (eds), *Social Ethics: Morality and Social Policy*, 4th ed., New York, McGraw-Hill, 1992; D. Archard, "Exploited Consent", *Journal of Social Philosophy*, 1994, vol. 25.
49 K. Burgess-Jackson, op.cit., p. 100.
50 L. May and R. Strikwerda, "Men in Groups: Collective Responsibility for Rape", *Hypatia*, 1994, vol. 9.
51 K. Burgess-Jackson, loc.cit.
52 See L. May and R. Strikwerda, op.cit., pp. 146–8.
53 A treatment of rape more comprehensive than can be attempted here would include a discussion of the way the *mens rea* in the crime of rape is to be defined, and the related, topical issue of date rape. On the former, see M.T. Thornton, "Rape and Mens Rea", HS; E.M. Curley, "Excusing Rape", *Philosophy & Public Affairs*, 1975/6, vol. 5; L. Bienen, "Mistakes", ibid., 1977/8, vol. 7; K. Burgess-Jackson, op.cit., ch. 8. On the latter, see L. Pineau, "Date Rape: A Feminist Analysis", HS; L. Francis (ed.), *Date Rape: Feminism, Philosophy, and the Law*, University Park, PA, The Pennsylvania State University Press, 1996.

12 CONCLUDING REMARKS

1 See R.D. Mohr, *Gays/Justice: A Study of Ethics, Society, and Law*, New York, Columbia University Press, 1988, pp. 24–5.
2 L.L. Fuller, *The Morality of Law*, revised ed., New Haven, Yale University Press, 1977, p. 10.
3 O. O'Neill, "Between Consenting Adults", *Philosophy & Public Affairs*, 1985, vol. 14, pp. 269–70.
4 Ibid., p. 270.
5 On intimacy in this latter, richer sense, see G. Graham and H. LaFollette, "Honesty and Intimacy", in G. Graham and H. LaFollette (eds), *Person to Person*, Philadelphia, Temple University Press, 1989.
6 G.E.M. Anscombe, "Contraception and Chastity", HS, p. 44.
7 R. Scruton, *Sexual Desire: A Philosophical Investigation*, London, Weidenfeld & Nicolson, 1986, p. 337.

SELECT BIBLIOGRAPHY

Altman, A., "Making Sense of Sexual Harassment Law", *Philosophy & Public Affairs*, 1996, vol. 25. Reprinted in HS

Anscombe, G.E.M., "Contraception and Chastity", *The Human World*, 1972, no. 7. Reprinted in HS

Archard, D., "Sex for Sale: The Morality of Prostitution", *Cogito*, 1989, vol. 3

—— *Children: Rights and Childhood*, London, Routledge, 1993

—— "Exploited Consent", *Journal of Social Philosophy*, 1994, vol. 25

Atkinson, R., *Sexual Morality*, London, Hutchinson, 1965

Augustine, St., *The City of God against the Pagans*, trans. P. Levine, Cambridge, MA, Harvard University Press, 1966

—— "The Good of Marriage", trans. C.T. Wilcox, M.M., *Treatises on Marriage and Other Subjects*, ed. R.J. Deferrari, Washington, DC, The Catholic University of America Press, 1969

Baker, R., " 'Pricks' and 'Chicks': A Plea for 'Persons'", P&S1. Reprinted in P&S2

Baumrin, B.H., "Sexual Morality Delineated", P&S1. Reprinted in P&S2

Bayles, M.D., "Coercive Offers and Public Benefits", *The Personalist*, 1974, vol. 55

—— "Marriage, Love and Procreation", P&S1. Reprinted in P&S2

Belliotti, R.A., *Good Sex: Perspectives on Sexual Ethics*, Lawrence, University Press of Kansas, 1993

Bentham, J., "Offences against One's Self: Paederasty", *Journal of Homosexuality*, 1977/8, vol. 3, and 1978/9, vol. 4. Reprinted in P&S2

Bertocci, P.A., *The Human Venture in Sex, Love, and Marriage*, New York, Association Press, 1949

Blackmun, H.A., Justice, "Dissenting Opinion in *Bowers vs. Hardwick*", in T.A. Mappes and J.S. Zembaty (eds), *Social Ethics*, 4th ed., New York, McGraw-Hill, 1992

Brison, S.J., "Surviving Sexual Violence: A Philosophical Perspective", *Journal of Social Philosophy*, 1993, vol. 24

Burgess-Jackson, K., *Rape: A Philosophical Investigation*, Aldershot, Dartmouth Publishing Co., 1996

Califia, P., "Man/Boy Love and the Lesbian/Gay Movement", in D. Tsang (ed.), *The Age Taboo: Gay Male Sexuality, Power and Consent*, Boston, Alyson Publications, 1981

Card, C., "Rape as a Terrorist Institution", in R.G. Frey and C.W. Morris (eds), *Violence, Terrorism, and Justice*, Cambridge, Cambridge University Press, 1991

Cohen, C., "Sex, Birth Control, and Human Life", *Ethics*, 1968/9, vol. 79. Reprinted in P&S1 and P&S2

Crosthwaite, J., and Swanton, C., "On the Nature of Sexual Harassment", *Australasian Journal of Philosophy*, 1986, supplem. to vol. 64. Reprinted in HS

Davis, K., "The Sociology of Prostitution", in S. Dinitz, R.R. Dynes, and A.C. Clare (eds), *Deviance*, 2nd ed., New York, Oxford University Press, 1975

Davis, M., "Setting Penalties: What Does Rape Deserve?", *Law and Philosophy*, 1984, vol. 3. Reprinted in Davis's *To Make the Punishment Fit the Crime*, Boulder, CO, Westview Press, 1992

Dynes, W. (ed.), *Encyclopedia of Homosexuality*, Chicago, St. James Press, 1990, 2 vols.

Earle, W.J., "Depersonalized Sex and Moral Perfection", *International Journal of Moral and Social Studies*, 1987, vol. 2. Reprinted in HS

Ehman, R., "Adult-Child Sex", P&S2

Ellis, A., "Casual Sex", *International Journal of Moral and Social Studies*, 1986, vol. 1. Reprinted in HS

Elliston, F., "In Defense of Promiscuity", P&S1

—— "Gay Marriage", P&S2

Engels, F., *The Origins of the Family, Private Property and the State*, trans. A. West, Harmondsworth, Penguin Books, 1985

Ericsson, L.O., "Charges against Prostitution: An Attempt at a Philosophical Assessment", *Ethics*, 1979/80, vol. 90

Eskridge, W.N., Jr., *The Case for Same-Sex Marriage*, New York, Free Press, 1996

Farrell, D.M., "Of Jealousy and Envy", in G. Graham and H. LaFollette (eds), *Person to Person*, Philadelphia, Temple University Press, 1989

Feinberg, J., *Harm to Self*, New York, Oxford University Press, 1986

Ferenczi, S., "Sprachverwirrung zwischen den Erwachsenen und dem Kind (Die Sprache der Zaertlichkeit und der Leidenschaft)", *Bausteine zur Psychoanalyse*, 2. Aufl., Bern, Verlag Hans Huber, 1964

Finkelhor, D., "What's Wrong with Sex between Adults and Children?", *American Journal of Orthopsychiatry*, 1979, vol. 49

Finnis, J.M., "Natural Law and Unnatural Acts", *Heythrop Journal*, 1970, vol. 11. Reprinted in HS

—— "Law, Morality, and 'Sexual Orientation'", *Notre Dame Law Review*, 1993/4, vol. 69

Foa, P., "What's Wrong with Rape", in M. Vetterling-Braggin, F.A. Elliston, and J. English (eds), *Feminism and Philosophy*, Totowa, NJ, Rowman & Littlefield, 1985

Fortunata, J., "Masturbation and Women's Sexuality", POS1

Frankel Paul, E., "Bared Buttocks and Federal Cases", *Society*, 1990/91, vol. 28. Reprinted in SH

Frye, M., "Critique" [of R. Ehman's "Adult-Child Sex"], P&S2

George, R.P., and Bradley, G.V., "Marriage and the Liberal Imagination", *Georgetown Law Journal*, 1995/6, vol. 84

Godwin, W., *An Enquiry Concerning Political Justice*, ed. M. Philip, London, William Pickering, 1993

Goldman, A., "Plain Sex", *Philosophy & Public Affairs*, 1976/7, vol. 6. Reprinted in HS, POS1, and POS3

Gray, R., "Sex and Sexual Perversion", *Journal of Philosophy*, 1978, vol. 75. Reprinted in POS1 and POS3

Griffin, S., "Rape: The All-American Crime", *Ramparts*, September 1971. Reprinted in M. Vetterling-Braggin, F.A. Elliston, and J. English (eds), op.cit.

Grisez, G., *Living a Christian Life*, Quincy, IL, Franciscan Press, 1993

Hajdin, M., "Sexual Harassment in the Law: The Demarcation Problem", *Journal of Social Philosophy*, 1994, vol. 25. Reprinted in HS and POS3
—— "Sexual Harassment and Negligence", *Journal of Social Philosophy*, 1997, vol. 28

Herman, B., "Could it Be Worth Thinking about Kant on Sex and Marriage?", in L.M. Antony and C. Witt (eds), *A Mind of One's Own: Feminist Essays on Reason and Objectivity*, Boulder, Westview Press, 1993

Hughes, J.C., and May, L., "Sexual Harassment", *Social Theory and Practice*, 1980, vol. 6

Humber, J.M., "Sexual Perversion and Human Nature", *Philosophy Research Archives*, 1987/8, vol. 13. Reprinted in HS

Hume, D., "Of Polygamy and Divorces", *Essays Literary, Moral and Political*, London, George Routledge & Sons, s.a.

Ingram, M., "Participating Victims: A Study of Sexual Offenses with Boys", in L.L. Constantine and F.M. Martinson (eds), *Children and Sex: New Findings, New Perspectives*, Boston, Little, Brown & Co., 1981

Jaggar, A.M., "Prostitution", POS1

John Paul II, Pope, *Letter to Families*, Vatican, Libreria Editrice Vaticana, 1994

Johnson, E., "Inscrutable Desires", *Philosophy of the Social Sciences*, 1990, vol. 20. Reprinted in HS
—— "Lovesexpressed", SLF

Kant, I., *Lectures on Ethics*, trans. L. Infield, London, Methuen, 1930
—— *The Metaphysics of Morals*, trans. and ed. M. Gregor, Cambridge, Cambridge University Press, 1996

Ketchum, S.A., "The Good, the Bad, and the Perverted: Sexual Paradigms Revisited", POS1

LeMoncheck, L., and Hajdin, M., *Sexual Harassment: A Debate*, Lanham, MD, Rowman & Littlefield, 1997

Lesser, A.H., "Love and Lust", *Journal of Value Inquiry*, 1980, vol. 14. Reprinted in HS

Levy, D., "Perversion and the Unnatural as Moral Categories", *Ethics*, 1979/80, vol. 90. Reprinted in POS1

Luther, M., "The Natural Place of Women", in D.P. Verene (ed.), *Sexual Love and Western Morality*, 2nd ed., Boston, Jones & Bartlett, 1995

Macedo, S., "Homosexuality and the Conservative Mind", *Georgetown Law Journal*, 1995/6, vol. 84

—— "Reply to Critics", ibid.

MacKinnon, C.A., *Sexual Harassment of Working Women*, New Haven, CT, Yale University Press, 1979

—— *Feminism Unmodified*, Cambridge, MA, Harvard University Press, 1987

—— *Toward a Feminist Theory of the State*, Cambridge, MA, Harvard University Press, 1989

—— *Only Words*, London, Harper/Collins, 1994

McMurtry, J., "Monogamy: A Critique", *The Monist*, 1972, vol. 56. Reprinted in P&S1 and P&S2

Mandeville, B., *The Fable of the Bees*, ed. F.B. Kaye, Oxford, Oxford University Press, 1957

Mappes, T.A., "Sexual Morality and the Concept of Using Another Person", in T.A. Mappes and J.S. Zembaty (eds), op.cit.

Margolis, J., "Perversion", *Negativities: The Limits of Life*, Columbus, Charles E. Merrill, 1975

—— and Margolis, C., "The Separation of Marriage and Family", in M. Vetterling-Braggin, F.A. Elliston, and J. English (eds), op.cit.

May, L., and Hughes, J., "Is Sexual Harassment Coercive?", in G. Ezorsky (ed.), *Moral Rights in the Workplace*, New York, State University of New York Press, 1987. Reprinted in SH

May, L., and Strikwerda, R., "Men in Groups: Collective Responsibility for Rape", *Hypatia*, 1994, vol. 9

Mendus, S., "Marital Faithfulness", *Philosophy*, 1984, vol. 59

Missner, M., "Why Have Children?", *International Journal of Applied Philosophy*, 1987, vol. 3

Mohr, R.D., *Gays/Justice: A Study of Ethics, Society, and Law*, New York, Columbia University Press, 1988

—— "The Case for Gay Marriage", *Notre Dame Journal of Law, Ethics, and Public Policy*, 1995, vol. 9. Reprinted in HS

Morgan, R., "Theory and Practice: Pornography and Rape", in L. Lederer (ed.), *Take Back the Night: Women on Pornography*, New York, William Morrow & Co., 1980

Moulton, J., "Sex and Reference", P&S1

—— "Sexual Behavior: Another Position", *Journal of Philosophy*, 1976, vol. 73. Reprinted in HS, POS1, and POS3

Nagel, T., "Sexual Perversion", *Journal of Philosophy*, 1969, vol. 66. Reprinted in P&S1, P&S2, POS1, POS3, and Nagel's *Mortal Questions*, Cambridge, Cambridge University Press, 1979

Neu, J., "Jealous Thoughts", in A. Oksenberg Rorty (ed.), *Explaining Emotions*, Berkeley, University of California Press, 1980

Nussbaum, M.C., "Sex in the Head", *New York Review of Books*, December 18, 1986

—— "Objectification", *Philosophy & Public Affairs*, 1995, vol. 24. Reprinted in POS3

O'Carroll, T., *Paedophilia: The Radical Case*, London, Peter Owen, 1980

O'Neill, O., "Between Consenting Adults", *Philosophy & Public Affairs*, 1985, vol. 14

Palmer, D., "The Consolation of the Wedded", P&S1. Reprinted in P&S2

Pateman, C., "Defending Prostitution: Charges against Ericsson", *Ethics*, 1982/3, vol. 93

Paul VI, Pope, "Humanae Vitae", P&S1, P&S2

Peterson, S.R., "Coercion and Rape: The State as a Male Protection Racket", in M. Vetterling-Braggin, F.A. Elliston, and J. English (eds), op.cit.

Pheterson, G. (ed.), *A Vindication of the Rights of Whores*, Seattle, Seal Press, 1989

Plummer, K., "The Paedophile's Progress: A View from Below", in B. Taylor (ed.), *Perspectives on Paedophilia*, London, Batsford, 1981

—— "Pedophilia: Constructing a Sociological Baseline", in M. Cook and K. Howells (eds), *Adult Sexual Interest in Children*, London, Academic Press, 1981

Powell, G.E., and Chalkley, A.J., "The Effects of Paedophile Attention on the Child", in B. Taylor (ed.), op.cit.

Priest, G., "Sexual Perversion", *Australasian Journal of Philosophy*, 1997, vol. 75

Richards, D.A.J., *Sex, Drugs, Death and the Law: An Essay on Overcriminalization*, Totowa, NJ, Rowman & Littlefield, 1982

Richards, J.R., *The Sceptical Feminist: A Philosophical Inquiry*, Harmondsworth, Penguin Books, 1984

Righton, P., "The Adult", in B. Taylor (ed.), op.cit.

Rubin, L.J., and Borgers, S.B., "Sexual Harassment in Universities During the 1980s", SH

Ruddick, S., "Better Sex", P&S1. Reprinted in P&S2

Ruse, M., *Homosexuality: A Philosophical Inquiry*, Oxford, Basil Blackwell, 1988

Russell, B., *Marriage and Morals*, London, George Allen & Unwin, 1976

Sade, D.A.F. de, *Philosophy in the Bedroom*, in *The Complete Justine, Philosophy in the Bedroom and Other Writings*, ed. and trans. R. Seaver and A. Wainhouse, New York, Grove Press, 1965

Schopenhauer, A., "The Metaphysics of Sexual Love", *The World as Will and Representation*, trans. E.F.J. Payne, New York, Dover Publications, 1966, vol. 2

—— "On Women", *Parerga and Paralipomena*, trans. E.F.J. Payne, Oxford, Oxford University Press, 1974, vol. 1

Schwarzenbach, S., "Contractarians and Feminists Debate Prostitution", *New York University Review of Law & Social Change*, 1990/91, vol. 18. Reprinted in HS

Scruton, R., *Sexual Desire: A Philosophical Investigation*, London, Weidenfeld & Nicolson, 1986

Shafer, C.M., and Frye, M., "Rape and Respect", in M. Vetterling-Braggin, F.A. Elliston, and J. English (eds), op.cit.

Shaffer, J.A., "Sexual Desire", *Journal of Philosophy*, 1978, vol. 75. Reprinted in SLF

Shrage, L., "Should Feminists Oppose Prostitution?", *Ethics*, 1988/9, vol. 99. Reprinted in HS and POS3

—— *Moral Dilemmas in Feminism: Prostitution, Adultery, and Abortion*, New York, Routledge, 1994

Slote, M., "Inapplicable Concepts and Sexual Perversion", P&S1

Smilansky, S., "Is There a Moral Obligation to Have Children?", *Journal of Applied Philosophy*, 1995, vol. 12

Soble, A., "Masturbation", *Pacific Philosophical Quarterly*, 1980, vol. 61. Reprinted in HS

—— *Sexual Investigations*, New York, New York University Press, 1996

Solomon, R., "Sexual Paradigms", *Journal of Philosophy*, 1974, vol. 71. Reprinted in HS, POS1, and POS3

—— "Sexual Perversion", P&S1. Reprinted in Solomon's *From Hegel to Existentialism*, New York, Oxford University Press, 1994

Stafford, J.M., "On Distinguishing between Love and Lust", *Journal of Value Inquiry*, 1977, vol. 11. Reprinted in Stafford's *Essays on Sexuality and Ethics*, Solihull, Ismeron, 1995

—— "Love and Lust Revisited: Intentionality, Homosexuality and Moral Education", *Journal of Applied Philosophy*, 1988, vol. 5. Reprinted in HS and Stafford's *Essays on Sexuality and Ethics*

—— *Homosexuality and Education*, Manchester, J.M. Stafford, 1988

Stein, E., "The Relevance of Scientific Research about Sexual Orienation to Lesbian and Gay Rights", *Journal of Homosexuality*, 1994, vol. 27. Reprinted in HS

Sullivan, A., *Virtually Normal: An Argument about Homosexuality*, London, Picador, 1995

Superson, A.M., "A Feminist Definition of Sexual Harassment", *Journal of Social Philosophy*, 1993, vol. 24. Reprinted in HS

Suppe, F., "Curing Homosexuality", P&S2

Teichman, J., "Intention and Sex", in C. Diamond and J. Teichman (eds), *Intention and Intentionality: Essays in Honour of G.E.M. Anscombe*, Brighton, Harvester Press, 1979

Thomas Aquinas, St., *Summa Contra Gentiles*, trans. V.J. Bourke, Notre Dame, Notre Dame University Press, 1975, bk. III, pt. II

—— *The Summa Theologica*, trans. by fathers of the English Dominican Province, London, Burns Oates & Washbourne, s.a., vol. 13

Tuana, N., "Sexual Harassment in Academe: Issues of Power and Coercion", *College Teaching*, 1985, vol. 33. Reprinted in SH

—— "Sexual Harassment: Offers and Coercion", *Journal of Social Philosophy*, 1988, vol. 19

Vannoy, R., *Sex Without Love: A Philosophical Exploration*, Buffalo, NY, Prometheus Books, 1980

—— "Can Sex Express Love?", SLF

"Vatican Declaration on Some Questions of Sexual Ethics", in T.A. Mappes and J.S. Zembaty (eds), op.cit.

Wall, E., "The Definition of Sexual Harassment", *Public Affairs Quarterly*, 1991, vol. 5. Reprinted in SH

Wasserstrom, R., "Is Adultery Immoral?", in R. Wasserstrom (ed.), *Today's Moral Problems*, New York, Macmillan, 1975. Reprinted in P&S1 and P&S2

White, B.R., Justice, "Majority Opinion in *Bowers vs. Hardwick*", in T.A. Mappes and J.S. Zembaty (eds), op.cit.

Wilder, H.T., "The Language of Sex and the Sex of Language", POS1. Reprinted in SLF

Wilson, J., *Logic and Sexual Morality*, Harmondsworth, Penguin Books, 1965

—— "Can One Promise to Love Another?", *Philosophy*, 1989, vol. 64

Wreen, M., "What's Really Wrong with Adultery", *International Journal of Applied Philosophy*, 1986, vol. 3

INDEX

coercion: rape 161–5; sexual
harassment 148–50
commercial sex 40, 88
common law marriage 81
communication 47, 59; *see also*
language view of sex
consent: pedophilia 134–5,
139–42; rape 160–5
critical morality 89, 167

deception 78–9, 82–4
degradation 99–105
depth psychology 64, 65
Descartes, R. 5
discrimination: homosexuals 118,
119–27; sexual harassment
151–4
divorce 12, 71, 72, 81
double reciprocal incarnation 35
double standards 87, 89, 167–8
Durkheim, Emile 89
Dworkin, Andrea 106, 108
Dynes, Wayne R. 110

Earle, W.J. 27
Ehman, Robert 136–41
Elliston, Frederick 12
embodiment 23–4
employment: homosexuals 123–7;
sexual harassment 144–6, 151–6
Engels, Friedrich 75–6, 89–90
England, sodomy laws 120
ephebophilia 133–4, 136, 168
Epictetus 4–5
Equal Employment Opportunity
Commission (United States)
146, 147, 153, 155–6
Ericsson, Lars O. 93, 102
erotic love 25, 28, 74
Eskridge, William N., Jr, 128–9
ethnic identity 103–4
European Convention of Human
Rights 120
Evangelium Vitae 71
exclusivity 84–5; *see also* sexual
exclusivity
exhibitionism 50, 56, 60, 62, 63,
65
extramarital sex *see* adultery

fear of loss 87
Feinberg, Joel 163, 164
feminism 6; prostitution 99–109;
rape 156, 159–62, 165–6;
sexual harassment 144, 150–3
Ferenczi, Sandor 141
fetishism 50, 55, 60, 62, 63, 64,
65, 66
fidelity 26, 86
Finkelhor, David 141–2
Finnis, John M. 113–14, 131, 177
n9
Fletcher, Joseph 16–17
France 119–20
Frankel Paul, Ellen 147
Freud, S. 122, 137
friendship 84–5
Frye, Marilyn 140, 157–8
Fuller, Lon L. 171

gay 110, 111
gay liberation movement 6, 111,
118
Germany 120
Gert, Bernard 79
Godwin, William 4, 74–5
Goldman, Alan 7, 31, 41–6, 56–8
Grice, H.P. 35
Griffin, Susan 160
Grisez, Germain 113, 114, 177 n9
Groddeck, Georg 45–6

Haft, Marilyn G. 106
Hale, Lord Chief Justice Matthew
157
Hardwick, Michael 120–1
hedonist view of sex *see* plain sex
view, plainer sex view
Heraclitus 5
heresy 119
higher education, sexual
harassment in 144, 145, 146,
148–9, 153–6
homosexuality 26, 31, 63, 64,
110–32; age of consent 134,
136; discrimination 119–27,
132; ephebophilia 134, 136;
marriage 127–32; as minority
sexual behavior 65; morality and

Mill, John Stuart 94, 184 n11
modesty 26
Mohr, Richard D. 123, 124
monogamy 6, 71, 72, 73, 75–8
Montesquieu, C.L. de Secondat 111
moral positivism 89
Morgan, Robin 161, 162
Moulton, Janice 39

Nagel, Thomas 7, 34–5, 180 n10
natural sex 50–1, 53–4, 56
necrophilia 25–6, 50, 55, 57, 60,
    61–3, 65
Neu, Jerome 86–7
new natural law 113–16, 177 n9
New Zealand 120
Nietzsche, F.W. 5, 6
normal sex *see* natural sex
Northern Ireland 120
Nussbaum, Martha 117

obscenity 25–6
O'Carroll, Tom 136–41
Oncale, Joseph 154
O'Neill, Onora 174, 175
open marriage 81–2
oral sex 12, 26, 40, 52, 54
orgasm 24, 47, 93
original sin 10
outing 188 n57

Paley, W. 4
Palmer, David 77, 80
paradox of hedonism 42
paraphilia 181–2 n28
Pateman, Carole 103–4
paternalism 91–4
patriarchal marriage 75
Paul, St. 9–10
Paul VI, Pope 71, 112
pederasty 111, 133–4
pedophilia 53, 133–43, 173;
    positive morality 168; as sexual
    perversion 50, 55, 57, 60, 61,
    63, 65; terminology 133–4
persuasive definitions 28–9
perverse 59–60
perverted behavior 61
perverted sex *see* sexual perversion

petting 12, 52, 54
philosophers and sex 3–7
Pius XII, Pope 71
plain sex view 37, 41–3, 83–4, 98,
    100, 172; marriage 69;
    objections 35, 36, 43–9; sexual
    perversion 56–8
plainer sex view 43–9
Plato 3–4, 5, 111, 186 n3
pleasure 22, 42; bodily 46–7; moral
    innocence 115; *see also* sexual
    pleasure
Plummer, Kenneth 138–9
polyandry 70
polygamy 6, 70–1, 72
pornography 26, 45, 160
positive morality 88–91, 167–8
possessiveness 86
Powell, Graham A. 139
pre-marital sex 52
privacy 56, 120–1, 147, 153
private property 77–8
procreation: and marriage 80–1,
    90, 130–1; and sexual pleasure
    47–9
procreation view of sex 9–13,
    169–70; homosexual marriage
    130–1; homosexuality 111–16;
    marriage 9–13, 69–74;
    masturbation 44; objections
    13–20, 35, 41–2; prostitution
    96–8, 100; sexual perversion
    51–4
promiscuity 118–19
promise-breaking 79, 82
prostitutes 109; rape of 101,
    156–7, 158
prostitution 47, 48–9, 55, 88–109,
    172–3; degradation of women
    99–105; language view of sex
    40; and marriage 75, 89–91, 98,
    morality and prudence 91–2,
    169; oppression of women 99,
    105–9; paternalism 91–4;
    positive morality 88–91, 167–8;
    sex with love view 26, 98;
    things not for sale 94–8
Protestantism 71, 112